MEL'S STORY

Also by G. B. Trudeau

Wounded Warrior Series

The Long Road Home: One Step at a Time
Foreword by Senator John McCain

The War Within: One More Step at a Time
Foreword by General Richard B. Myers

Signature Wound: Rocking TBI
Foreword by General Peter Pace

Recent Collections

Red Rascal's War

Squared Away

Special Collections

Doonesbury.com's The Sandbox:
Dispatches from Troops in Iraq and Afghanistan

Doonesbury.com's The War in Quotes

"My Shorts R Bunching. Thoughts?" The Tweets of Roland Hedley

40: A Doonesbury Retrospective

MEL'S STORY
Surviving Military Sexual Assault

by **G. B. TRUDEAU**

.

Foreword by
CONGRESSWOMAN JACKIE SPEIER

Andrews McMeel
Publishing

Kansas City • Sydney • London

"Gee whiz, the hormone level created by nature sets in place the possibility for these types of things to occur."

—Sen. Saxby Chambliss at Senate Armed Services
Committee Hearing on Military Sexual Assault

Foreword
by Congresswoman Jackie Speier

The military's justice system hasn't stopped the epidemic of rape and sexual assault among the ranks. Responses by Congress and the White House fail our brave service members and jeopardize their health and safety every day. The Department of Defense continues to defend this age-old justice system that places total authority over rape cases into the hands of commanders with no legal expertise.

There are an estimated 26,000 sexual assaults a year in the military, but reporting is low, court-martials are rare, and the conviction rate is less than 2 percent under the chain of command. Only 5,000 reports were made in 2013 and only about 10 percent of those even went to trial. The reason is crystal clear—commanders have a built-in conflict of interest that undermines a soldier's due process rights.

Since 2011, I have shared thirty stories on the House floor of both men and women in our armed forces who were sexually assaulted. Many of these stories involved commanders who subverted investigations, refused to bring a case to court-martial, or overturned a case after a jury had found the perpetrator guilty and a jail sentence already issued.

It's a toxic culture that encourages our soldiers not to report rape because there is practically a guarantee they will not find justice, that they will face fierce retaliation, and often see their assailants promoted. Many rape and sexual assault survivors have their careers destroyed and suffer with Post-Traumatic Stress Disorder. Some of these survivors even end up in homeless shelters or on the streets.

In response to this epidemic, I introduced the bipartisan Sexual Assault Training Oversight and Prevention (STOP) Act, which would strip the chain of command of its authority to pursue sexual assault cases. But the DOD is against this vital reform measure despite the multiple black eyes it has gotten related to high-profile sexual assault trials. One of the most significant is that of a brigadier general who carried on a three-year relationship with a subordinate. Most of the charges against him, however, were dropped and his sentence was a slap on the wrist in relation to what he did plead guilty to.

In testimony, the female captain reported she was forced to perform sex acts with the general even after she tried to call off the relationship.

This is known as "command rape" and is part of the narrative of Melissa, the *Doonesbury* character featured in Garry Trudeau's latest book about wounded warriors. Mel's choice while serving in Iraq was either to sleep with her commander or be taken off the flight line as a Chinook helicopter mechanic for garbage duty. When she wants out, the commander threatens to write her up, and when she attempts to report, she is told it could put lives at risk in a war zone. In the aftermath, we meet Mel in counseling, feeling isolated, detached, zoned out, and refusing to take her prescription medication. She distrusts men and feels stalked by other wounded warriors who take a sincere interest in her story and recovery. Mel's story mirrors so many of the survivor stories I've shared in the Congress.

Survivors often suffer through deep depression, but many do not let being raped or sexually assaulted define their stories going forward. Many remain proud they donned the uniforms of the world's greatest military. This is the story of Mel, a young woman who you root for as Trudeau unfolds her story. You want her to succeed and grow suspicious with her outcome as she faces her next obstacles. Trudeau holds your interest throughout and informs the reader on what military sexual assault is through a diverse set of characters who each have their own military stories and secrets to share. *Mel's Story: Surviving Military Sexual Assault* is yet another of Trudeau's testaments to our service members and wounded warriors who sacrifice so much to keep our country safe.

MEL'S STORY

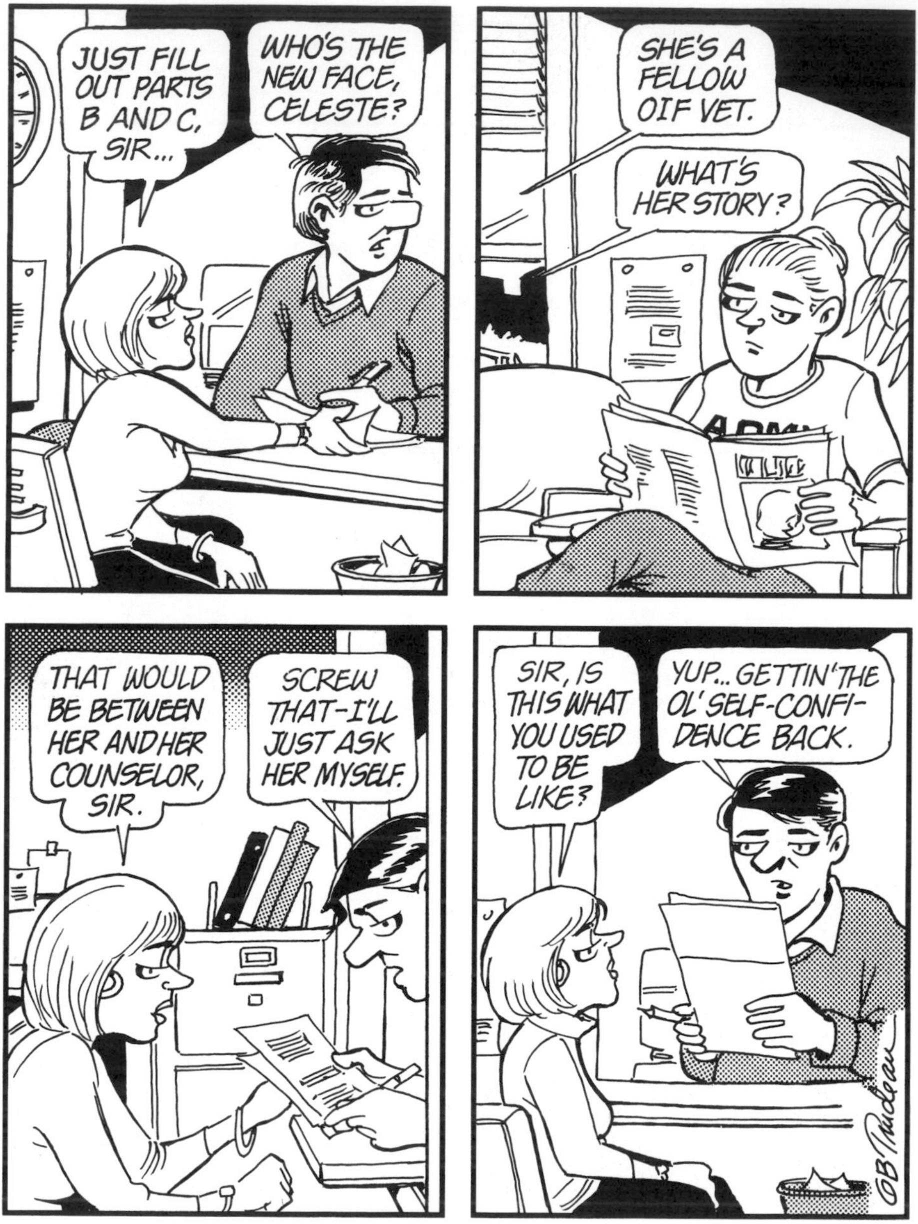

JUST FILL OUT PARTS B AND C, SIR...
WHO'S THE NEW FACE, CELESTE?
SHE'S A FELLOW OIF VET.
WHAT'S HER STORY?
THAT WOULD BE BETWEEN HER AND HER COUNSELOR, SIR.
SCREW THAT–I'LL JUST ASK HER MYSELF.
SIR, IS THIS WHAT YOU USED TO BE LIKE?
YUP... GETTIN' THE OL' SELF-CONFIDENCE BACK.

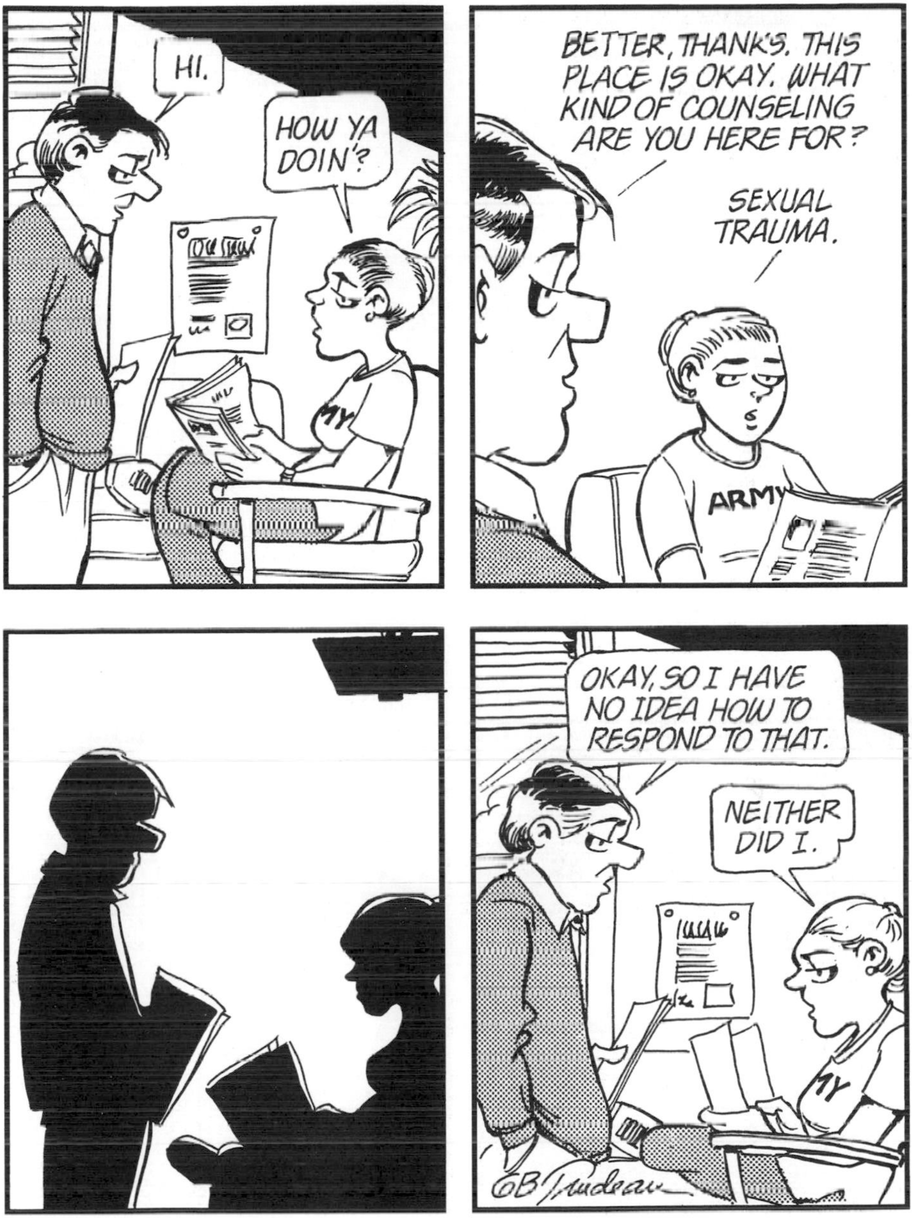
HI.
HOW YA DOIN'?
BETTER, THANKS. THIS PLACE IS OKAY. WHAT KIND OF COUNSELING ARE YOU HERE FOR?
SEXUAL TRAUMA.
ARMY
OKAY, SO I HAVE NO IDEA HOW TO RESPOND TO THAT.
NEITHER DID I.
©B Trudeau

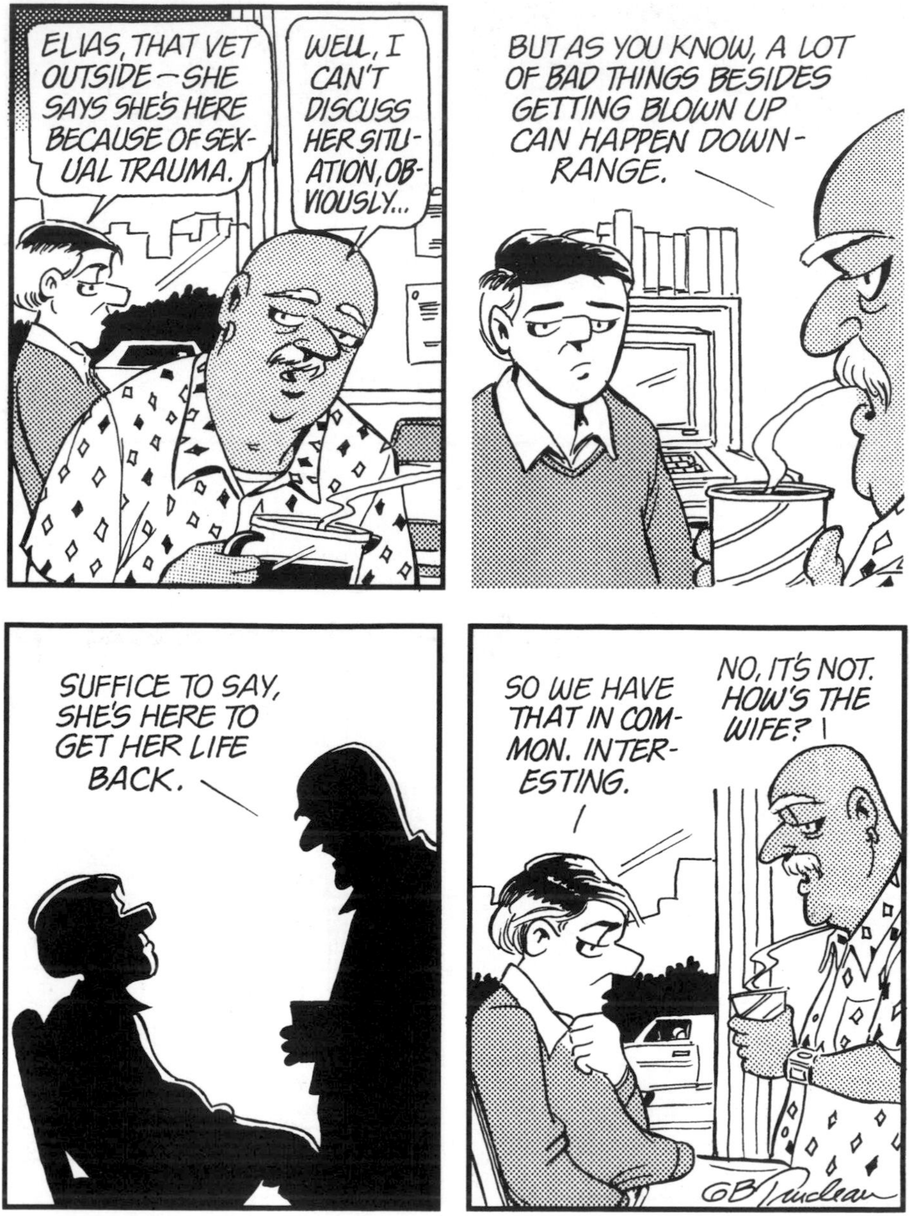
ELIAS, THAT VET OUTSIDE — SHE SAYS SHE'S HERE BECAUSE OF SEX-UAL TRAUMA.
WELL, I CAN'T DISCUSS HER SITU-ATION, OB-VIOUSLY...
BUT AS YOU KNOW, A LOT OF BAD THINGS BESIDES GETTING BLOWN UP CAN HAPPEN DOWN-RANGE.
SUFFICE TO SAY, SHE'S HERE TO GET HER LIFE BACK.
SO WE HAVE THAT IN COM-MON. INTER-ESTING.
NO, IT'S NOT. HOW'S THE WIFE?
GB Trudeau

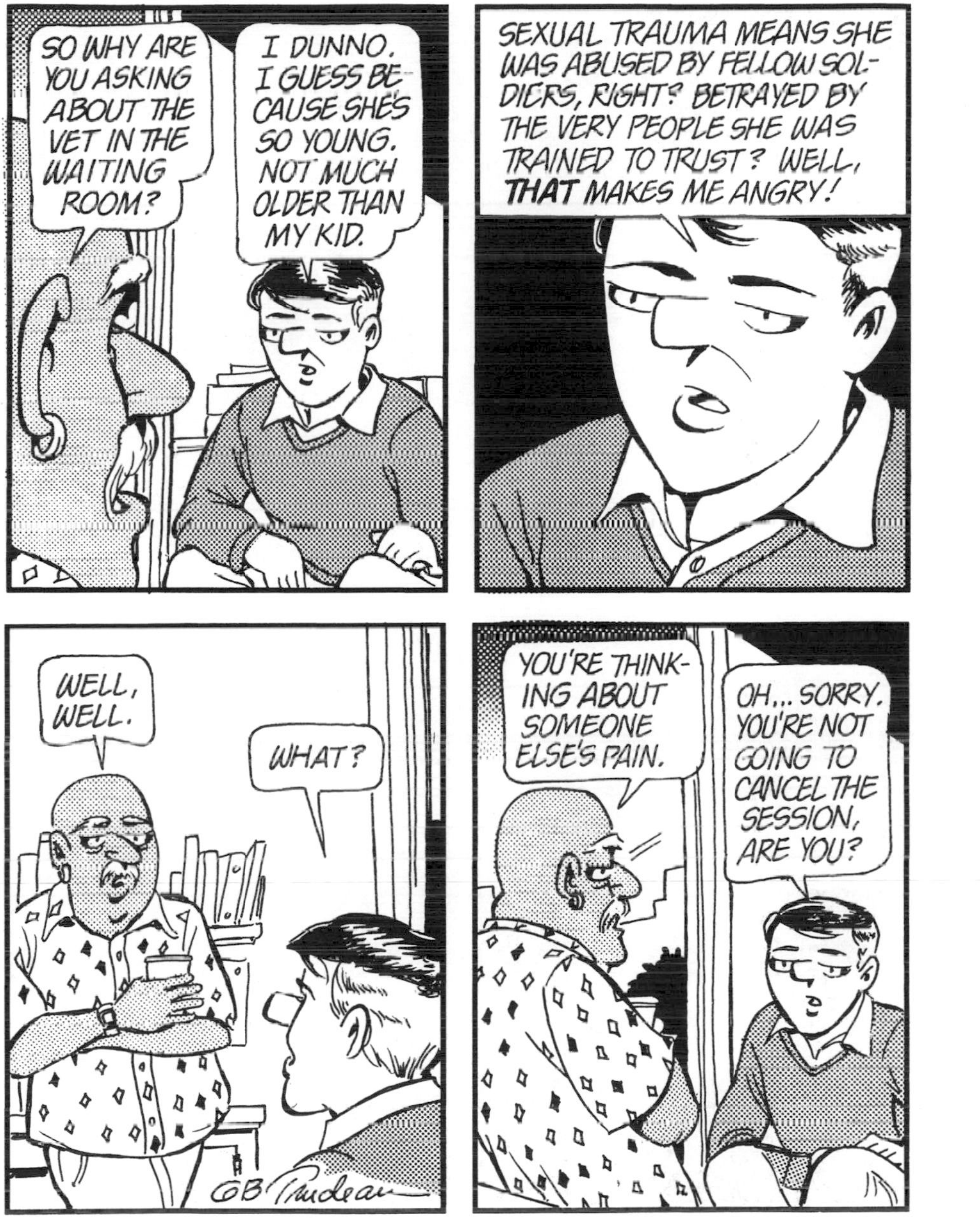
SO WHY ARE YOU ASKING ABOUT THE VET IN THE WAITING ROOM?
I DUNNO. I GUESS BECAUSE SHE'S SO YOUNG. NOT MUCH OLDER THAN MY KID.
SEXUAL TRAUMA MEANS SHE WAS ABUSED BY FELLOW SOLDIERS, RIGHT? BETRAYED BY THE VERY PEOPLE SHE WAS TRAINED TO TRUST? WELL, THAT MAKES ME ANGRY!
WELL, WELL.
WHAT?
GB Trudeau
YOU'RE THINKING ABOUT SOMEONE ELSE'S PAIN.
OH... SORRY. YOU'RE NOT GOING TO CANCEL THE SESSION, ARE YOU?

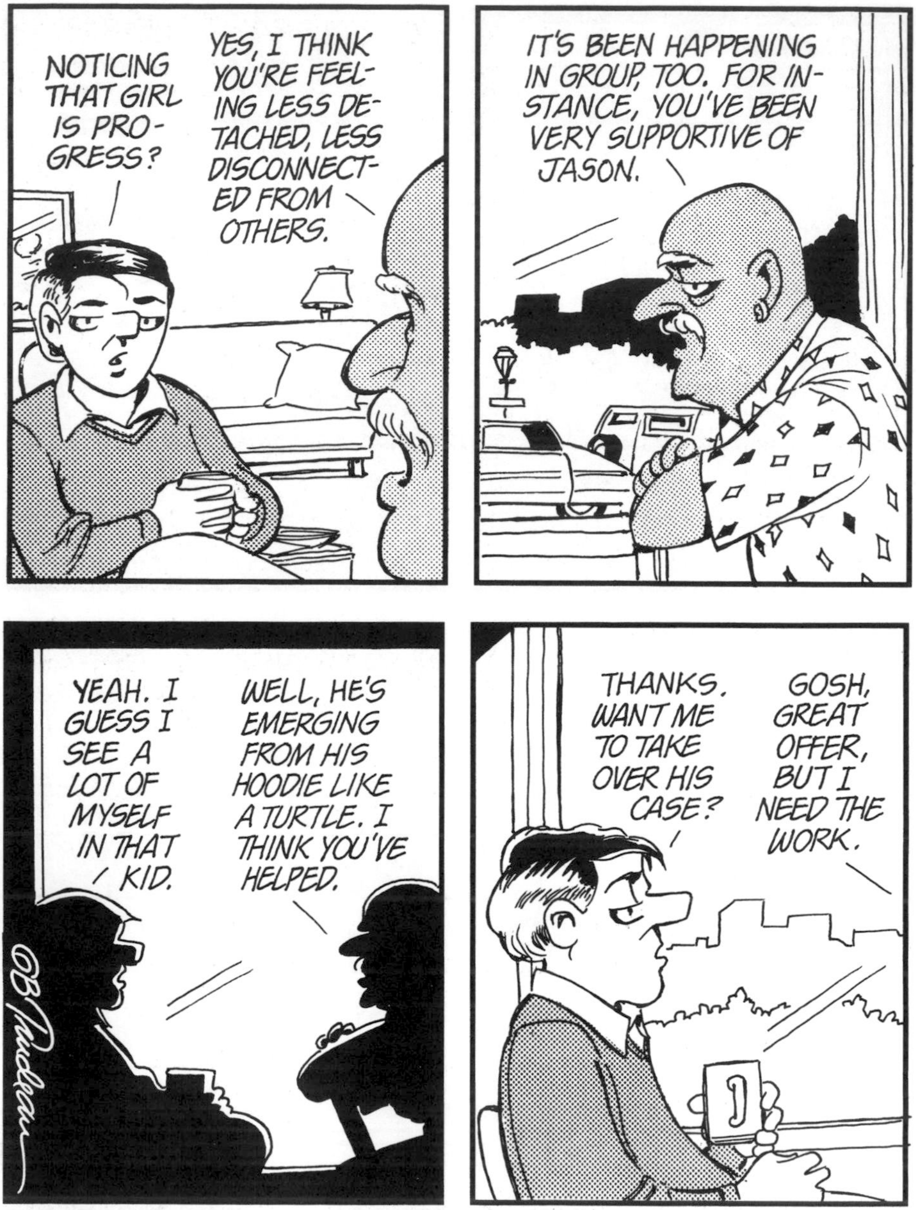

NOTICING THAT GIRL IS PROGRESS?
YES, I THINK YOU'RE FEELING LESS DETACHED, LESS DISCONNECTED FROM OTHERS.
IT'S BEEN HAPPENING IN GROUP, TOO. FOR INSTANCE, YOU'VE BEEN VERY SUPPORTIVE OF JASON.
YEAH. I GUESS I SEE A LOT OF MYSELF IN THAT KID.
WELL, HE'S EMERGING FROM HIS HOODIE LIKE A TURTLE. I THINK YOU'VE HELPED.
©B. Trudeau
THANKS. WANT ME TO TAKE OVER HIS CASE?
GOSH, GREAT OFFER, BUT I NEED THE WORK.

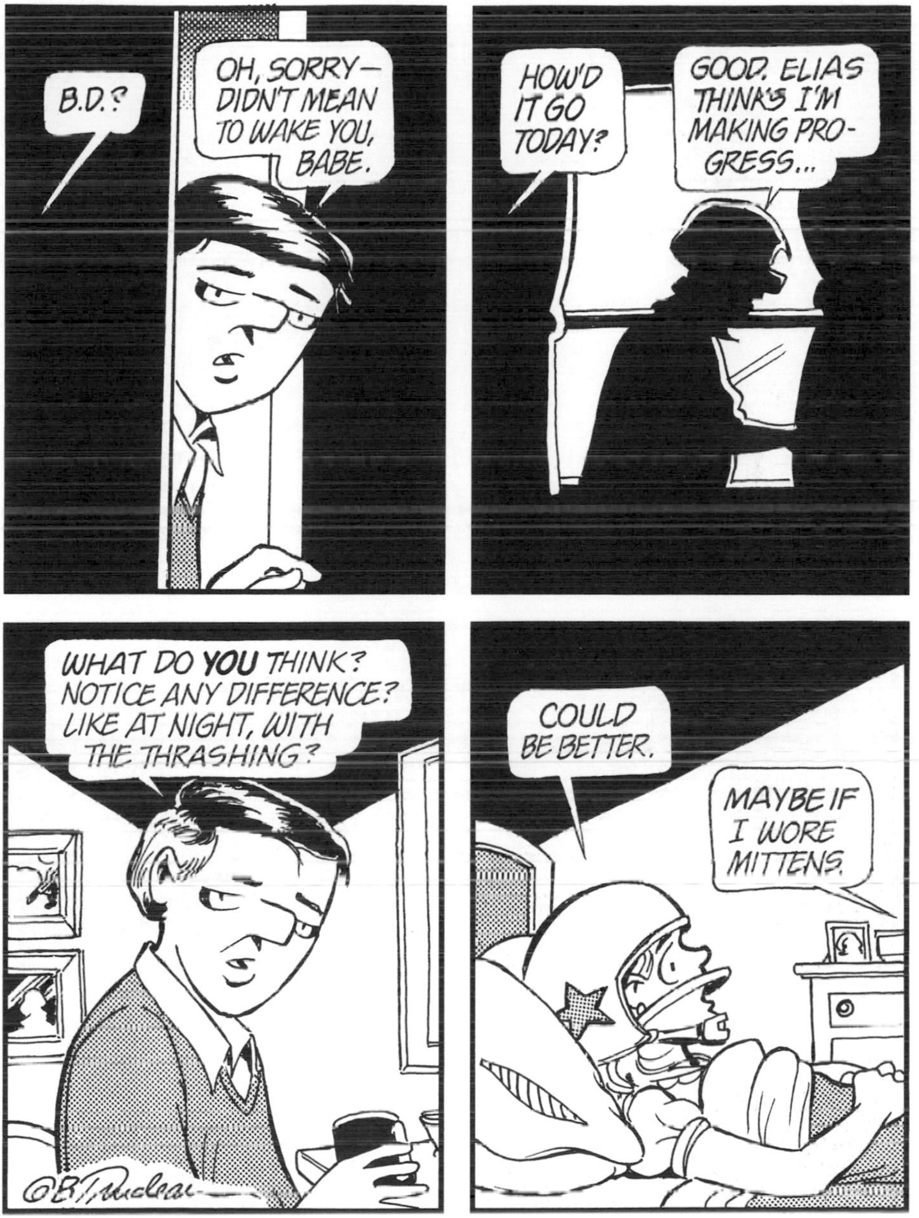
B.D.?
OH, SORRY— DIDN'T MEAN TO WAKE YOU, BABE.
HOW'D IT GO TODAY?
GOOD. ELIAS THINKS I'M MAKING PRO-GRESS...
WHAT DO **YOU** THINK? NOTICE ANY DIFFERENCE? LIKE AT NIGHT, WITH THE THRASHING?
COULD BE BETTER.
MAYBE IF I WORE MITTENS.

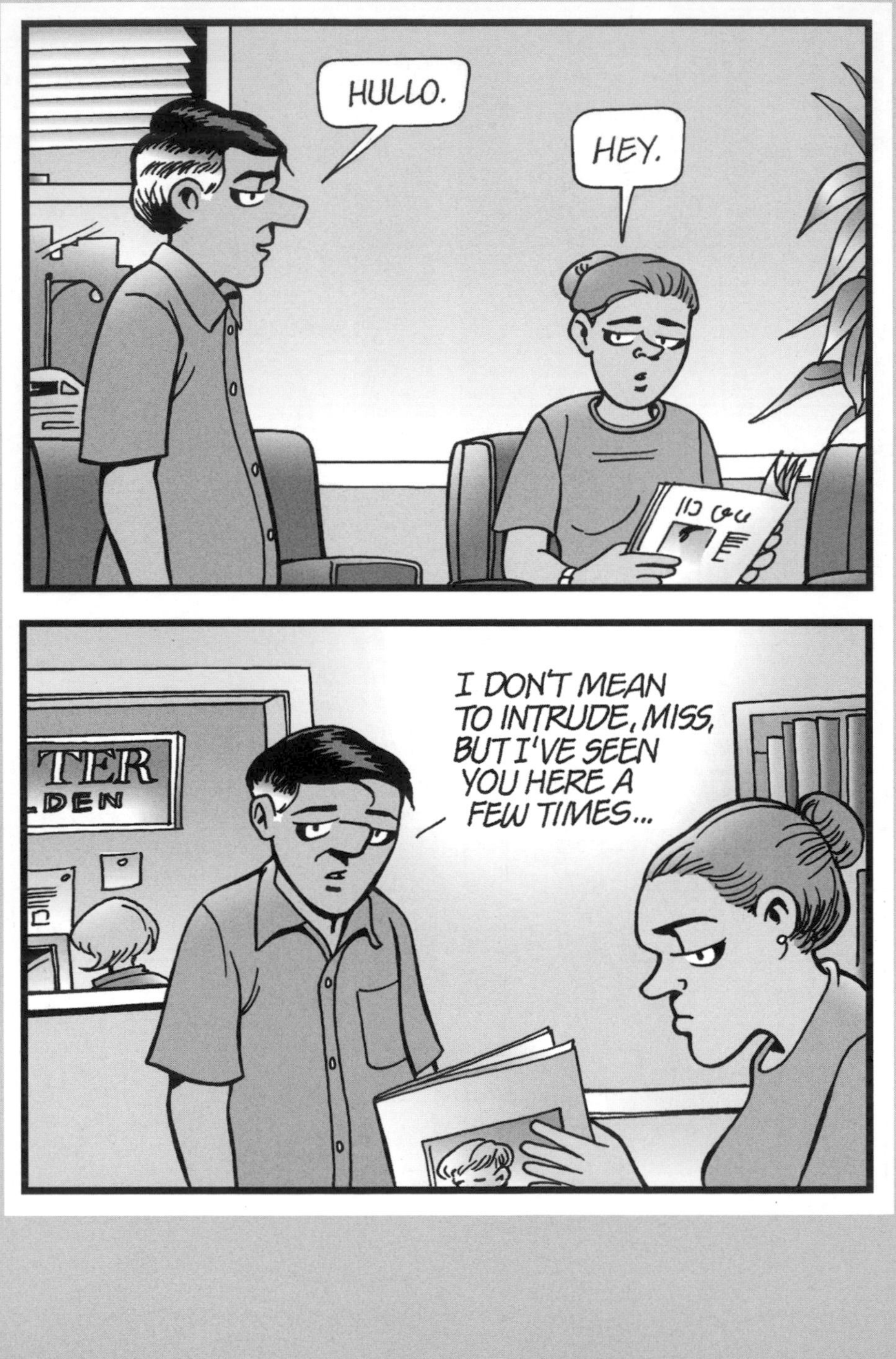
HULLO.
HEY.
TER
LDEN
I DON'T MEAN TO INTRUDE, MISS, BUT I'VE SEEN YOU HERE A FEW TIMES...

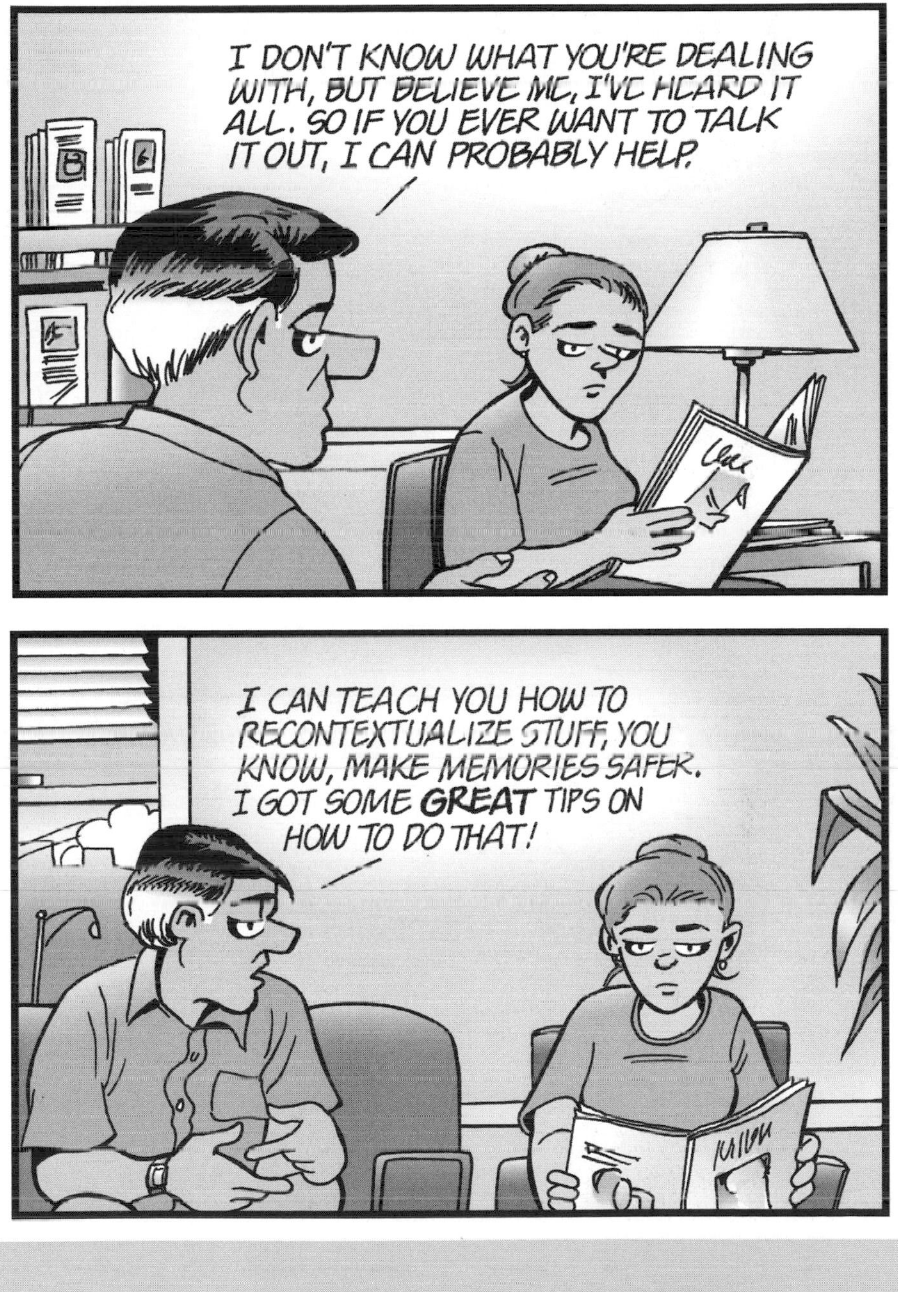
I DON'T KNOW WHAT YOU'RE DEALING WITH, BUT BELIEVE ME, I'VE HEARD IT ALL. SO IF YOU EVER WANT TO TALK IT OUT, I CAN PROBABLY HELP.
I CAN TEACH YOU HOW TO RECONTEXTUALIZE STUFF, YOU KNOW, MAKE MEMORIES SAFER. I GOT SOME **GREAT** TIPS ON HOW TO DO THAT!

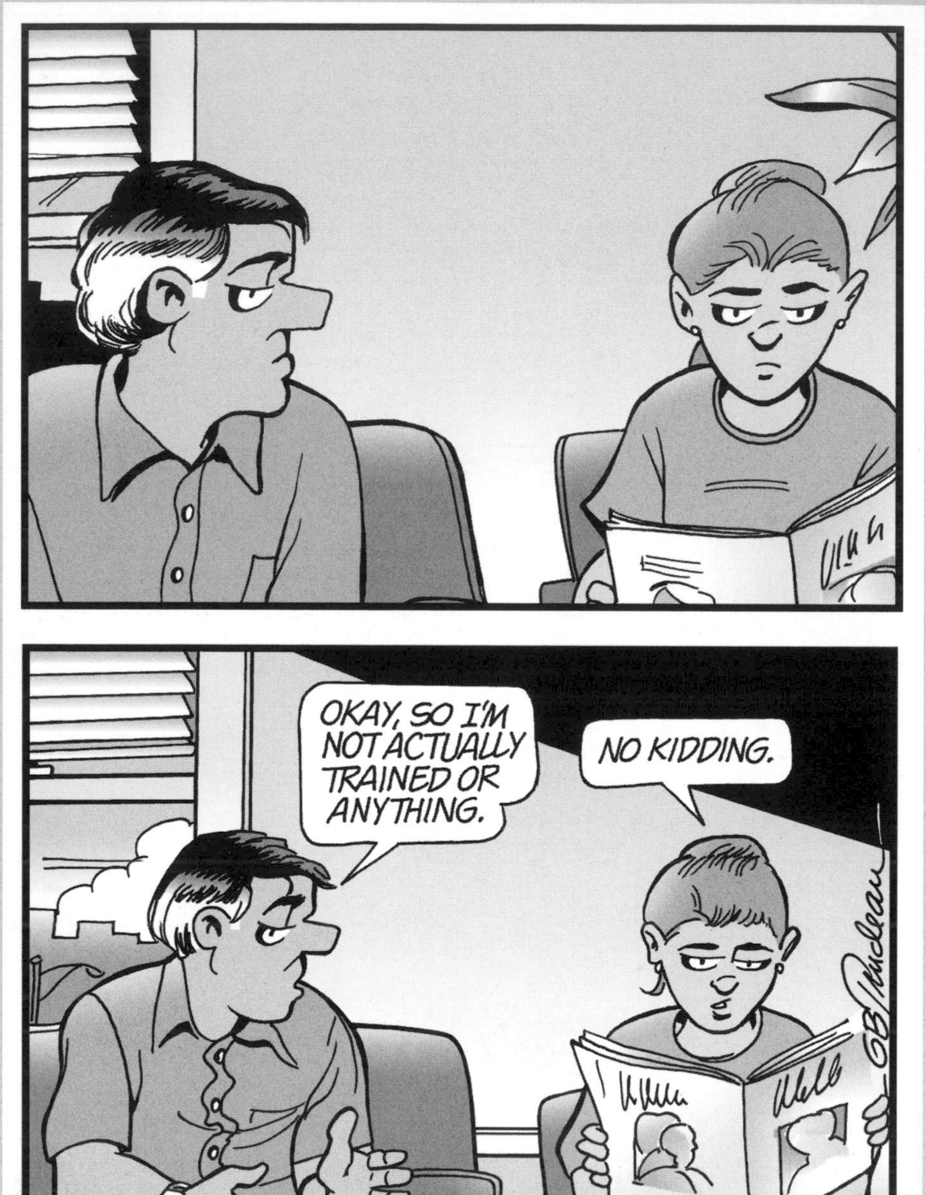
OKAY, SO I'M NOT ACTUALLY TRAINED OR ANYTHING.
NO KIDDING.

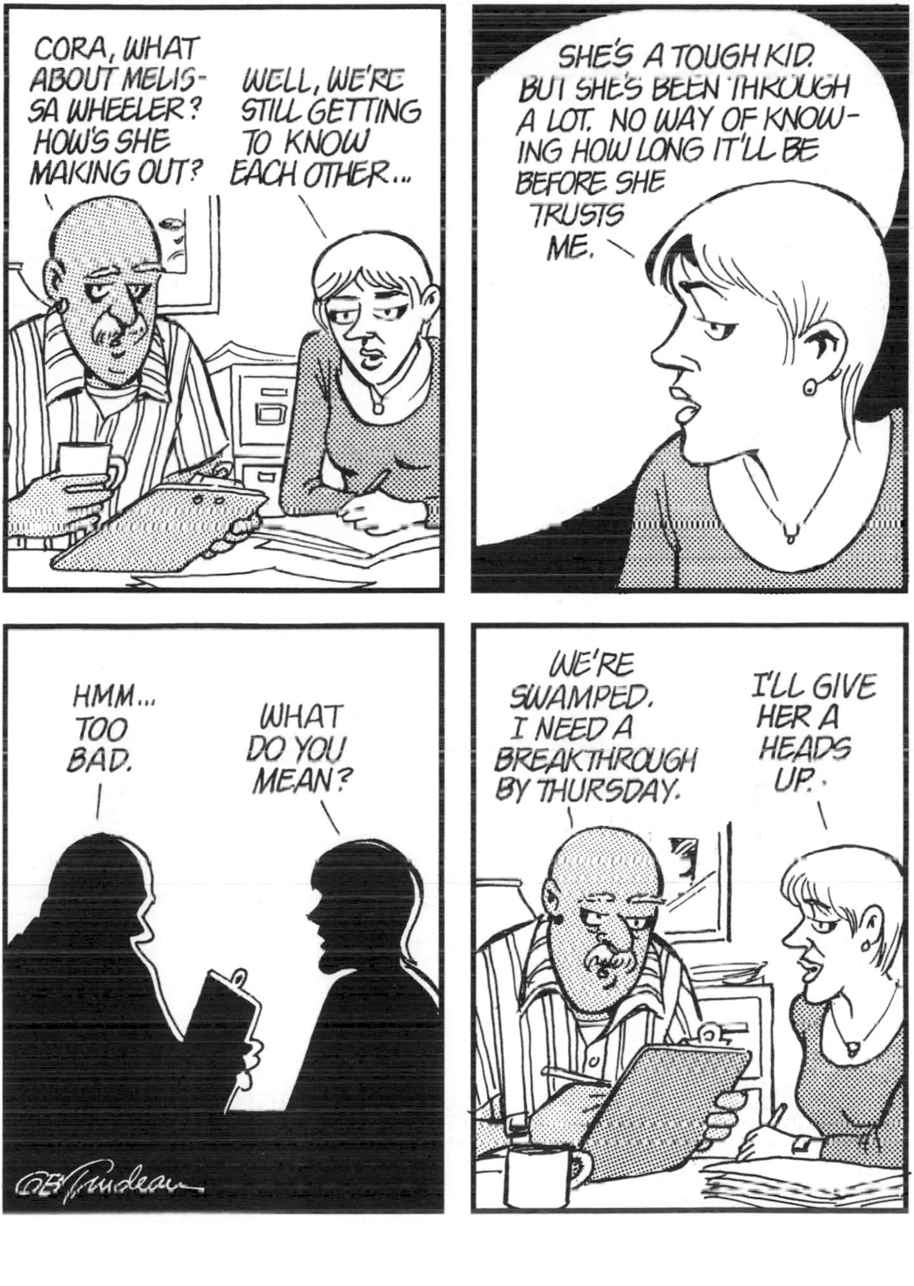
CORA, WHAT ABOUT MELISSA WHEELER? HOW'S SHE MAKING OUT?
WELL, WE'RE STILL GETTING TO KNOW EACH OTHER...
SHE'S A TOUGH KID. BUT SHE'S BEEN THROUGH A LOT. NO WAY OF KNOWING HOW LONG IT'LL BE BEFORE SHE TRUSTS ME.
HMM... TOO BAD.
WHAT DO YOU MEAN?
WE'RE SWAMPED. I NEED A BREAKTHROUGH BY THURSDAY.
I'LL GIVE HER A HEADS UP.

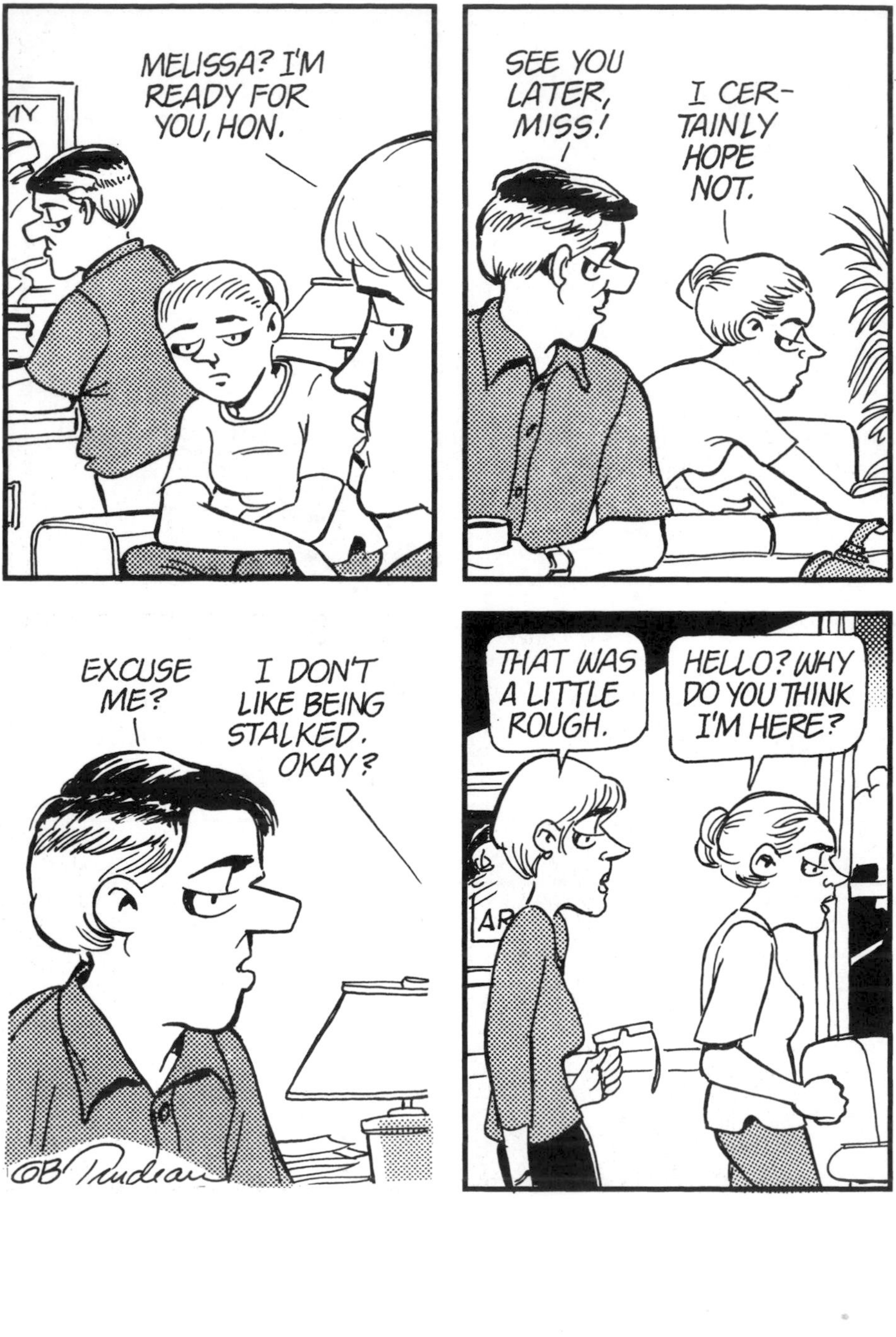
MELISSA? I'M READY FOR YOU, HON.
SEE YOU LATER, MISS!
I CER-TAINLY HOPE NOT.
EXCUSE ME?
I DON'T LIKE BEING STALKED. OKAY?
THAT WAS A LITTLE ROUGH.
HELLO? WHY DO YOU THINK I'M HERE?
©B Trudeau

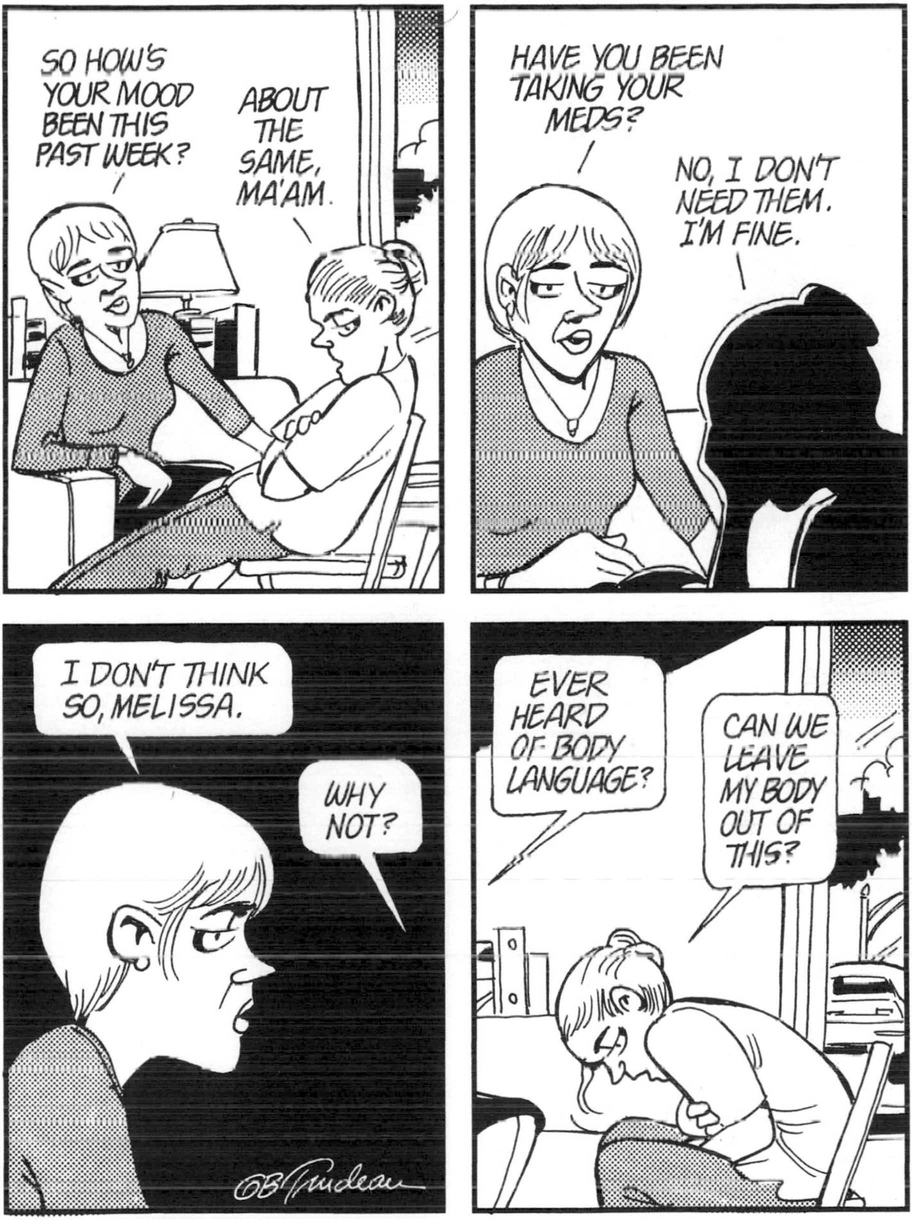
SO HOW'S YOUR MOOD BEEN THIS PAST WEEK?
ABOUT THE SAME, MA'AM.
HAVE YOU BEEN TAKING YOUR MEDS?
NO, I DON'T NEED THEM. I'M FINE.
I DON'T THINK SO, MELISSA.
WHY NOT?
©B Trudeau
EVER HEARD OF BODY LANGUAGE?
CAN WE LEAVE MY BODY OUT OF THIS?

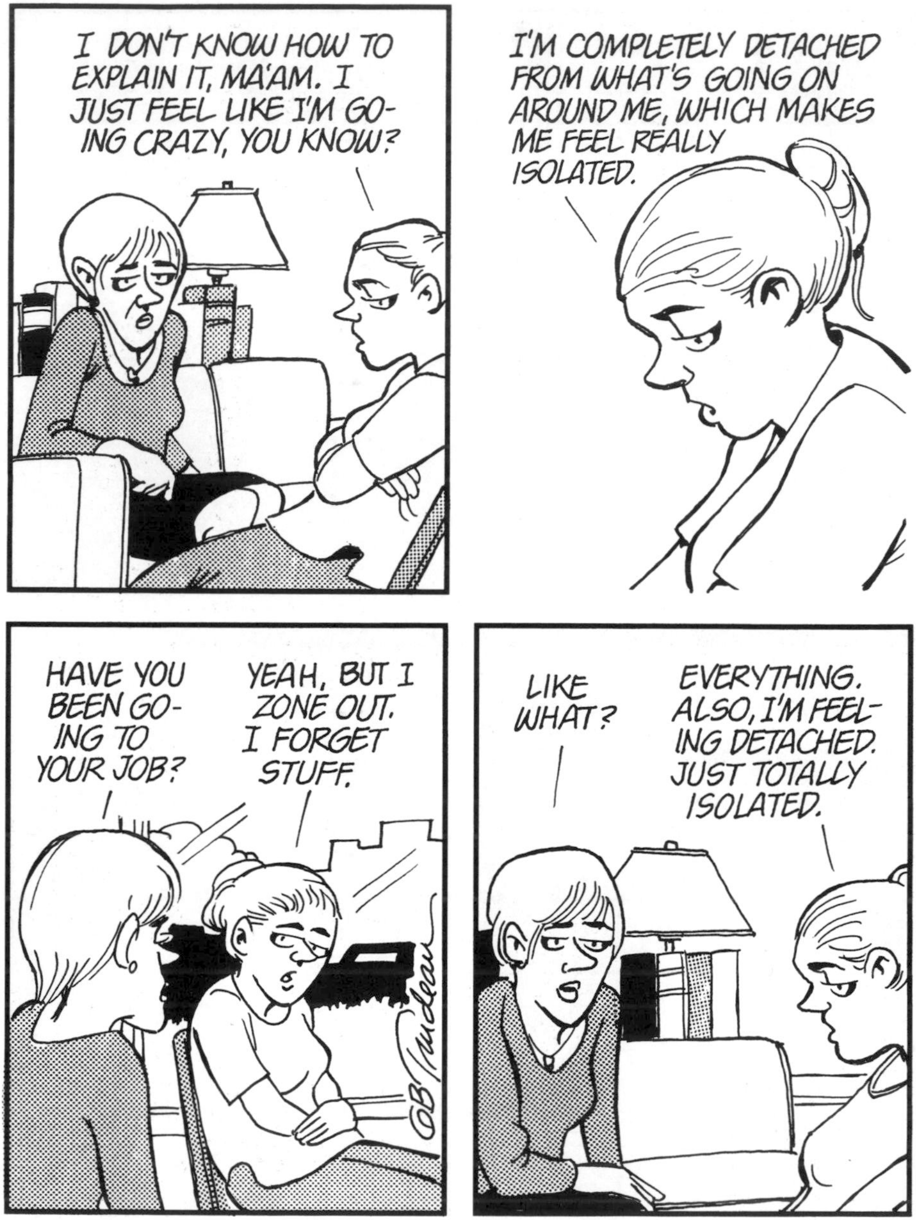
I DON'T KNOW HOW TO EXPLAIN IT, MA'AM. I JUST FEEL LIKE I'M GOING CRAZY, YOU KNOW?
I'M COMPLETELY DETACHED FROM WHAT'S GOING ON AROUND ME, WHICH MAKES ME FEEL REALLY ISOLATED.
HAVE YOU BEEN GOING TO YOUR JOB?
YEAH, BUT I ZONE OUT. I FORGET STUFF.
LIKE WHAT?
EVERYTHING. ALSO, I'M FEELING DETACHED. JUST TOTALLY ISOLATED.
©B Trudeau

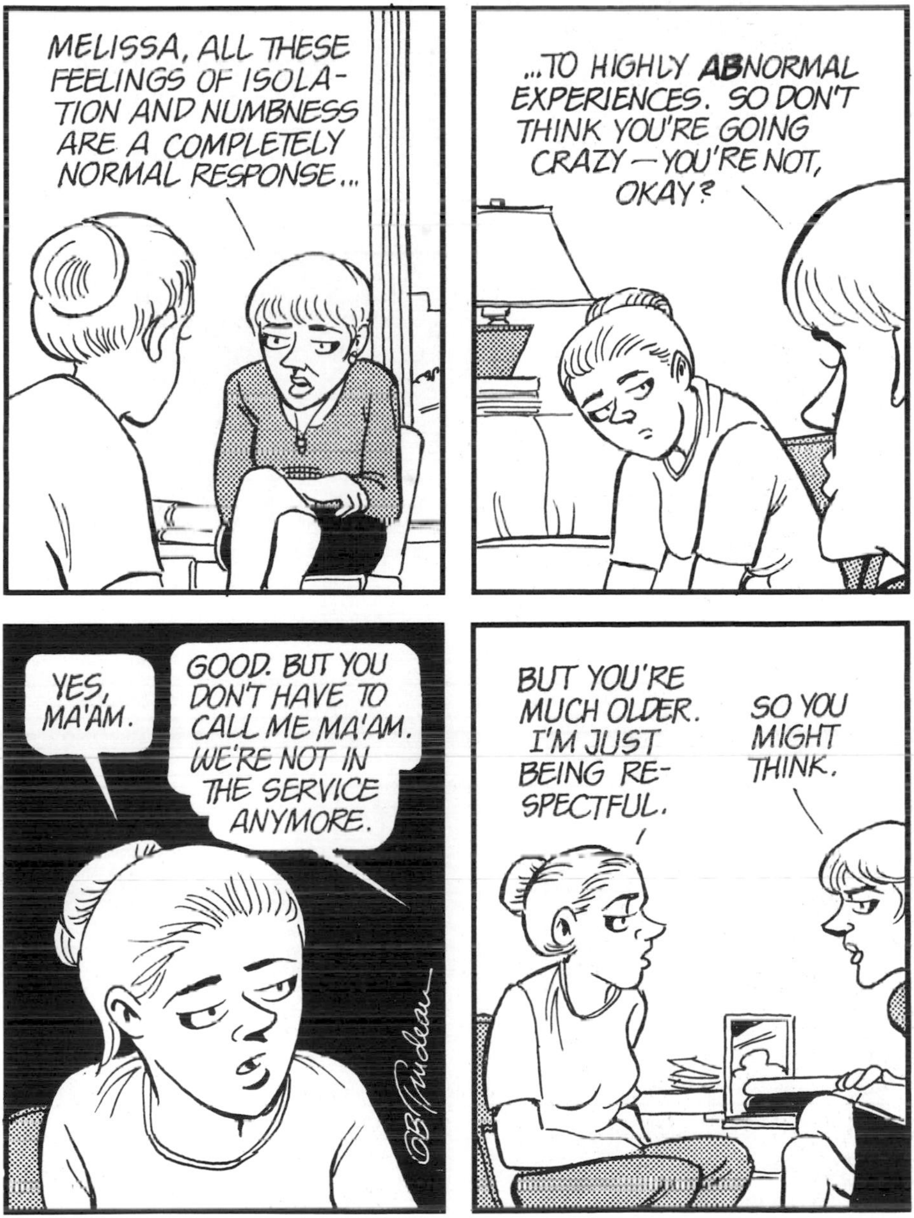
MELISSA, ALL THESE FEELINGS OF ISOLATION AND NUMBNESS ARE A COMPLETELY NORMAL RESPONSE...
...TO HIGHLY ABNORMAL EXPERIENCES. SO DON'T THINK YOU'RE GOING CRAZY—YOU'RE NOT, OKAY?
YES, MA'AM.
GOOD. BUT YOU DON'T HAVE TO CALL ME MA'AM. WE'RE NOT IN THE SERVICE ANYMORE.
©B Trudeau
BUT YOU'RE MUCH OLDER. I'M JUST BEING RESPECTFUL.
SO YOU MIGHT THINK.

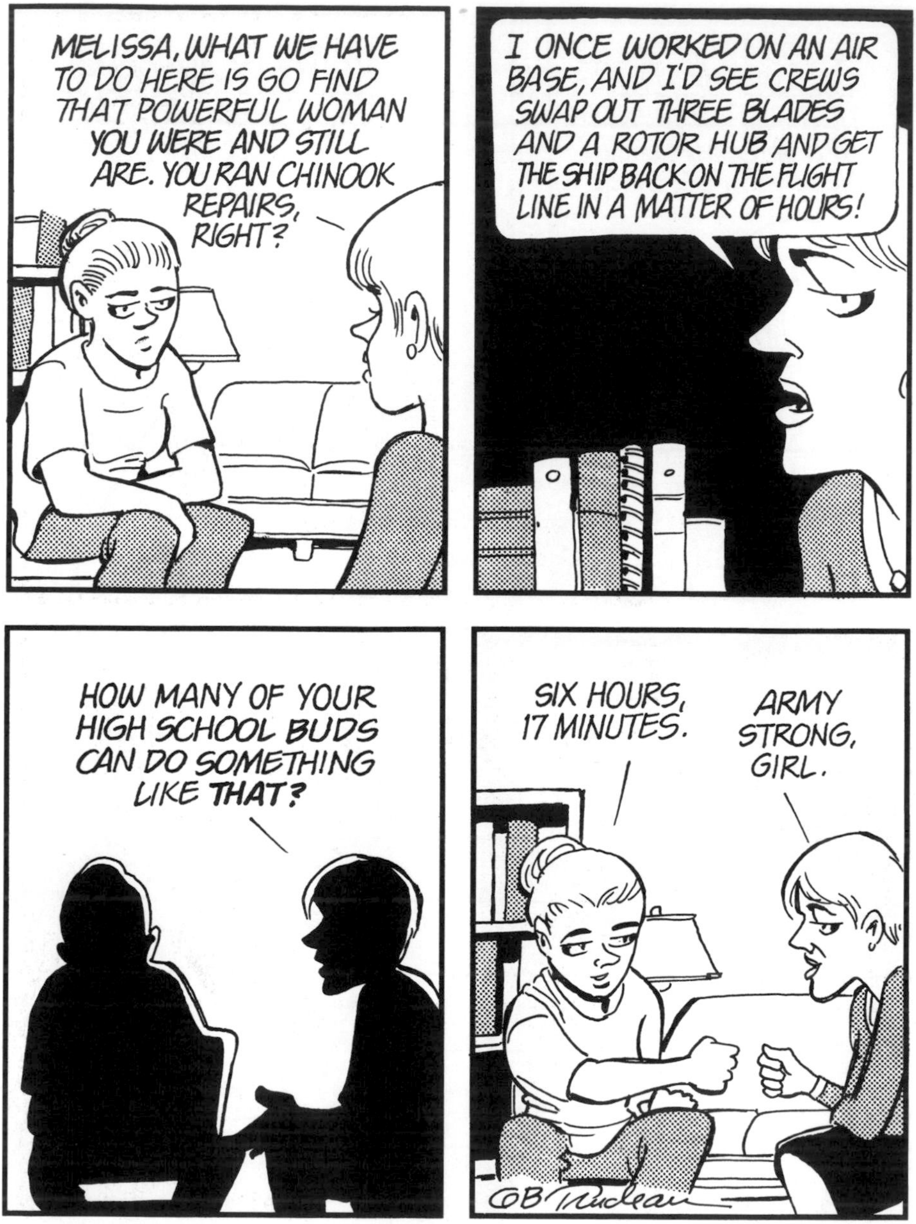
MELISSA, WHAT WE HAVE TO DO HERE IS GO FIND THAT POWERFUL WOMAN YOU WERE AND STILL ARE. YOU RAN CHINOOK REPAIRS, RIGHT?
I ONCE WORKED ON AN AIR BASE, AND I'D SEE CREWS SWAP OUT THREE BLADES AND A ROTOR HUB AND GET THE SHIP BACK ON THE FLIGHT LINE IN A MATTER OF HOURS!
HOW MANY OF YOUR HIGH SCHOOL BUDS CAN DO SOMETHING LIKE THAT?
SIX HOURS, 17 MINUTES.
ARMY STRONG, GIRL.
©B Trudeau

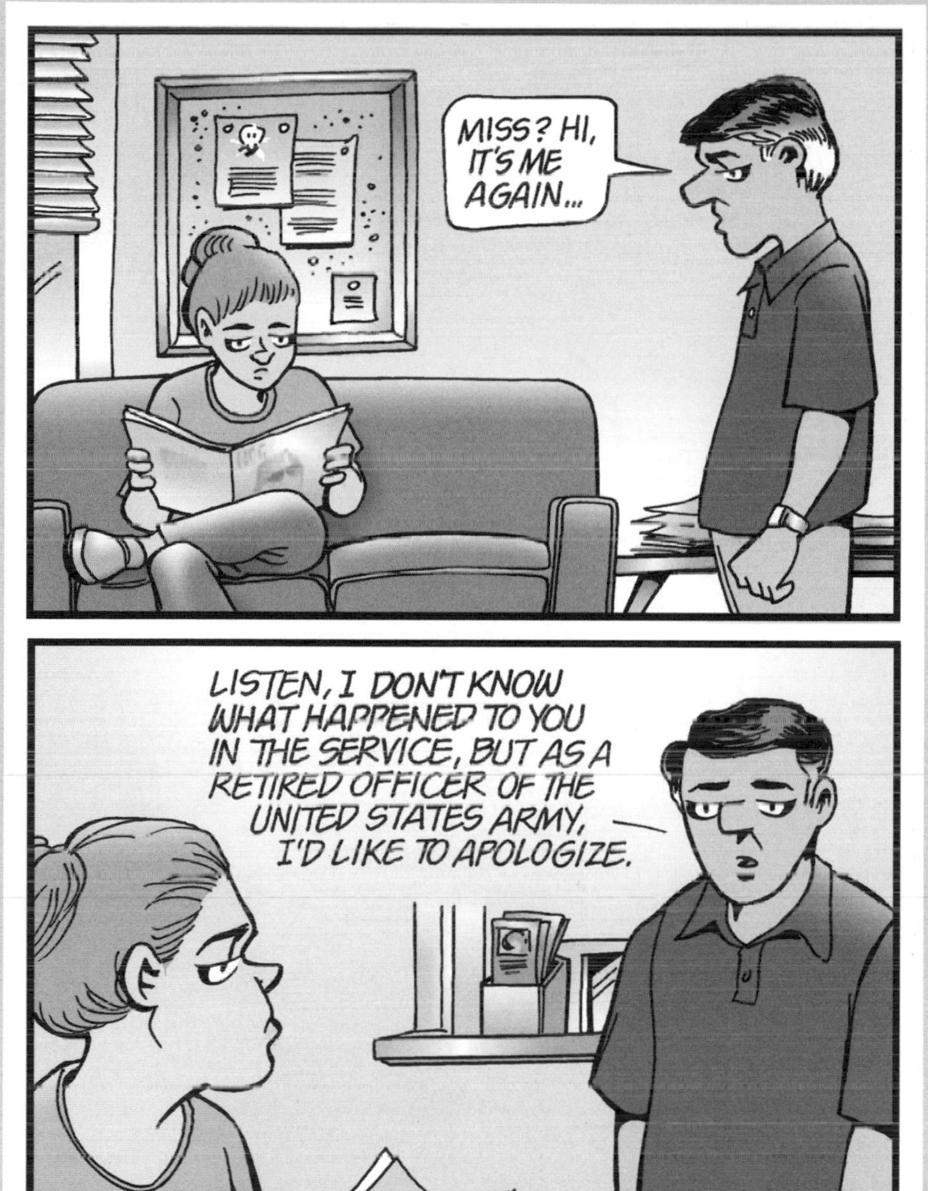
MISS? HI, IT'S ME AGAIN...
LISTEN, I DON'T KNOW WHAT HAPPENED TO YOU IN THE SERVICE, BUT AS A RETIRED OFFICER OF THE UNITED STATES ARMY, I'D LIKE TO APOLOGIZE.

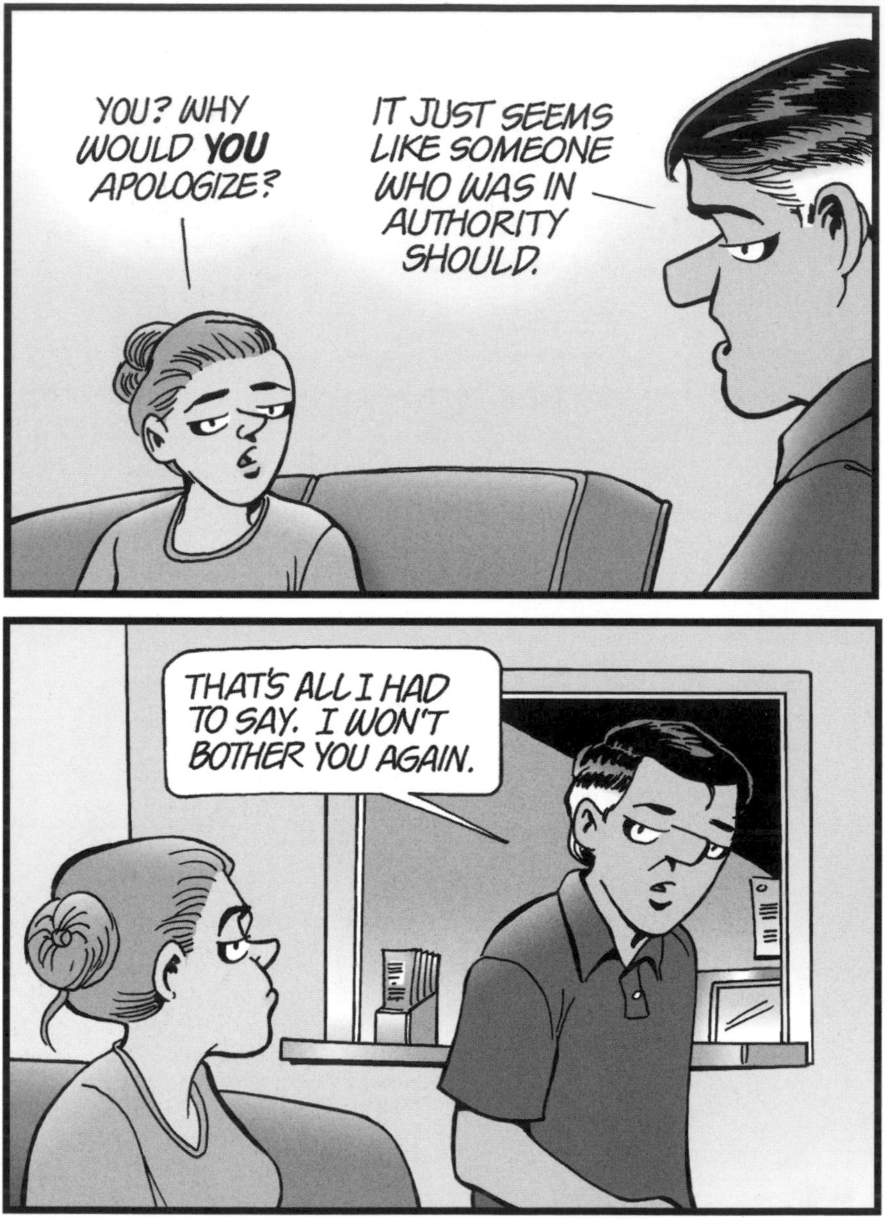
YOU? WHY WOULD **YOU** APOLOGIZE?
IT JUST SEEMS LIKE SOMEONE WHO WAS IN AUTHORITY SHOULD.
THAT'S ALL I HAD TO SAY. I WON'T BOTHER YOU AGAIN.

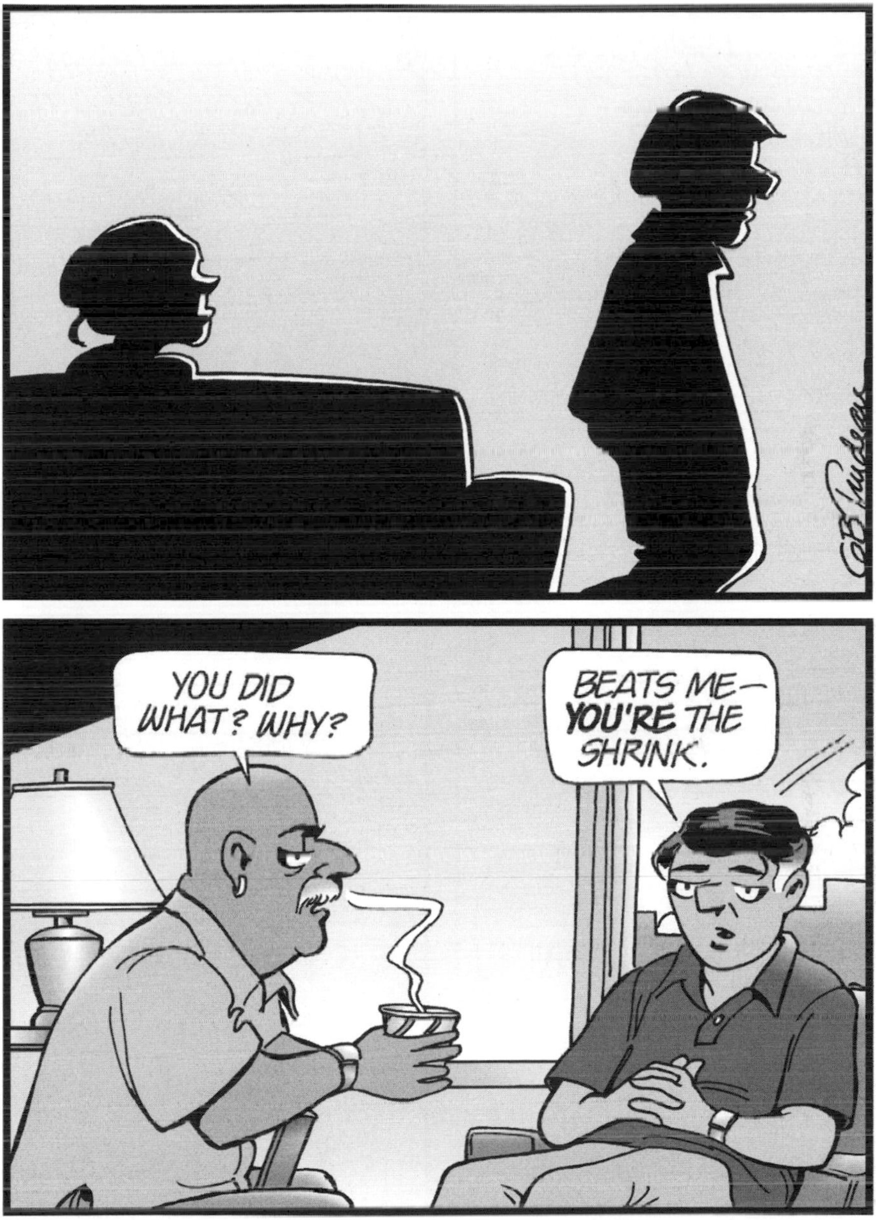
YOU DID WHAT? WHY?
BEATS ME— **YOU'RE** THE SHRINK.

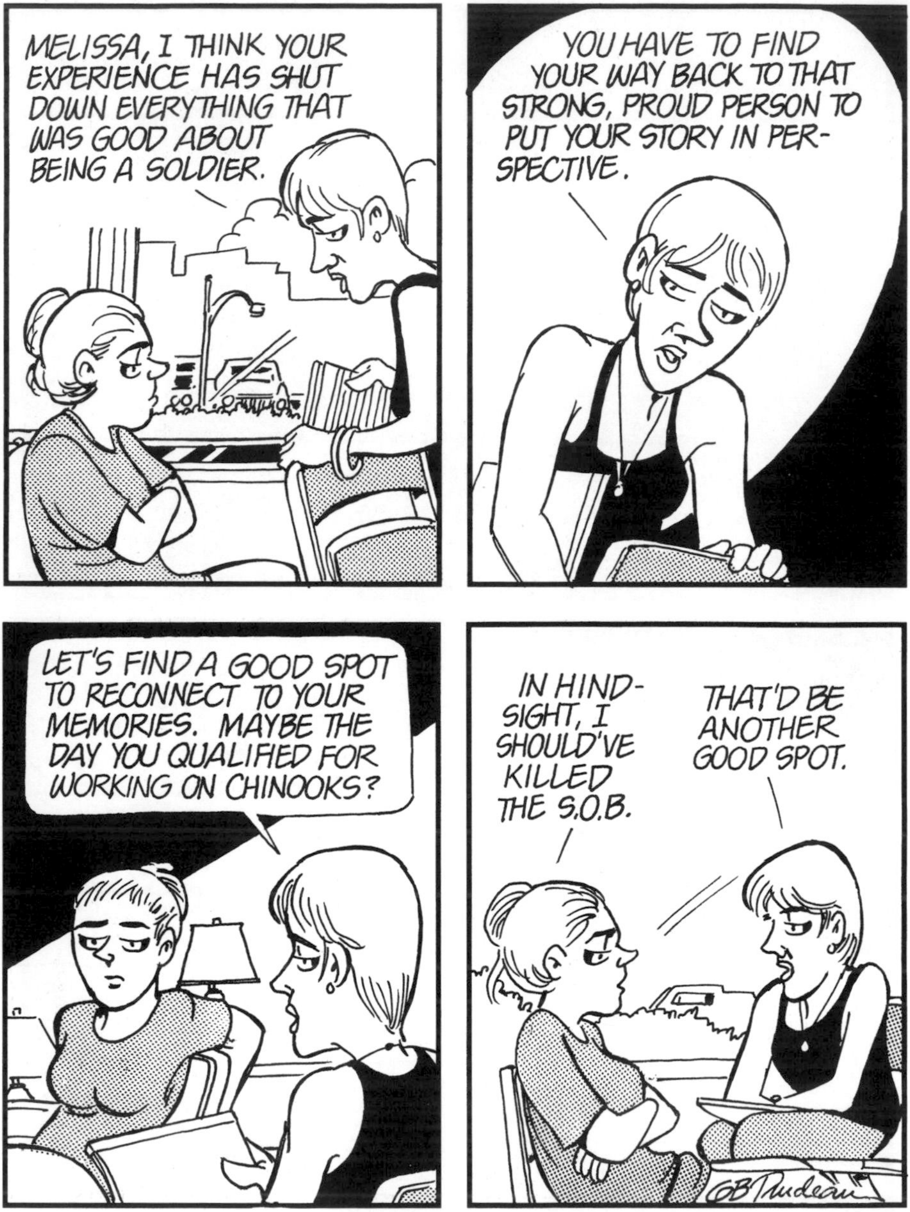
MELISSA, I THINK YOUR EXPERIENCE HAS SHUT DOWN EVERYTHING THAT WAS GOOD ABOUT BEING A SOLDIER.
YOU HAVE TO FIND YOUR WAY BACK TO THAT STRONG, PROUD PERSON TO PUT YOUR STORY IN PER-SPECTIVE.
LET'S FIND A GOOD SPOT TO RECONNECT TO YOUR MEMORIES. MAYBE THE DAY YOU QUALIFIED FOR WORKING ON CHINOOKS?
IN HIND-SIGHT, I SHOULD'VE KILLED THE S.O.B.
THAT'D BE ANOTHER GOOD SPOT.
GB Trudeau

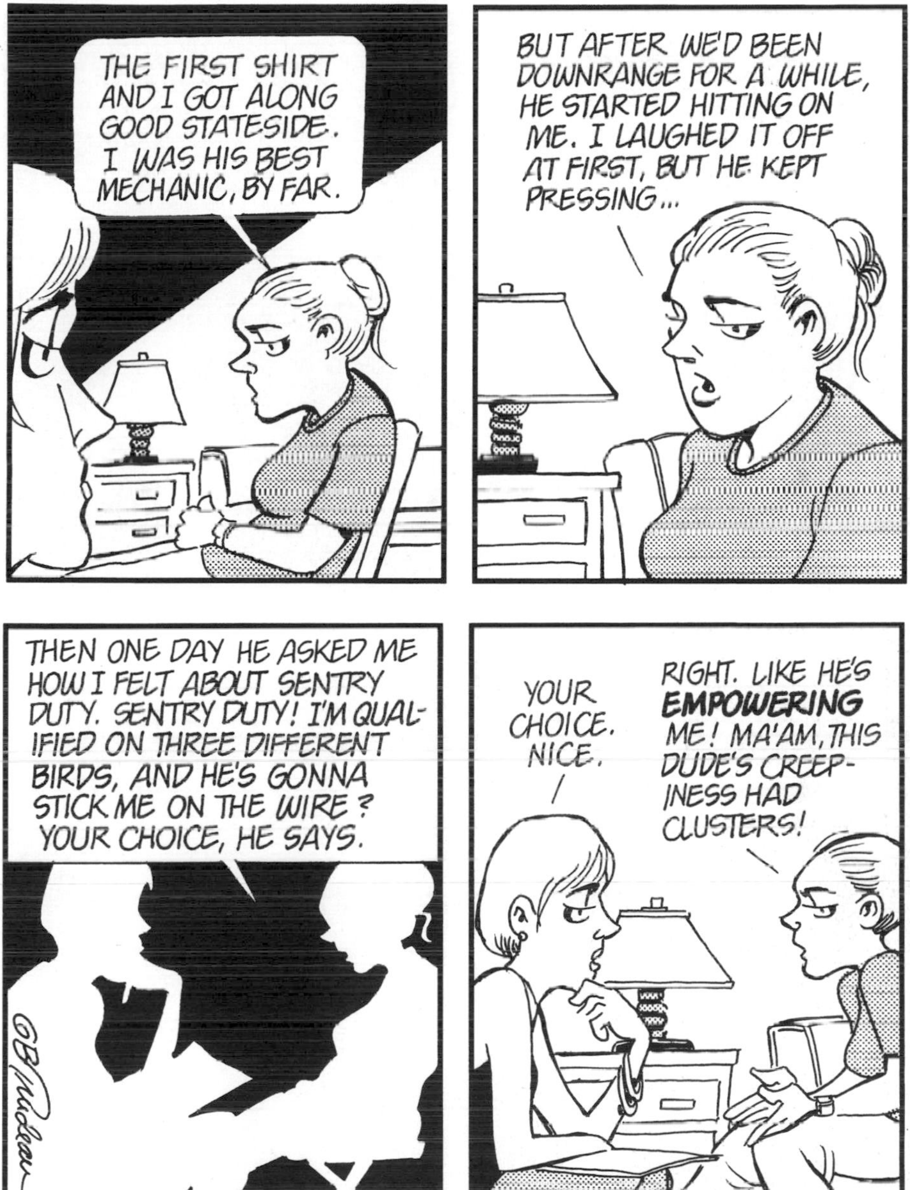
THE FIRST SHIRT AND I GOT ALONG GOOD STATESIDE. I WAS HIS BEST MECHANIC, BY FAR.
BUT AFTER WE'D BEEN DOWNRANGE FOR A WHILE, HE STARTED HITTING ON ME. I LAUGHED IT OFF AT FIRST, BUT HE KEPT PRESSING...
THEN ONE DAY HE ASKED ME HOW I FELT ABOUT SENTRY DUTY. SENTRY DUTY! I'M QUALIFIED ON THREE DIFFERENT BIRDS, AND HE'S GONNA STICK ME ON THE WIRE? YOUR CHOICE, HE SAYS.
YOUR CHOICE. NICE.
RIGHT. LIKE HE'S **EMPOWERING** ME! MA'AM, THIS DUDE'S CREEPINESS HAD CLUSTERS!
©BTrudeau

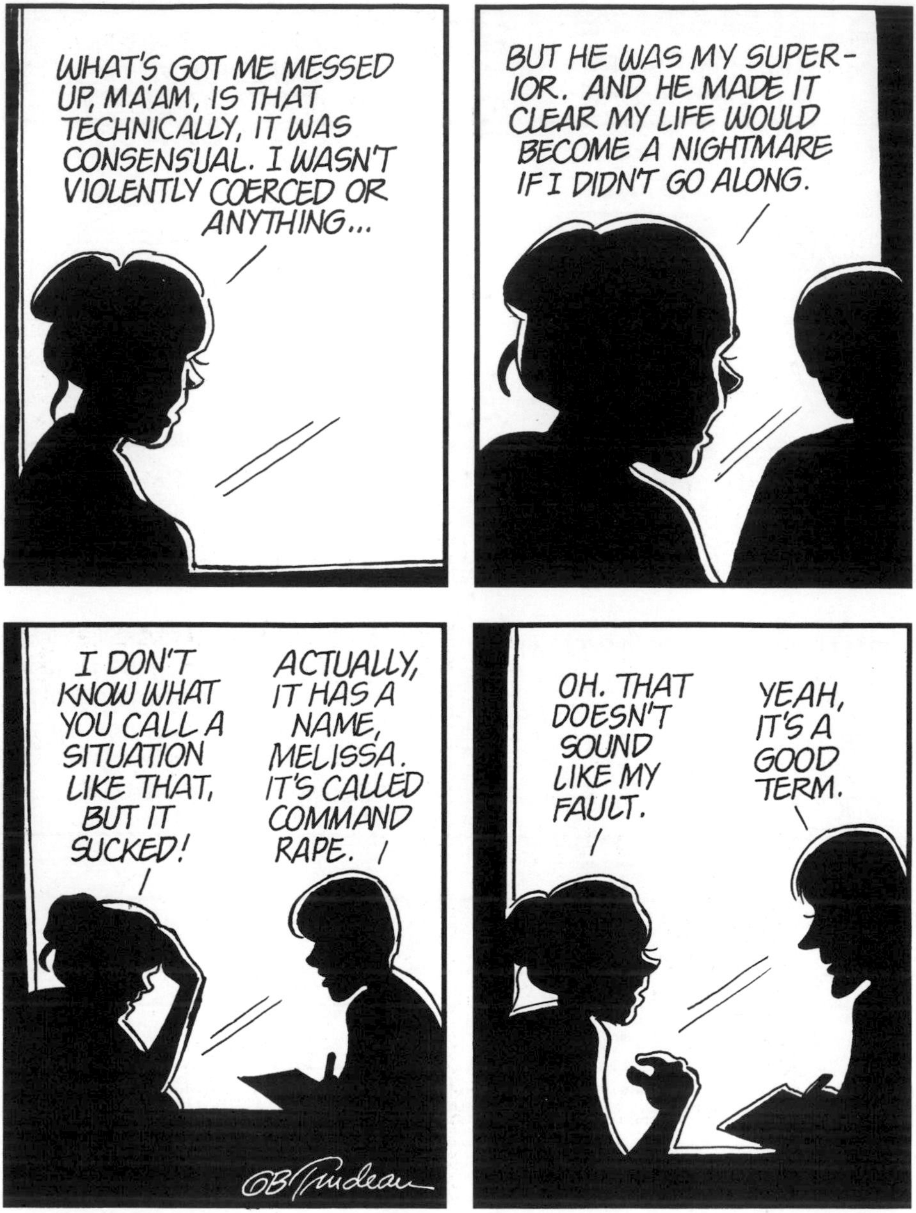
WHAT'S GOT ME MESSED UP, MA'AM, IS THAT TECHNICALLY, IT WAS CONSENSUAL. I WASN'T VIOLENTLY COERCED OR ANYTHING...
BUT HE WAS MY SUPERIOR. AND HE MADE IT CLEAR MY LIFE WOULD BECOME A NIGHTMARE IF I DIDN'T GO ALONG.
I DON'T KNOW WHAT YOU CALL A SITUATION LIKE THAT, BUT IT SUCKED!
ACTUALLY, IT HAS A NAME, MELISSA. IT'S CALLED COMMAND RAPE.
GB Trudeau
OH. THAT DOESN'T SOUND LIKE MY FAULT.
YEAH, IT'S A GOOD TERM.

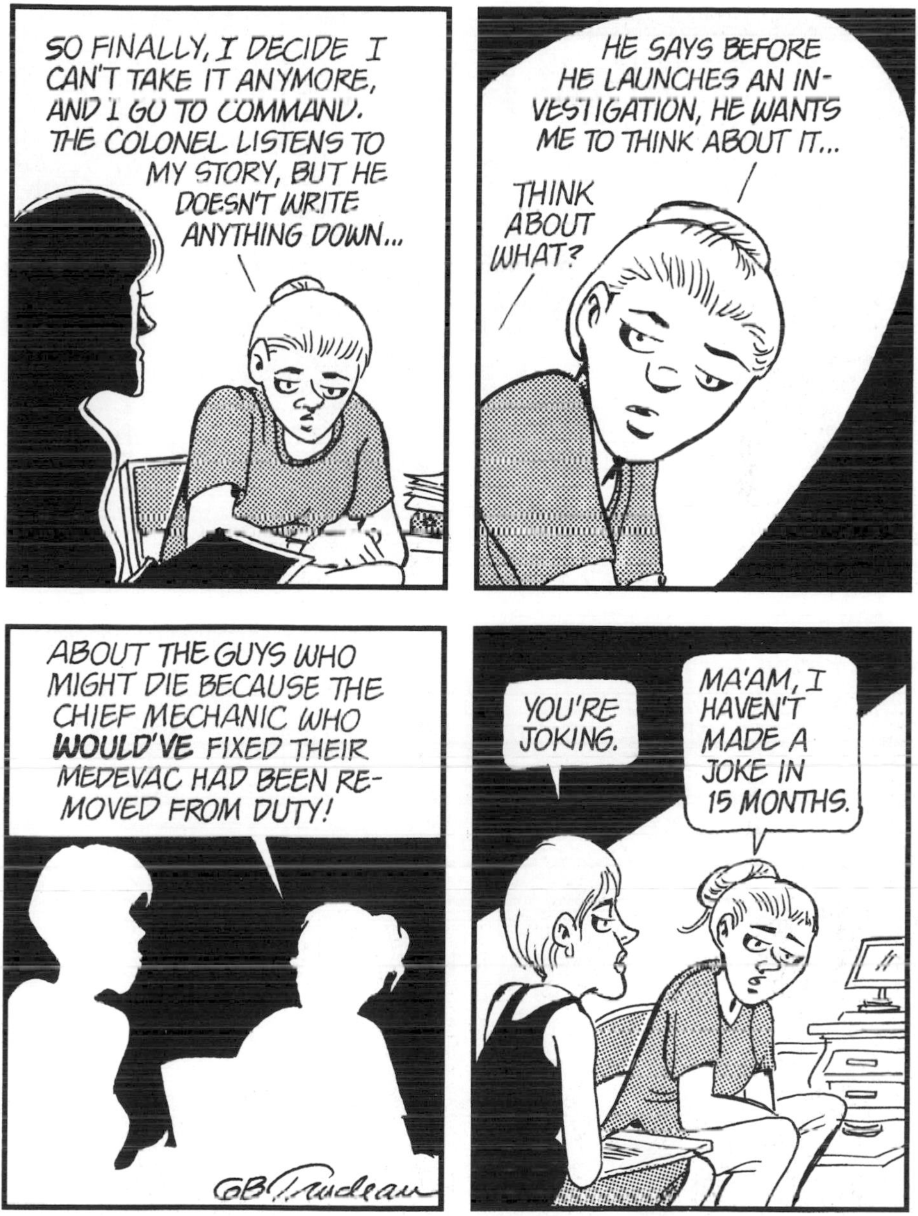
SO FINALLY, I DECIDE I CAN'T TAKE IT ANYMORE, AND I GO TO COMMAND. THE COLONEL LISTENS TO MY STORY, BUT HE DOESN'T WRITE ANYTHING DOWN...
HE SAYS BEFORE HE LAUNCHES AN INVESTIGATION, HE WANTS ME TO THINK ABOUT IT...
THINK ABOUT WHAT?
ABOUT THE GUYS WHO MIGHT DIE BECAUSE THE CHIEF MECHANIC WHO **WOULD'VE** FIXED THEIR MEDEVAC HAD BEEN REMOVED FROM DUTY!
YOU'RE JOKING.
MA'AM, I HAVEN'T MADE A JOKE IN 15 MONTHS.
GB Trudeau

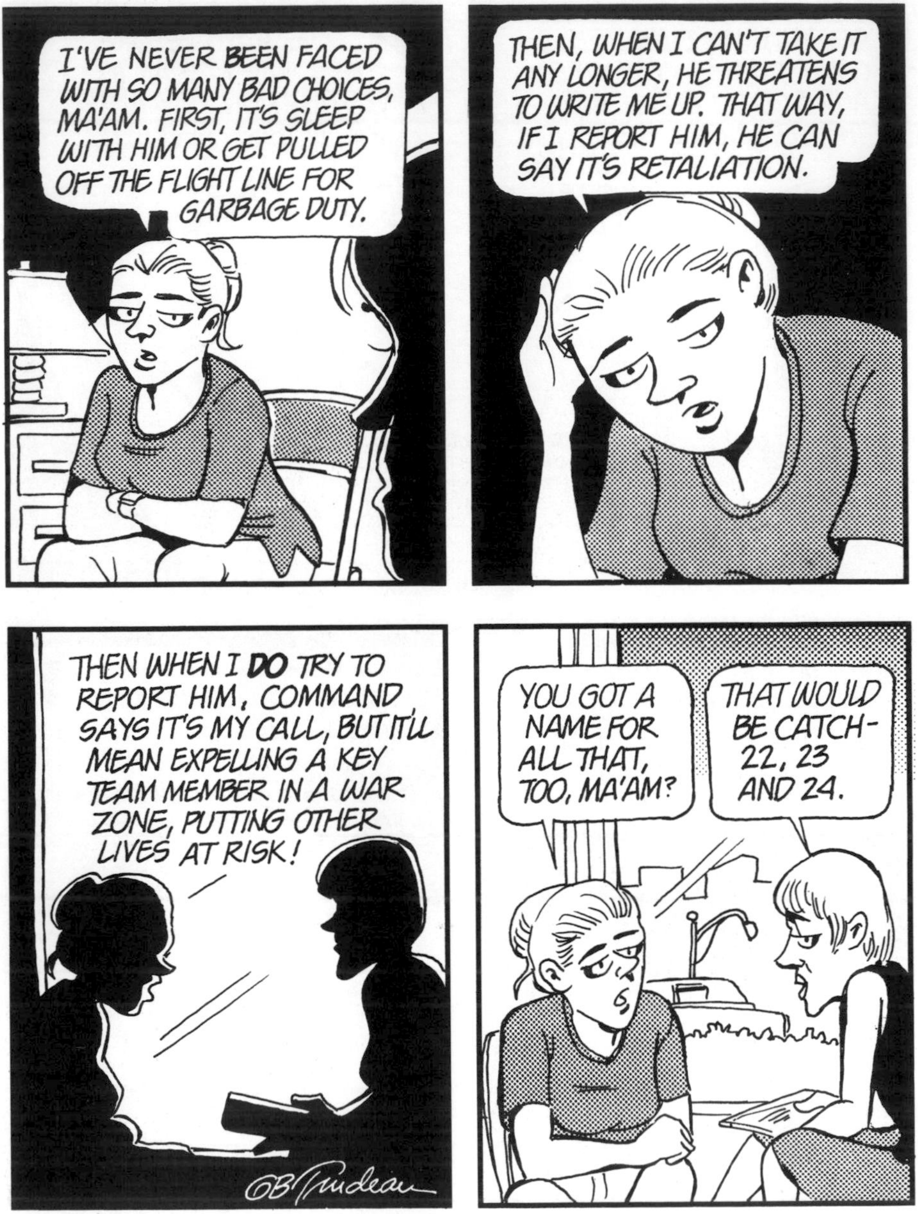
I'VE NEVER BEEN FACED WITH SO MANY BAD CHOICES, MA'AM. FIRST, IT'S SLEEP WITH HIM OR GET PULLED OFF THE FLIGHT LINE FOR GARBAGE DUTY.
THEN, WHEN I CAN'T TAKE IT ANY LONGER, HE THREATENS TO WRITE ME UP. THAT WAY, IF I REPORT HIM, HE CAN SAY IT'S RETALIATION.
THEN WHEN I **DO** TRY TO REPORT HIM, COMMAND SAYS IT'S MY CALL, BUT IT'LL MEAN EXPELLING A KEY TEAM MEMBER IN A WAR ZONE, PUTTING OTHER LIVES AT RISK!
©B. Trudeau
YOU GOT A NAME FOR ALL THAT, TOO, MA'AM?
THAT WOULD BE CATCH-22, 23 AND 24.

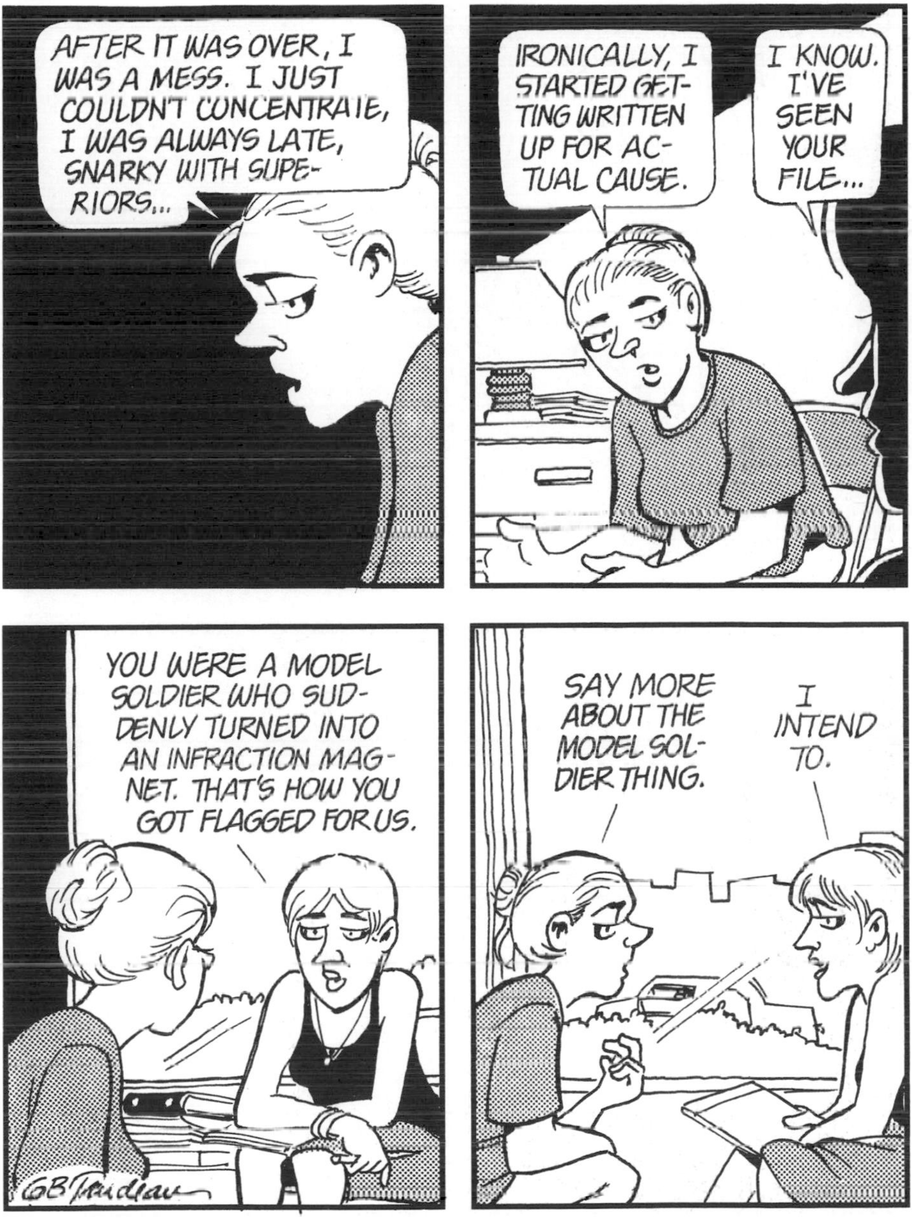
AFTER IT WAS OVER, I WAS A MESS. I JUST COULDN'T CONCENTRATE, I WAS ALWAYS LATE, SNARKY WITH SUPE-RIORS...
IRONICALLY, I STARTED GET-TING WRITTEN UP FOR AC-TUAL CAUSE.
I KNOW. I'VE SEEN YOUR FILE...
YOU WERE A MODEL SOLDIER WHO SUD-DENLY TURNED INTO AN INFRACTION MAG-NET. THAT'S HOW YOU GOT FLAGGED FOR US.
GB Trudeau
SAY MORE ABOUT THE MODEL SOL-DIER THING.
I INTEND TO.

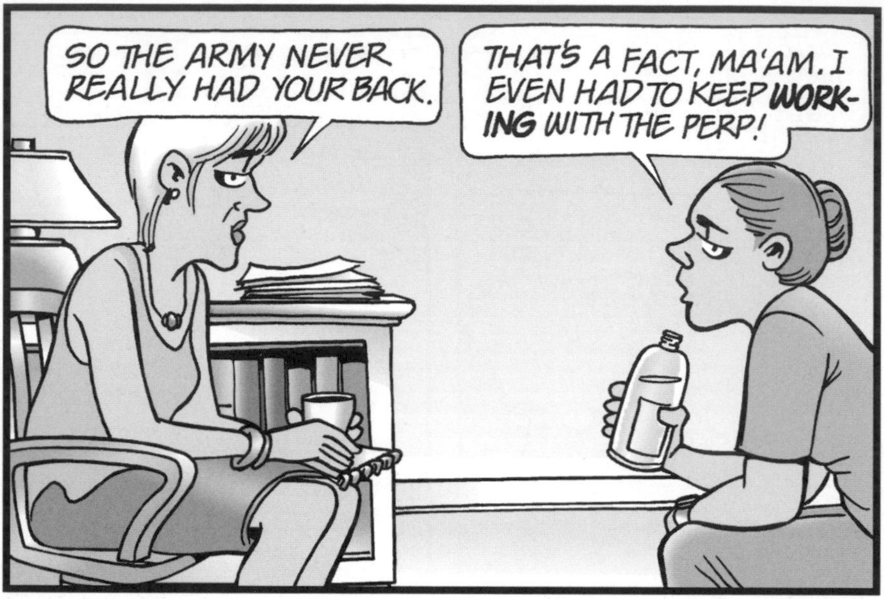
SO THE ARMY NEVER REALLY HAD YOUR BACK.
THAT'S A FACT, MA'AM. I EVEN HAD TO KEEP **WORKING** WITH THE PERP!

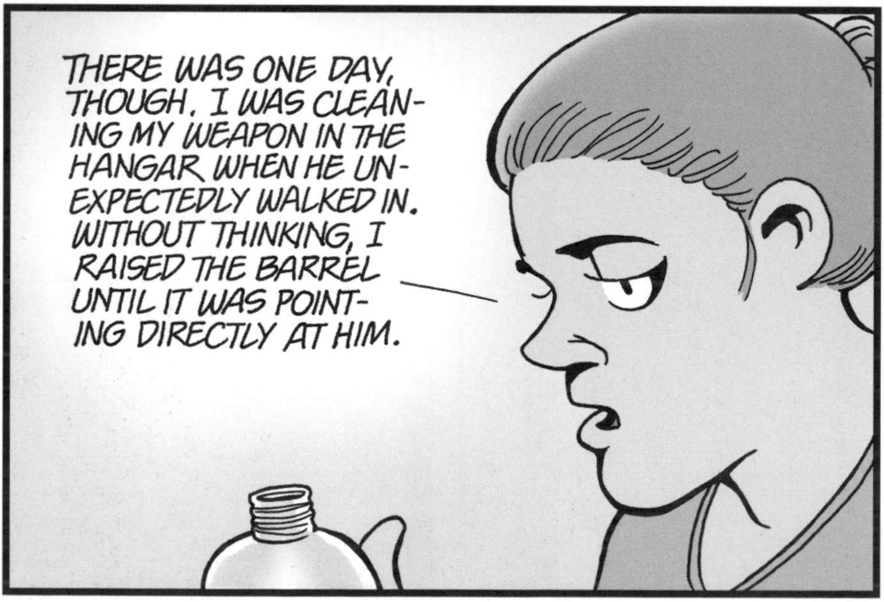
THERE WAS ONE DAY, THOUGH. I WAS CLEANING MY WEAPON IN THE HANGAR WHEN HE UNEXPECTEDLY WALKED IN. WITHOUT THINKING, I RAISED THE BARREL UNTIL IT WAS POINTING DIRECTLY AT HIM.

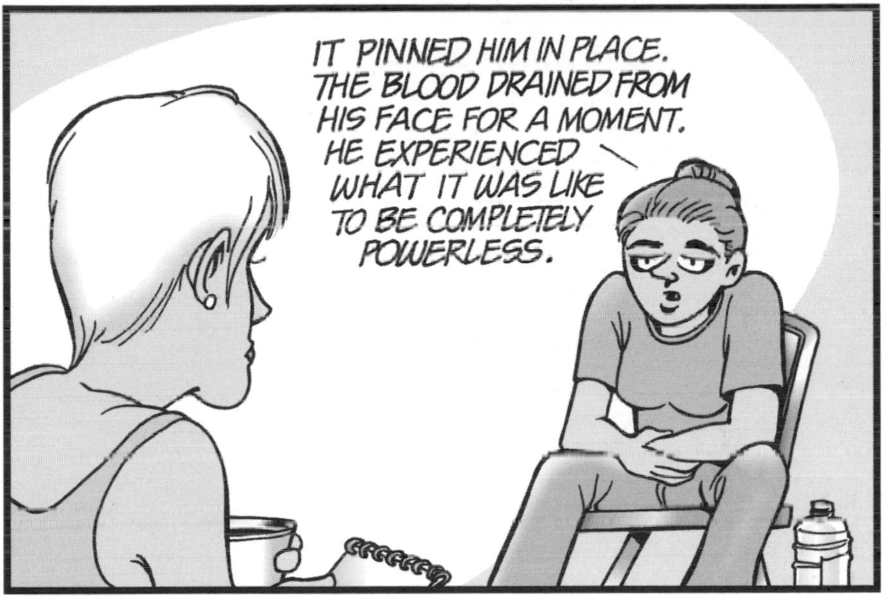
IT PINNED HIM IN PLACE. THE BLOOD DRAINED FROM HIS FACE FOR A MOMENT. HE EXPERIENCED WHAT IT WAS LIKE TO BE COMPLETELY POWERLESS.

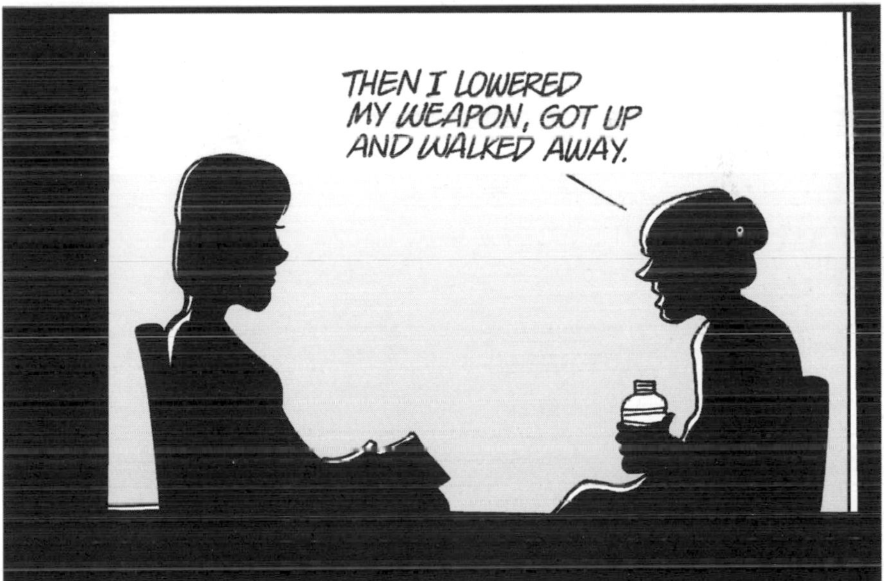
THEN I LOWERED MY WEAPON, GOT UP AND WALKED AWAY.

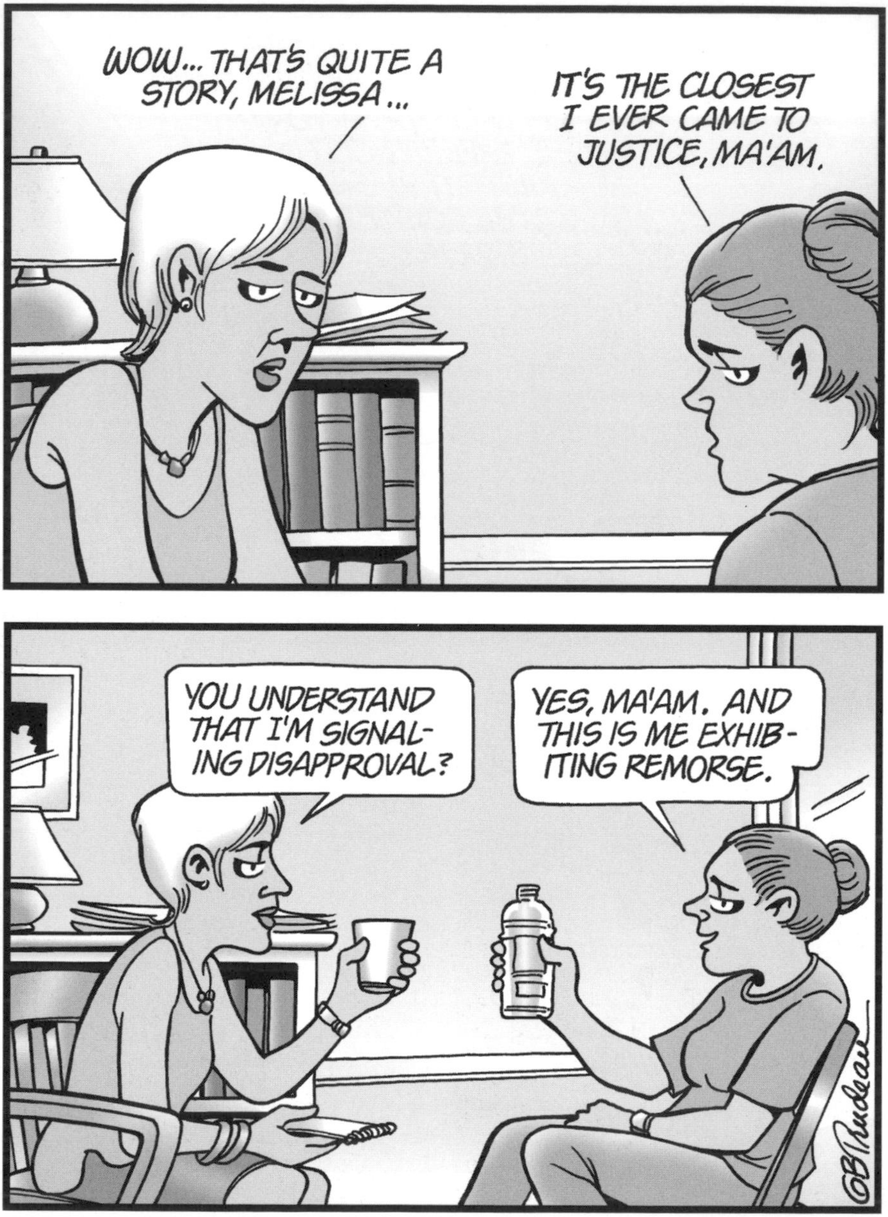
WOW... THAT'S QUITE A STORY, MELISSA...
IT'S THE CLOSEST I EVER CAME TO JUSTICE, MA'AM.
YOU UNDERSTAND THAT I'M SIGNALING DISAPPROVAL?
YES, MA'AM. AND THIS IS ME EXHIBITING REMORSE.
©B Trudeau

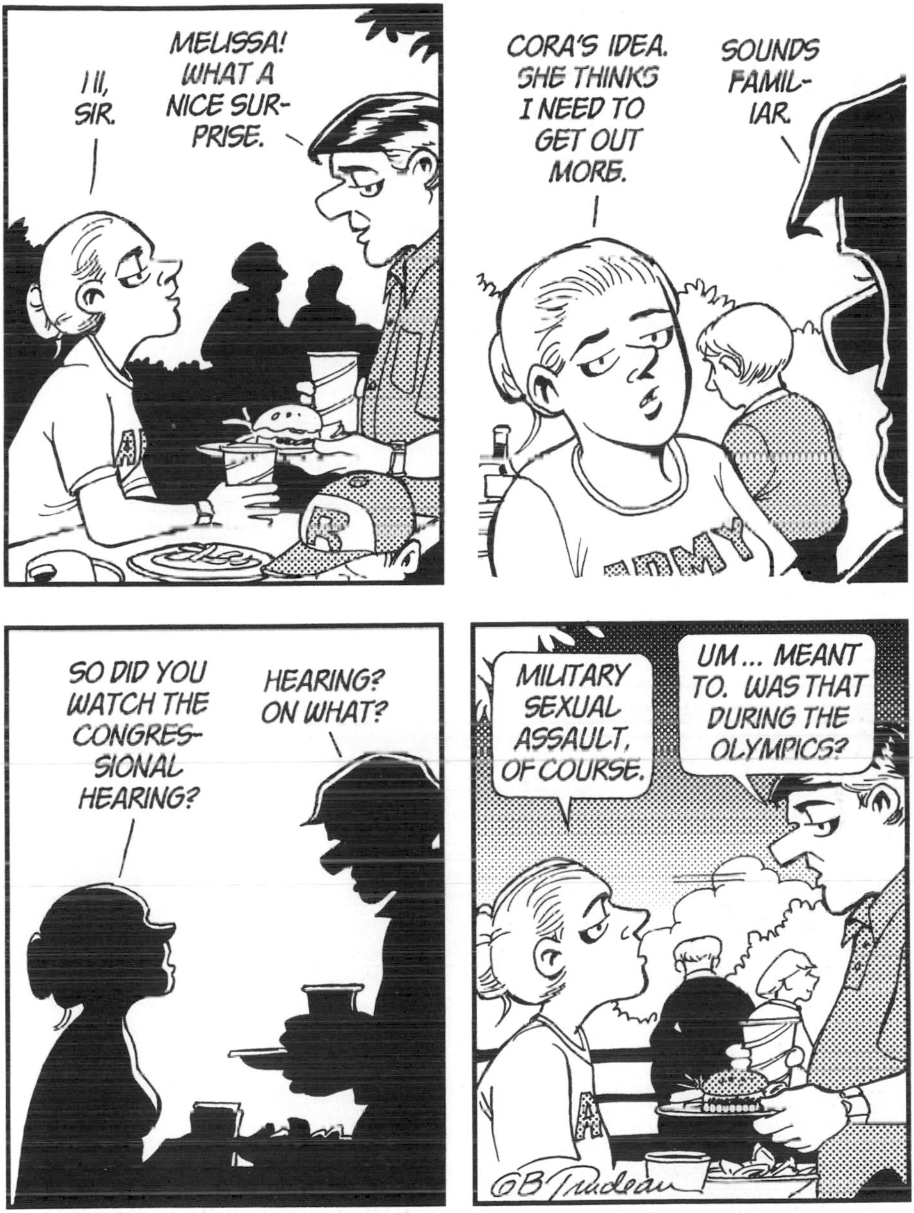
HI, SIR.
MELISSA! WHAT A NICE SURPRISE.
CORA'S IDEA. SHE THINKS I NEED TO GET OUT MORE.
SOUNDS FAMILIAR.
ARMY
SO DID YOU WATCH THE CONGRESSIONAL HEARING?
HEARING? ON WHAT?
MILITARY SEXUAL ASSAULT, OF COURSE.
UM ... MEANT TO. WAS THAT DURING THE OLYMPICS?
©B Trudeau

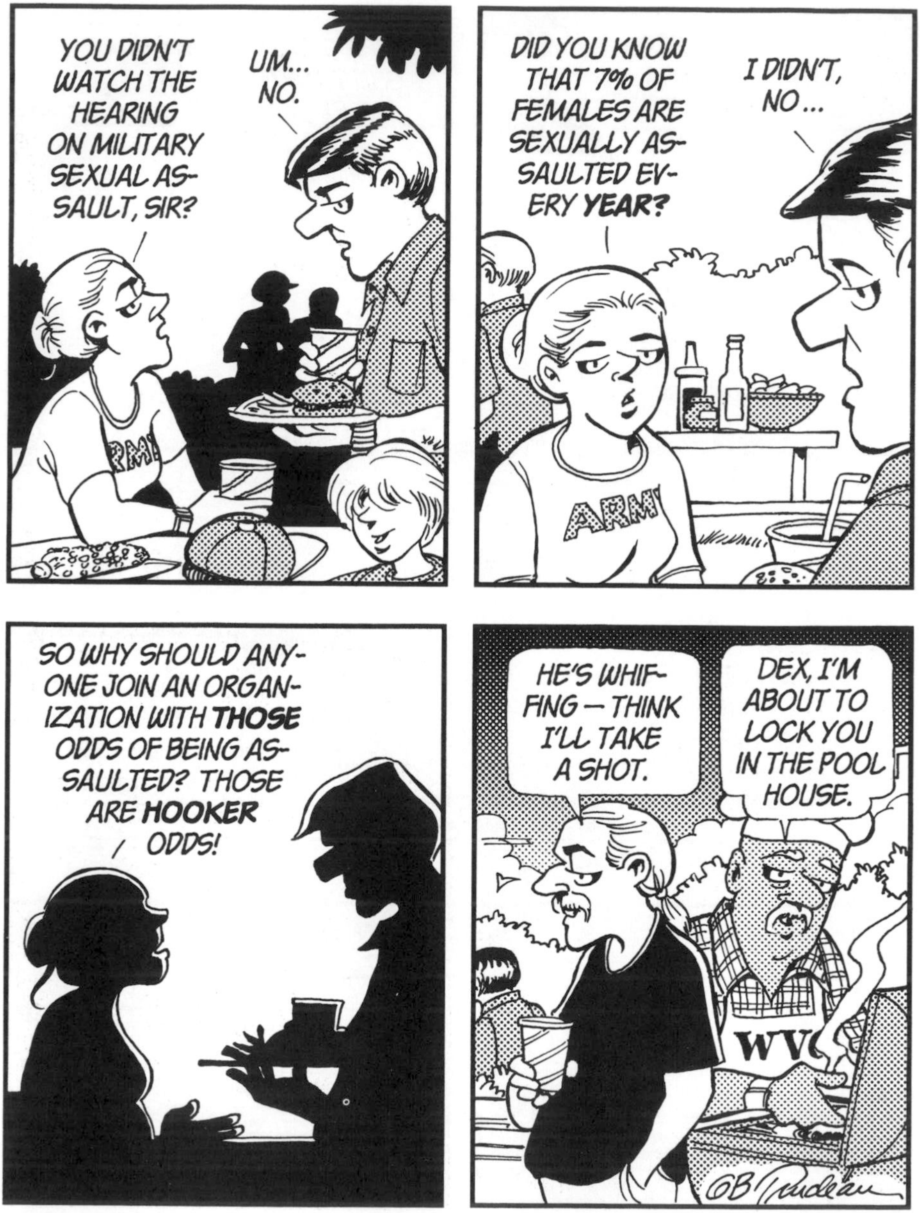
YOU DIDN'T WATCH THE HEARING ON MILITARY SEXUAL AS-SAULT, SIR?
UM... NO.
DID YOU KNOW THAT 7% OF FEMALES ARE SEXUALLY AS-SAULTED EV-ERY YEAR?
I DIDN'T, NO...
SO WHY SHOULD ANY-ONE JOIN AN ORGAN-IZATION WITH THOSE ODDS OF BEING AS-SAULTED? THOSE ARE HOOKER ODDS!
HE'S WHIF-FING — THINK I'LL TAKE A SHOT.
DEX, I'M ABOUT TO LOCK YOU IN THE POOL HOUSE.
ARMY
ARMY
WVC
GB Trudeau

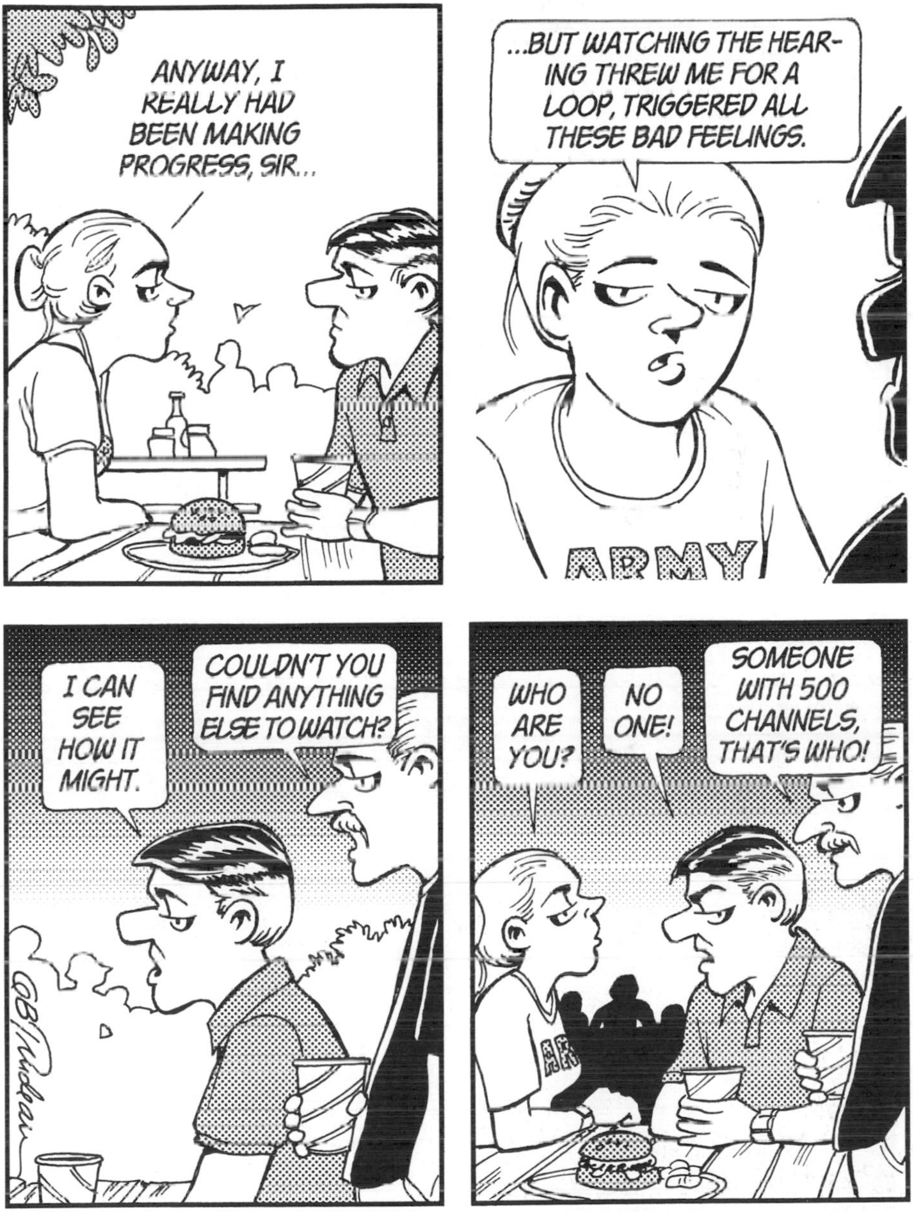
ANYWAY, I REALLY HAD BEEN MAKING PROGRESS, SIR...
...BUT WATCHING THE HEAR-ING THREW ME FOR A LOOP, TRIGGERED ALL THESE BAD FEELINGS.
ARMY
I CAN SEE HOW IT MIGHT.
COULDN'T YOU FIND ANYTHING ELSE TO WATCH?
WHO ARE YOU?
NO ONE!
SOMEONE WITH 500 CHANNELS, THAT'S WHO!

GO ARMY
HEY THERE, MELISSA! CORA'S RUNNING A LITTLE LATE. SHOULD BE HERE ANY MINUTE.
HOPE SO, SIR. I'VE BEEN KIND OF A MESS LATELY...
MESS? YOU'RE NOT A MESS — YOU'RE A WOUNDED WARRIOR.

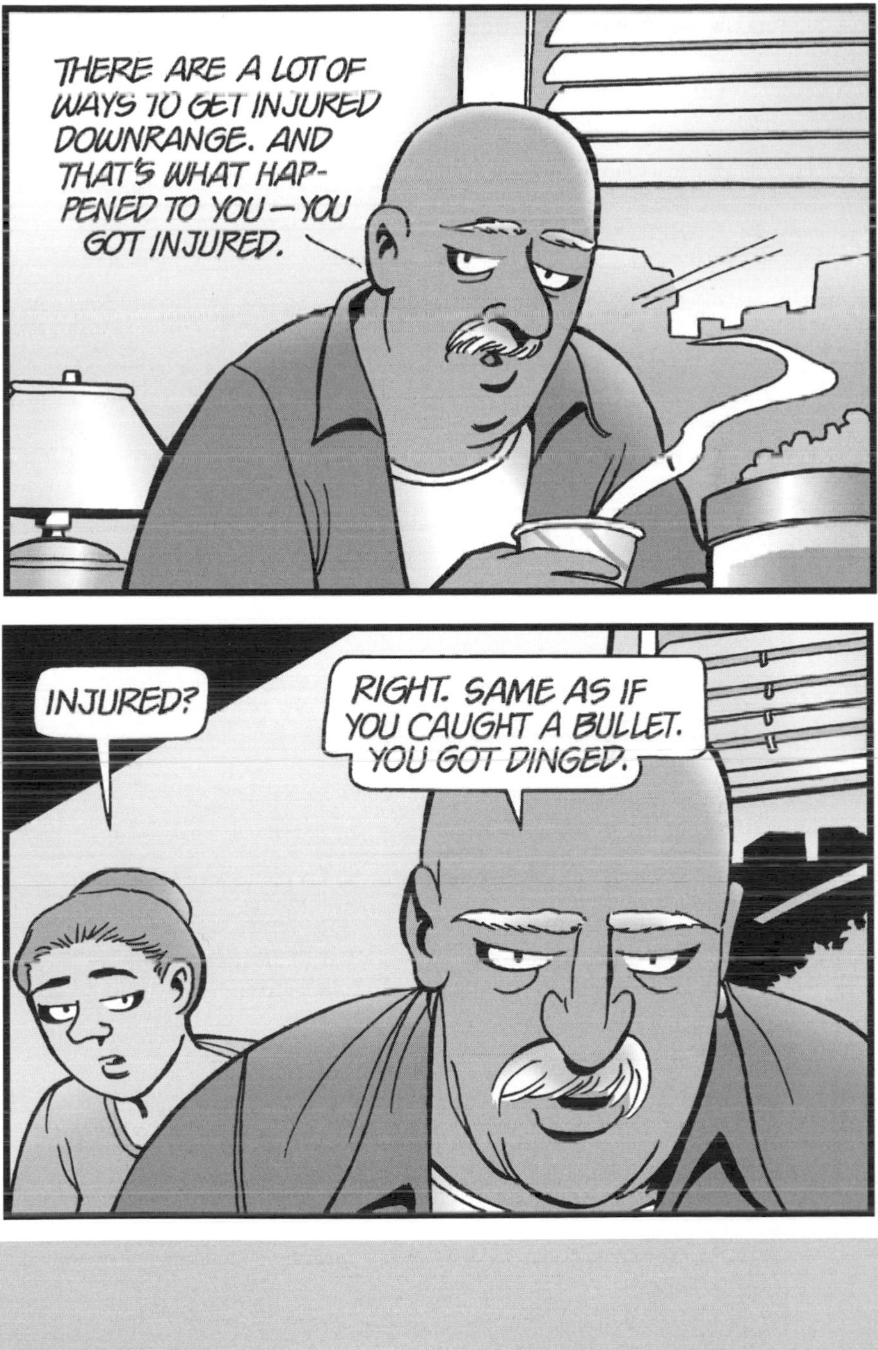
THERE ARE A LOT OF WAYS TO GET INJURED DOWNRANGE. AND THAT'S WHAT HAPPENED TO YOU—YOU GOT INJURED.
INJURED?
RIGHT. SAME AS IF YOU CAUGHT A BULLET. YOU GOT DINGED.

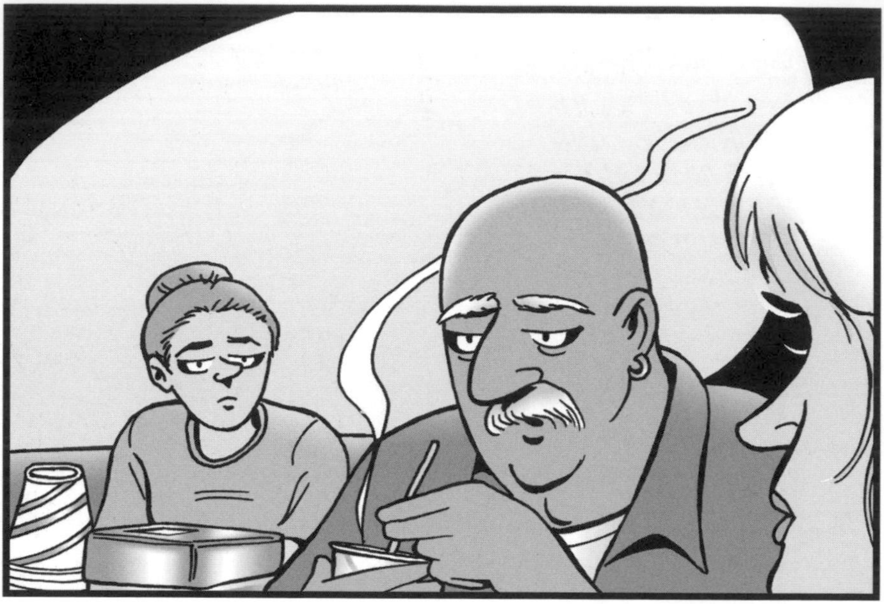

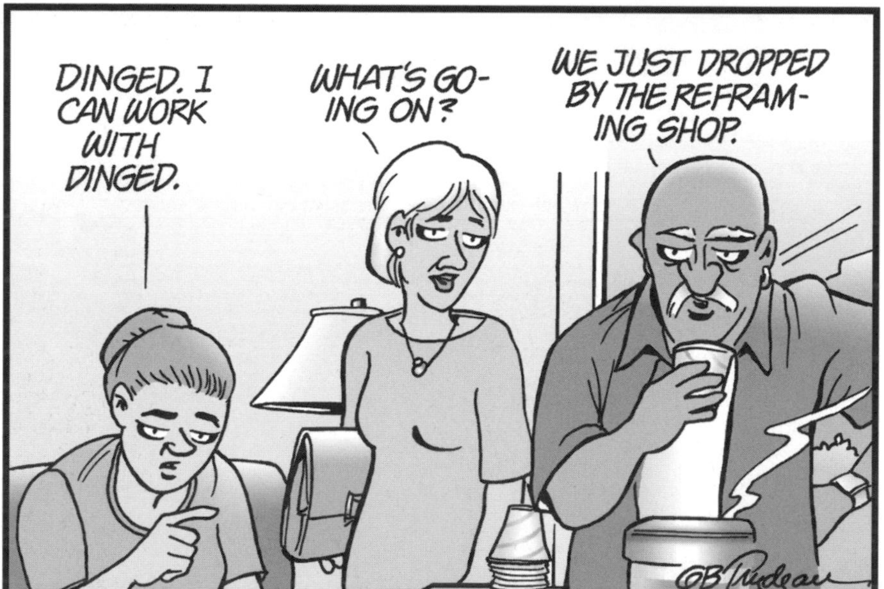
DINGED. I CAN WORK WITH DINGED.
WHAT'S GO-ING ON?
WE JUST DROPPED BY THE REFRAM-ING SHOP.
©B Trudeau

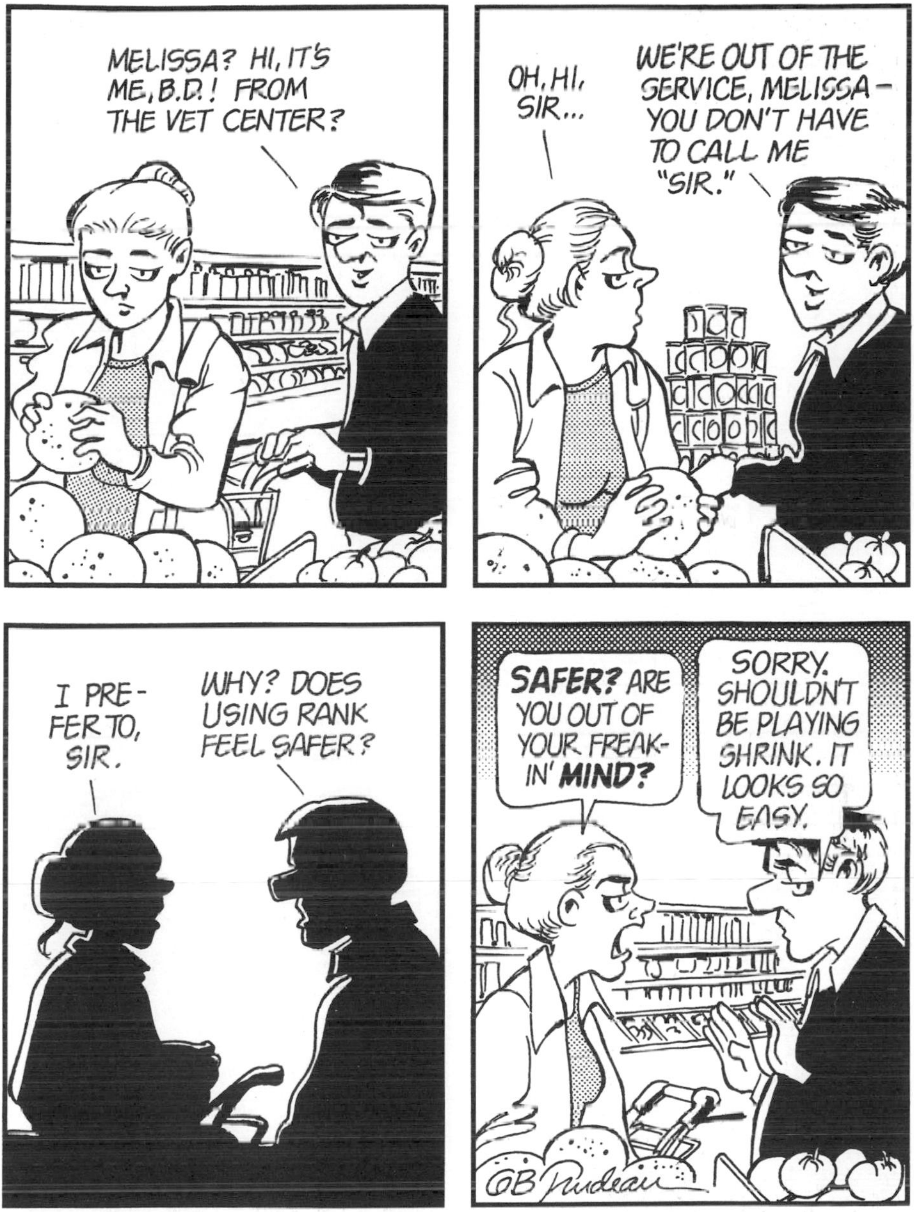
MELISSA? HI, IT'S ME, B.D.! FROM THE VET CENTER?
OH, HI, SIR...
WE'RE OUT OF THE SERVICE, MELISSA – YOU DON'T HAVE TO CALL ME "SIR."
I PRE-FER TO, SIR.
WHY? DOES USING RANK FEEL SAFER?
SAFER? ARE YOU OUT OF YOUR FREAK-IN' **MIND?**
SORRY. SHOULDN'T BE PLAYING SHRINK. IT LOOKS SO EASY.
©B Trudeau

QUITE A COINCIDENCE, ISN'T IT, SIR? BUMPING INTO YOU SHOPPING AT 2:00 A.M.?
NOT REALLY...
LOTS OF VETS SHOP AT THIS HOUR. CROWDED PLACES TEND TO FREAK US OUT.
SEE THAT BIG DUDE IN FROZEN FOOD? HE'S OIF, AND SO'S THAT GUY WALKING TOWARDS US IN THE BAKING PRODUCTS AISLE...
WELL, GREAT— I'M SURROUNDED.
OH... SORRY. YO, JASON! BACK OFF! TAKE AISLE 4!

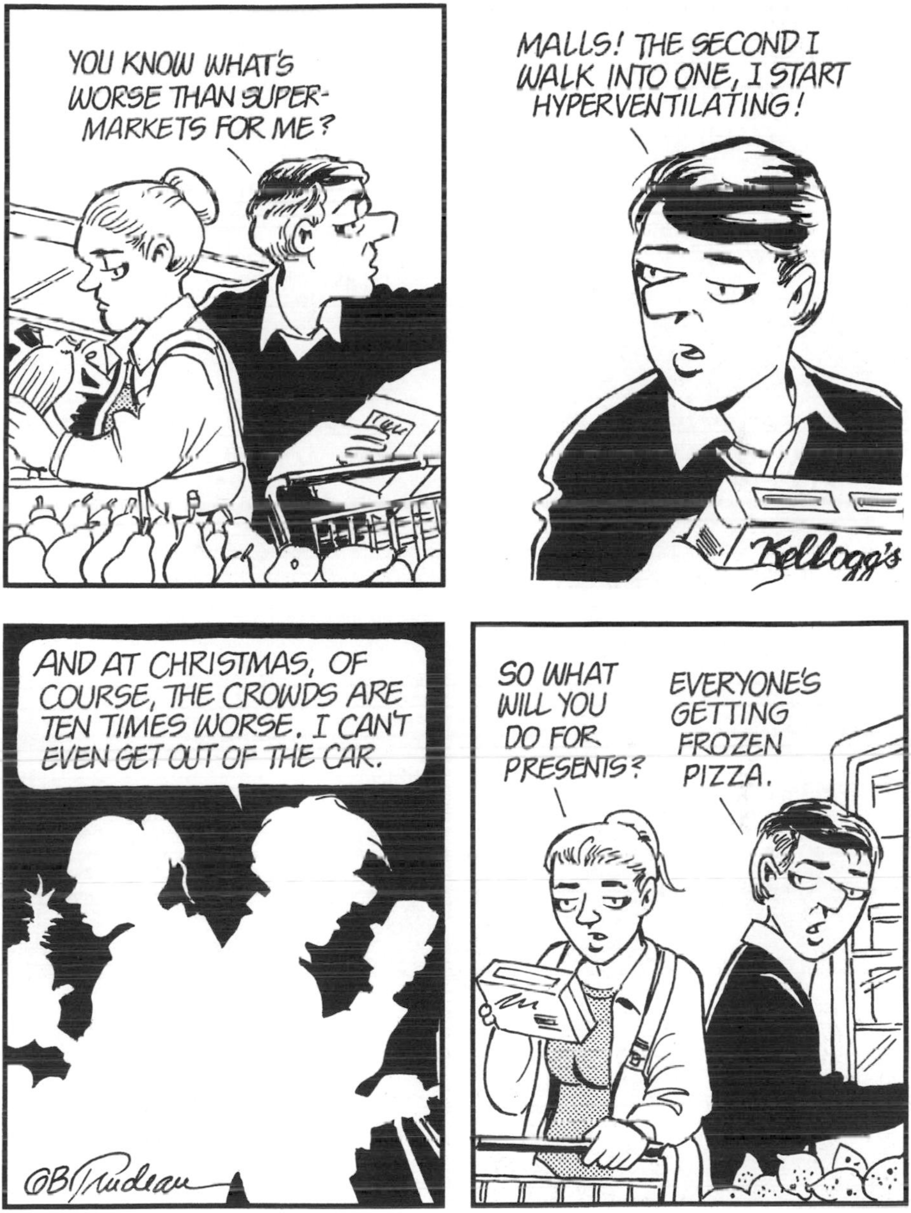
YOU KNOW WHAT'S WORSE THAN SUPER-MARKETS FOR ME?
MALLS! THE SECOND I WALK INTO ONE, I START HYPERVENTILATING!
Kellogg's
AND AT CHRISTMAS, OF COURSE, THE CROWDS ARE TEN TIMES WORSE. I CAN'T EVEN GET OUT OF THE CAR.
©B Trudeau
SO WHAT WILL YOU DO FOR PRESENTS?
EVERYONE'S GETTING FROZEN PIZZA.

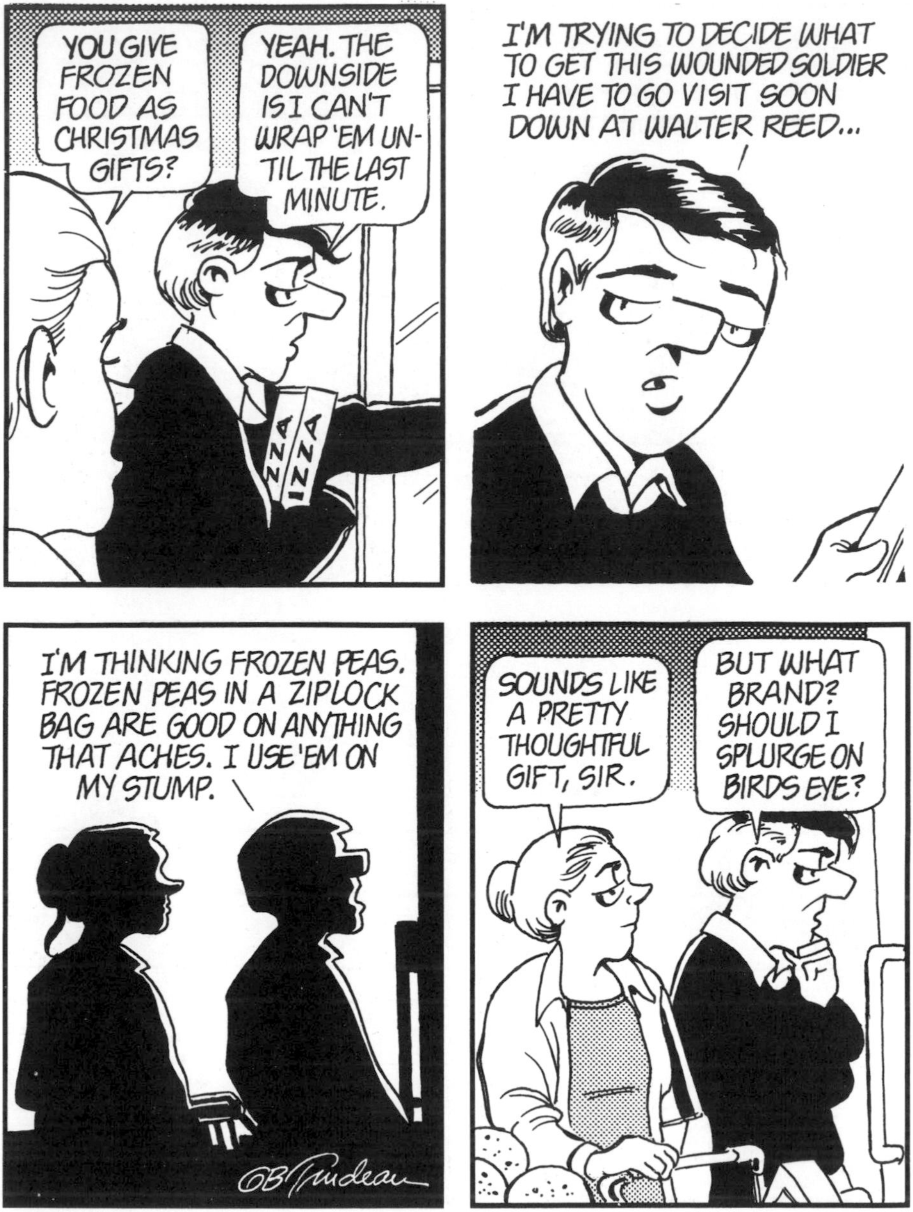
YOU GIVE FROZEN FOOD AS CHRISTMAS GIFTS?
YEAH. THE DOWNSIDE IS I CAN'T WRAP 'EM UN-TIL THE LAST MINUTE.
I'M TRYING TO DECIDE WHAT TO GET THIS WOUNDED SOLDIER I HAVE TO GO VISIT SOON DOWN AT WALTER REED...
I'M THINKING FROZEN PEAS. FROZEN PEAS IN A ZIPLOCK BAG ARE GOOD ON ANYTHING THAT ACHES. I USE 'EM ON MY STUMP.
SOUNDS LIKE A PRETTY THOUGHTFUL GIFT, SIR.
BUT WHAT BRAND? SHOULD I SPLURGE ON BIRDS EYE?
GBTrudeau

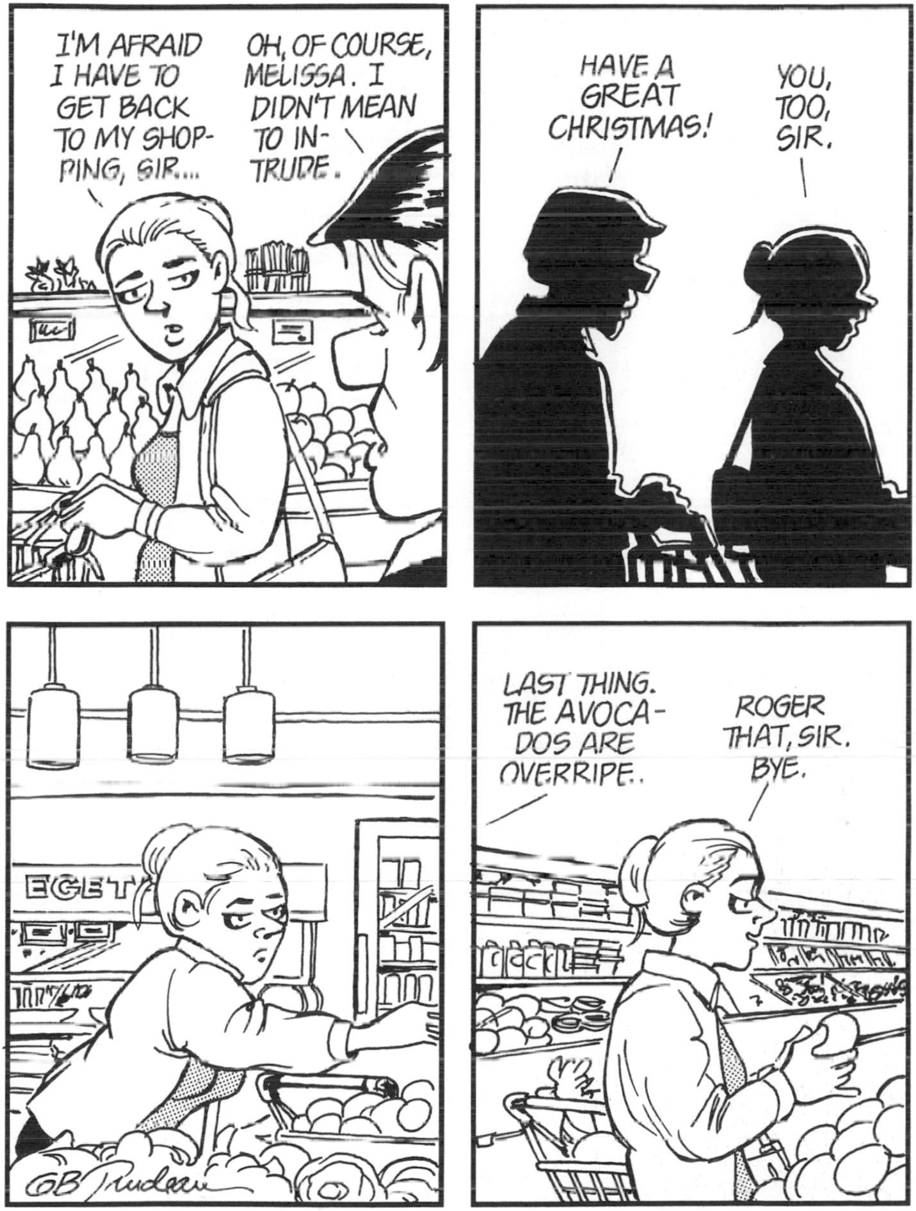
I'M AFRAID I HAVE TO GET BACK TO MY SHOP-PING, SIR...
OH, OF COURSE, MELISSA. I DIDN'T MEAN TO IN-TRUDE.
HAVE A GREAT CHRISTMAS!
YOU, TOO, SIR.
EGET
LAST THING. THE AVOCA-DOS ARE OVERRIPE..
ROGER THAT, SIR. BYE.
GB Trudeau

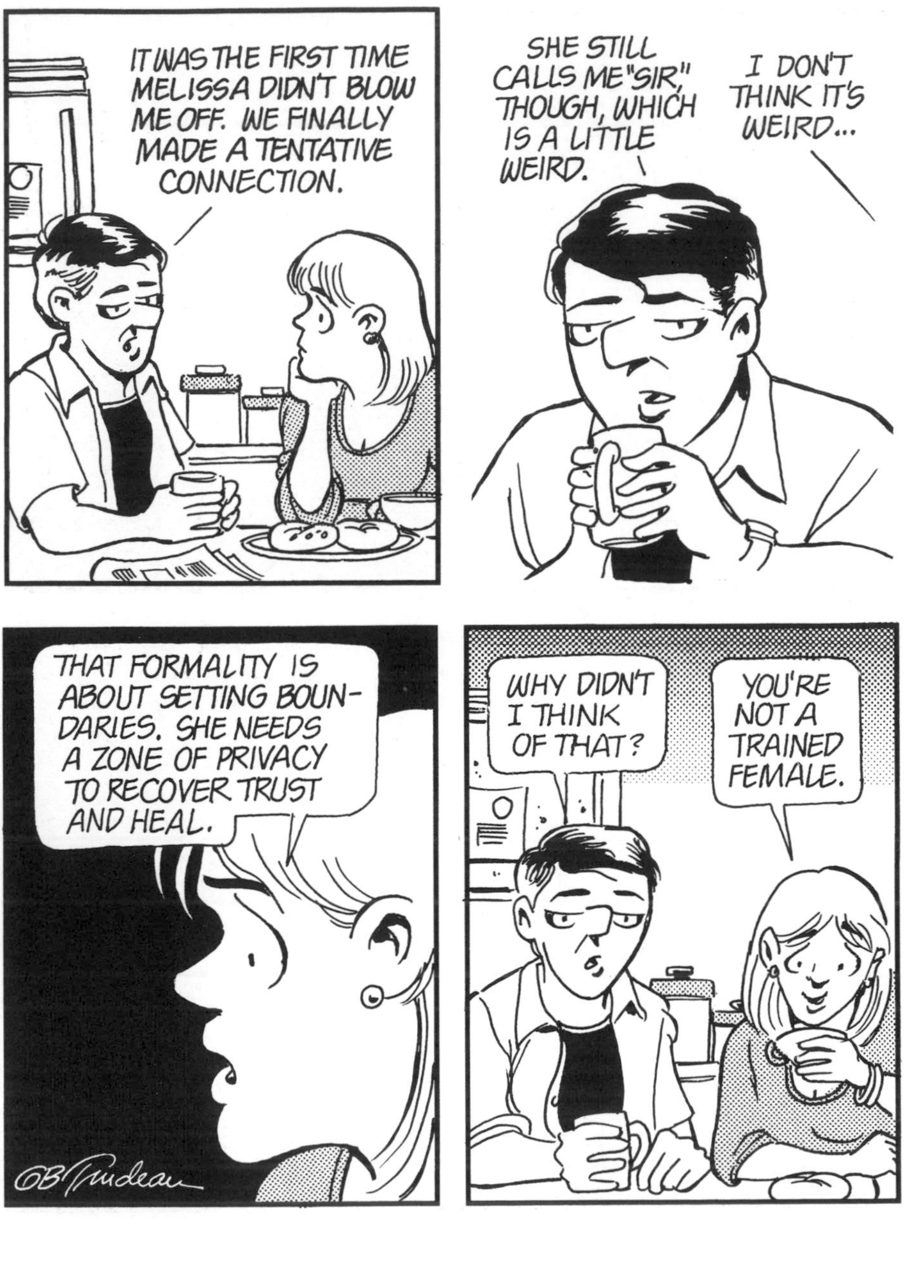
IT WAS THE FIRST TIME MELISSA DIDN'T BLOW ME OFF. WE FINALLY MADE A TENTATIVE CONNECTION.
SHE STILL CALLS ME "SIR," THOUGH, WHICH IS A LITTLE WEIRD.
I DON'T THINK IT'S WEIRD...
THAT FORMALITY IS ABOUT SETTING BOUNDARIES. SHE NEEDS A ZONE OF PRIVACY TO RECOVER TRUST AND HEAL.
WHY DIDN'T I THINK OF THAT?
YOU'RE NOT A TRAINED FEMALE.
GB Trudeau

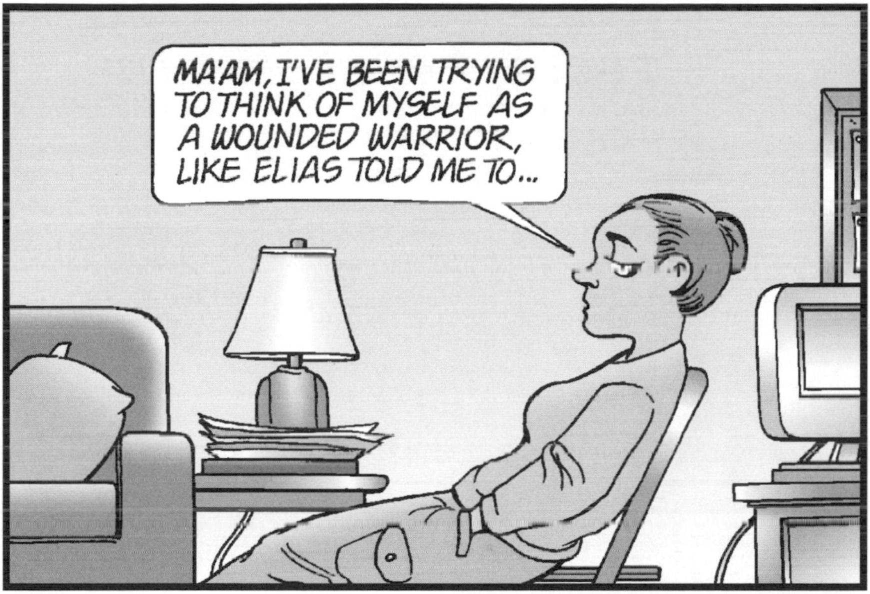
MA'AM, I'VE BEEN TRYING TO THINK OF MYSELF AS A WOUNDED WARRIOR, LIKE ELIAS TOLD ME TO...

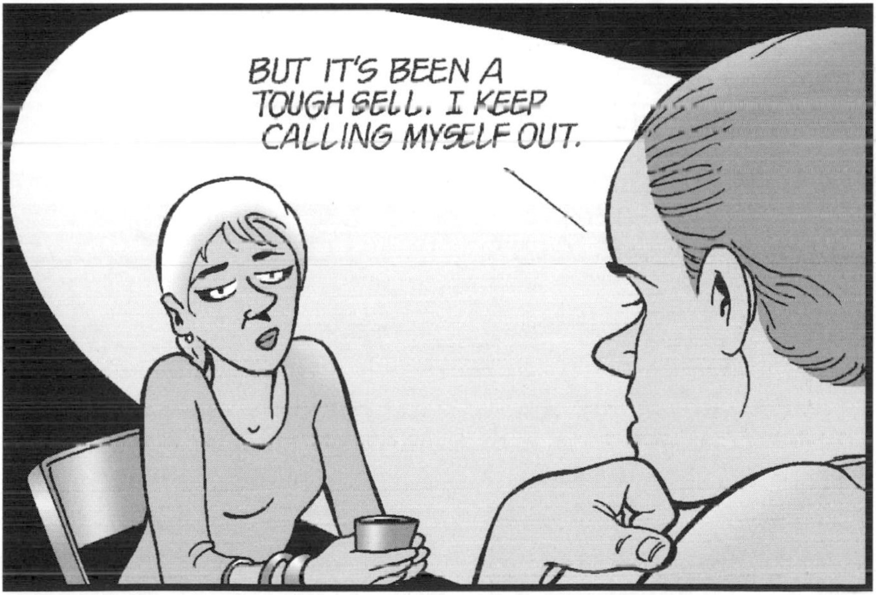
BUT IT'S BEEN A TOUGH SELL. I KEEP CALLING MYSELF OUT.

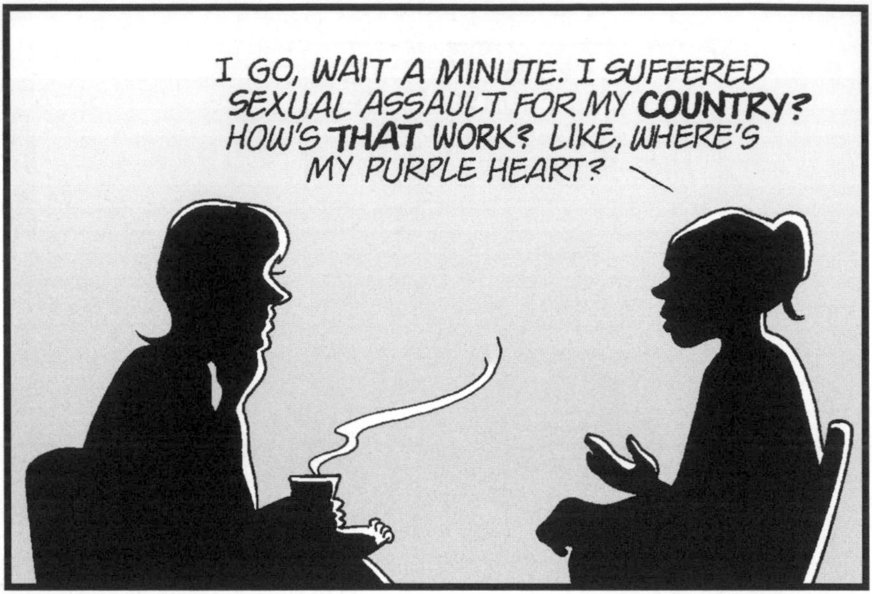
I GO, WAIT A MINUTE. I SUFFERED SEXUAL ASSAULT FOR MY **COUNTRY**? HOW'S **THAT** WORK? LIKE, WHERE'S MY PURPLE HEART?

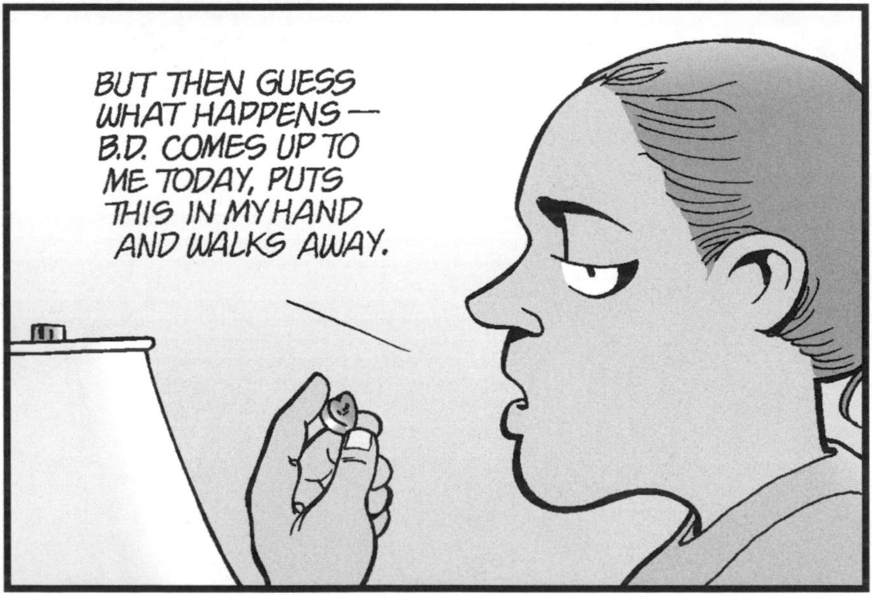
BUT THEN GUESS WHAT HAPPENS— B.D. COMES UP TO ME TODAY, PUTS THIS IN MY HAND AND WALKS AWAY.

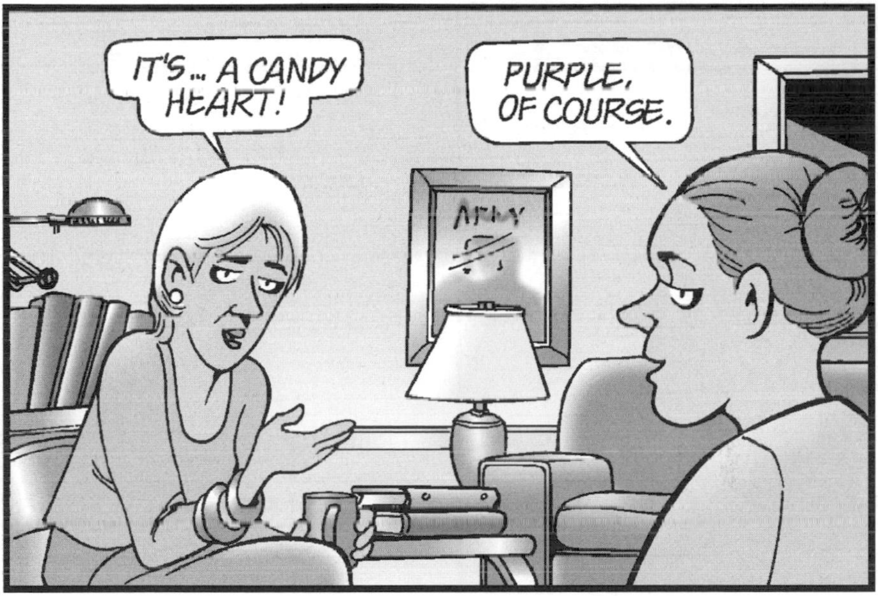
IT'S... A CANDY HEART!
PURPLE, OF COURSE.

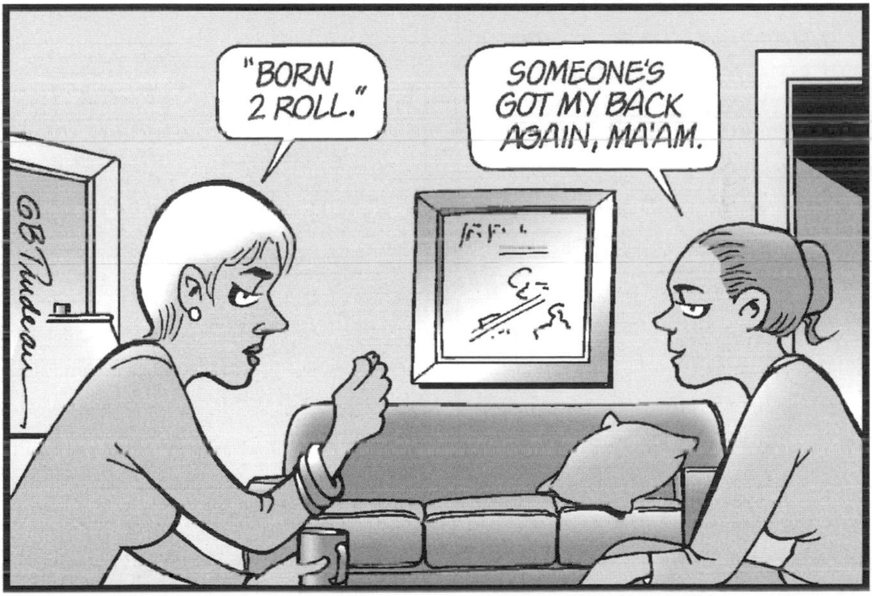
"BORN 2 ROLL."
SOMEONE'S GOT MY BACK AGAIN, MA'AM.
GB Trudeau

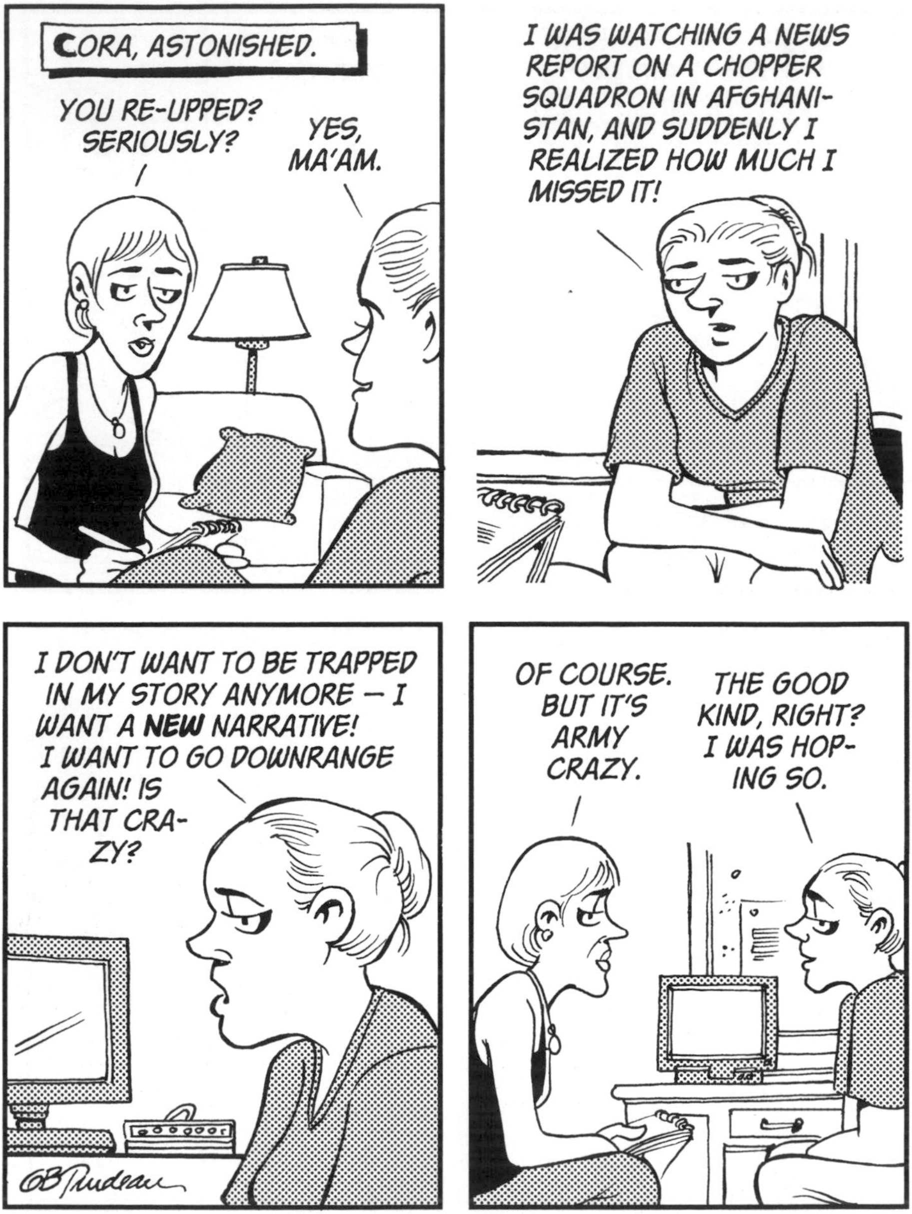
CORA, ASTONISHED.
YOU RE-UPPED? SERIOUSLY?
YES, MA'AM.
I WAS WATCHING A NEWS REPORT ON A CHOPPER SQUADRON IN AFGHANI-STAN, AND SUDDENLY I REALIZED HOW MUCH I MISSED IT!
I DON'T WANT TO BE TRAPPED IN MY STORY ANYMORE — I WANT A **NEW** NARRATIVE! I WANT TO GO DOWNRANGE AGAIN! IS THAT CRA-ZY?
OF COURSE. BUT IT'S ARMY CRAZY.
THE GOOD KIND, RIGHT? I WAS HOP-ING SO.
GBTrudeau

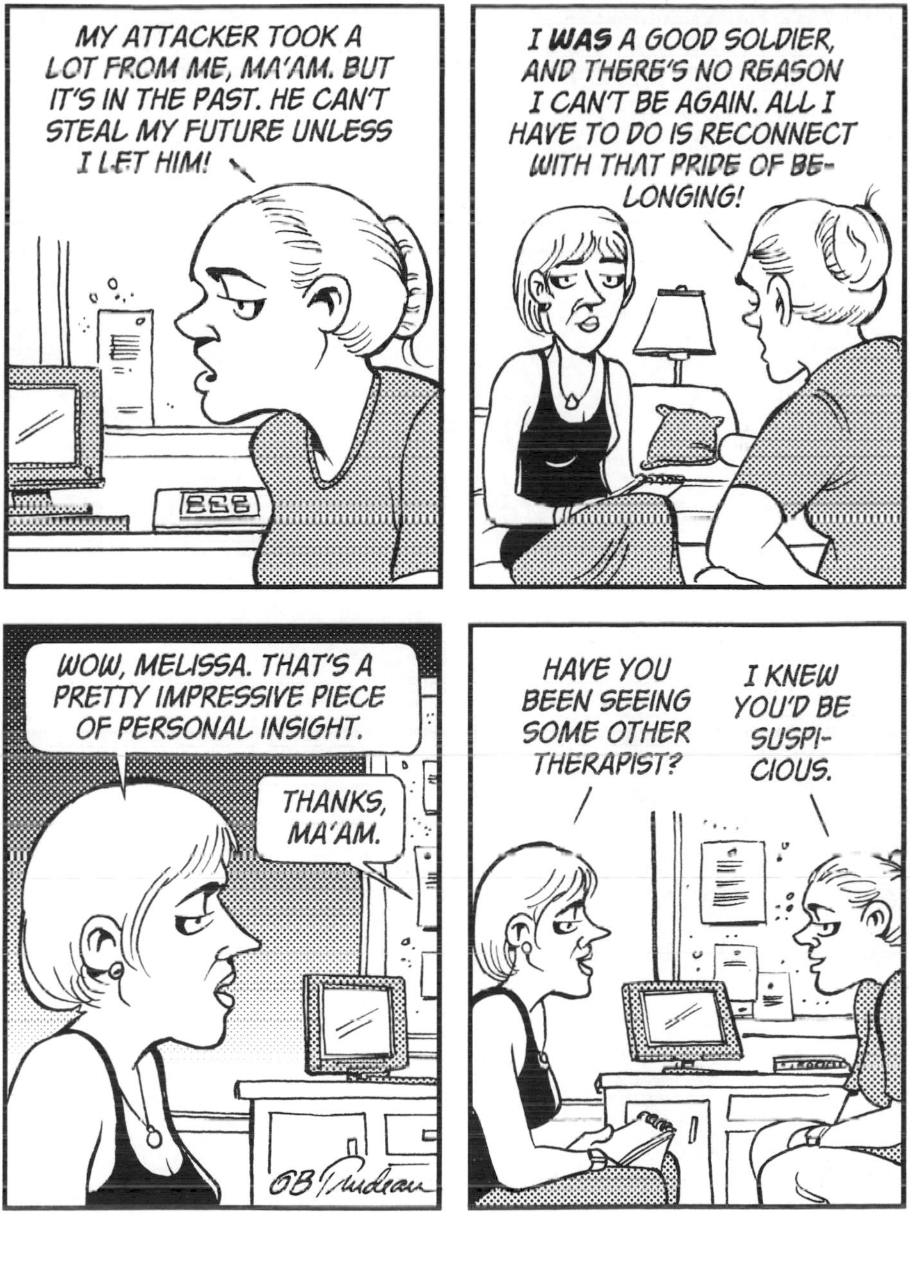
MY ATTACKER TOOK A LOT FROM ME, MA'AM. BUT IT'S IN THE PAST. HE CAN'T STEAL MY FUTURE UNLESS I LET HIM!
I *WAS* A GOOD SOLDIER, AND THERE'S NO REASON I CAN'T BE AGAIN. ALL I HAVE TO DO IS RECONNECT WITH THAT PRIDE OF BE-LONGING!
WOW, MELISSA. THAT'S A PRETTY IMPRESSIVE PIECE OF PERSONAL INSIGHT.
THANKS, MA'AM.
GB Trudeau
HAVE YOU BEEN SEEING SOME OTHER THERAPIST?
I KNEW YOU'D BE SUSPI-CIOUS.

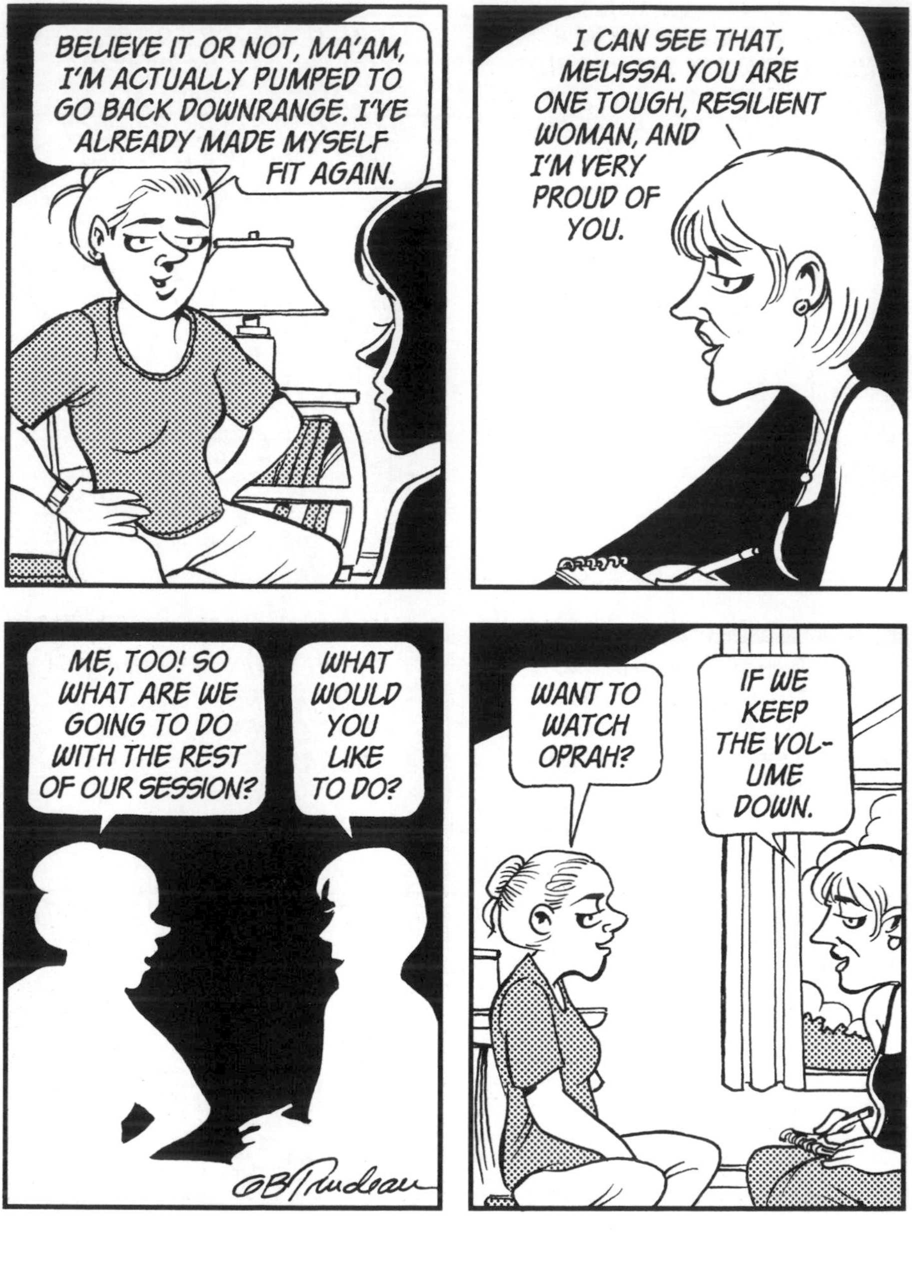
BELIEVE IT OR NOT, MA'AM, I'M ACTUALLY PUMPED TO GO BACK DOWNRANGE. I'VE ALREADY MADE MYSELF FIT AGAIN.
I CAN SEE THAT, MELISSA. YOU ARE ONE TOUGH, RESILIENT WOMAN, AND I'M VERY PROUD OF YOU.
ME, TOO! SO WHAT ARE WE GOING TO DO WITH THE REST OF OUR SESSION?
WHAT WOULD YOU LIKE TO DO?
WANT TO WATCH OPRAH?
IF WE KEEP THE VOL-UME DOWN.
©B Trudeau

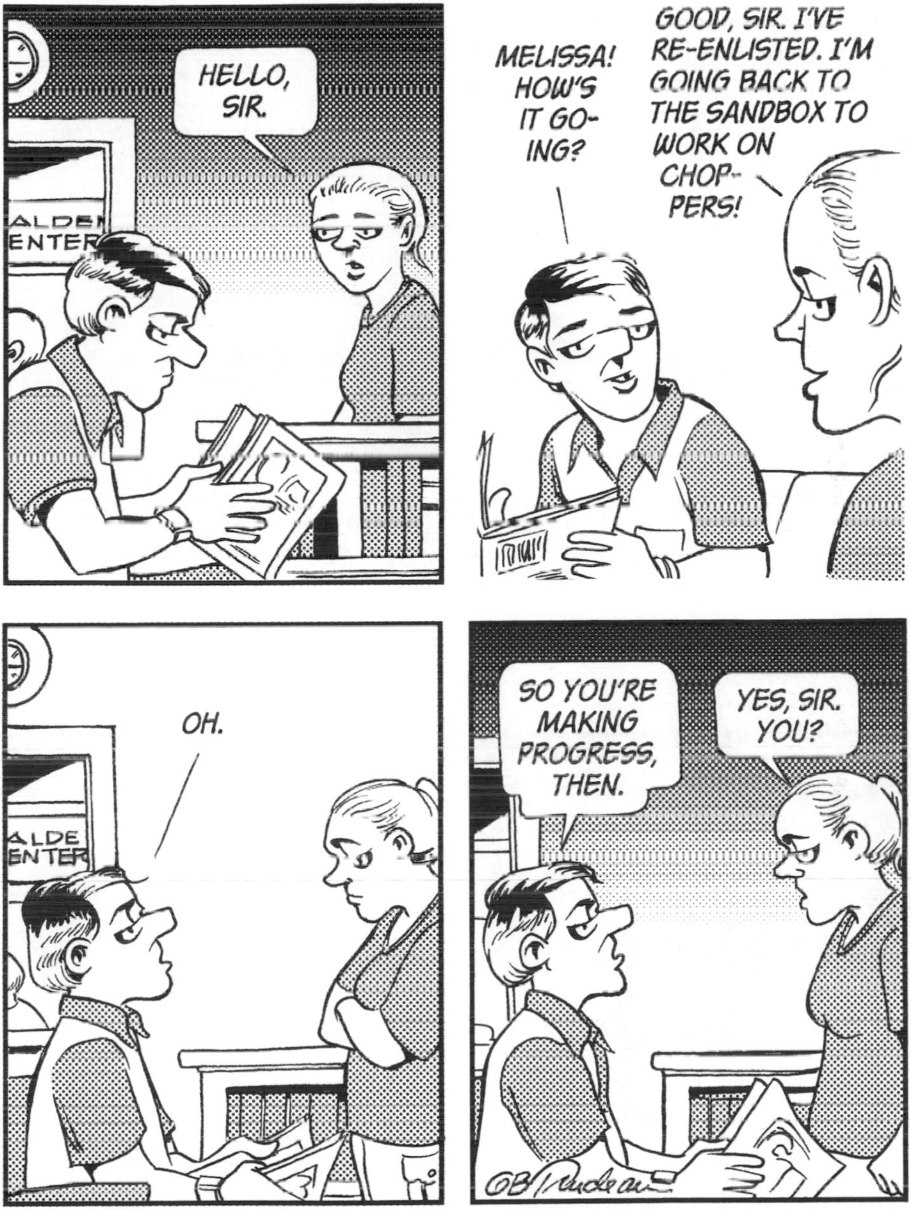
HELLO, SIR.
ALDE ENTER
MELISSA! HOW'S IT GO-ING?
GOOD, SIR. I'VE RE-ENLISTED. I'M GOING BACK TO THE SANDBOX TO WORK ON CHOP-PERS!
OH.
ALDE ENTER
SO YOU'RE MAKING PROGRESS, THEN.
YES, SIR. YOU?
©B. Trudeau

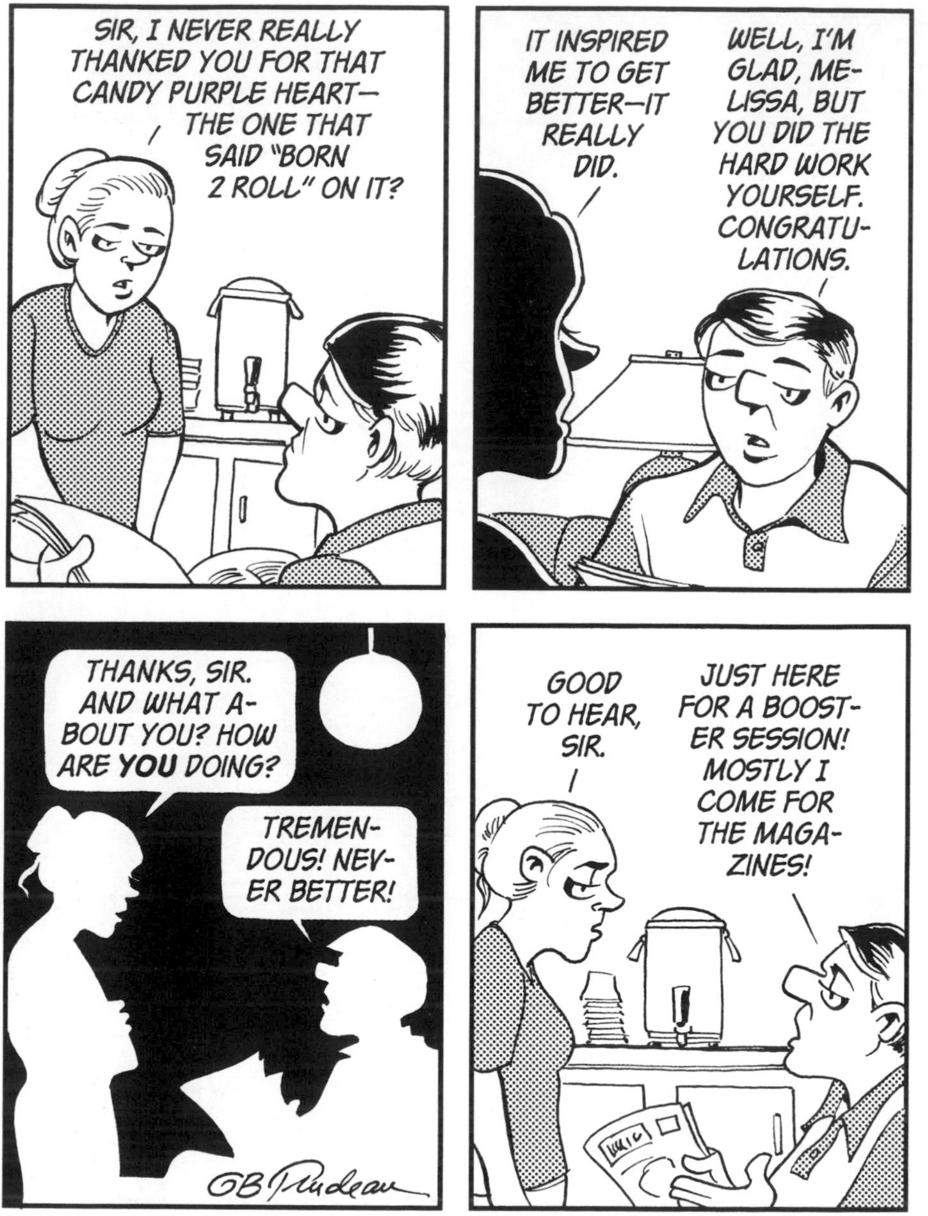
SIR, I NEVER REALLY THANKED YOU FOR THAT CANDY PURPLE HEART— THE ONE THAT SAID "BORN 2 ROLL" ON IT?
IT INSPIRED ME TO GET BETTER—IT REALLY DID.
WELL, I'M GLAD, MELISSA, BUT YOU DID THE HARD WORK YOURSELF. CONGRATULATIONS.
THANKS, SIR. AND WHAT ABOUT YOU? HOW ARE **YOU** DOING?
TREMENDOUS! NEVER BETTER!
GB Trudeau
GOOD TO HEAR, SIR.
JUST HERE FOR A BOOSTER SESSION! MOSTLY I COME FOR THE MAGAZINES!

I CAN'T EXPLAIN MY REACTION, MAN. BUT FOR SOME REASON, I WASN'T HAPPY FOR HER...

IT'S ALMOST LIKE I RESENTED MELISSA FOR GETTING BETTER. HOW WRONG IS **THAT?**

BUT THE FACT IS, ELIAS, SHE'S GETTING ON WITH HER LIFE, WHILE AFTER FOUR YEARS I'M STILL STUCK HERE WITH...WITH...

WITH ME. YEAH, I GET THAT COMPLAINT A LOT.

SO WHERE'S THE FAIRNESS IN **THAT?**

HOW'S IT GOING, MEL?
BEEN BETTER.
YEAH? WHAT'S UP?
SAME OLD. 200 HORN DOGS WATCHING ME EAT LUNCH.
OH, THAT...
YO, RYAN. PASS THE KETCHUP, WILLYA?
HOW BAD DO YOU WANT IT? THE KETCHUP, I MEAN!
HA!
WHAT A RIOT, DUDE.
I HATE MID-DEPLOYMENT.
GB Trudeau

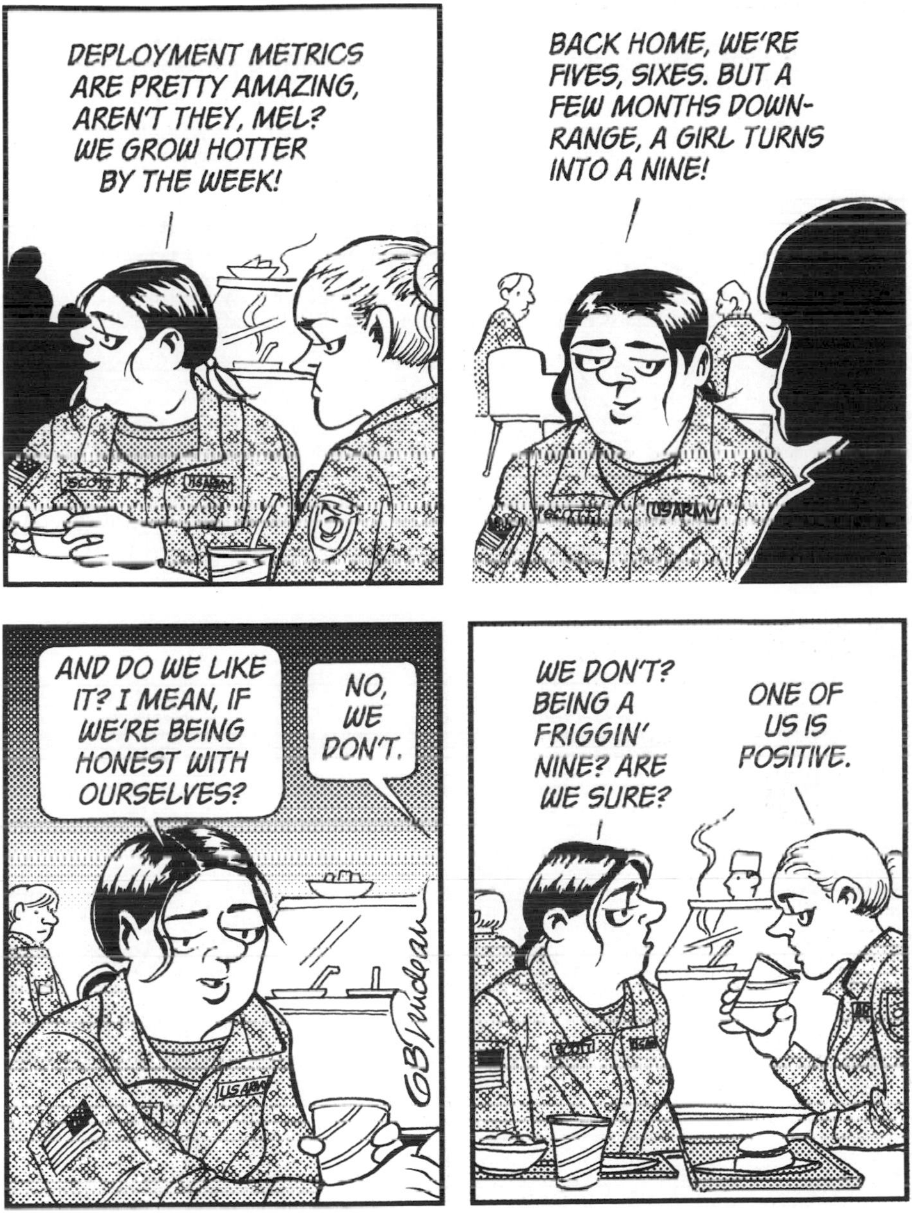
DEPLOYMENT METRICS ARE PRETTY AMAZING, AREN'T THEY, MEL? WE GROW HOTTER BY THE WEEK!
BACK HOME, WE'RE FIVES, SIXES. BUT A FEW MONTHS DOWN-RANGE, A GIRL TURNS INTO A NINE!
AND DO WE LIKE IT? I MEAN, IF WE'RE BEING HONEST WITH OURSELVES?
NO, WE DON'T.
WE DON'T? BEING A FRIGGIN' NINE? ARE WE SURE?
ONE OF US IS POSITIVE.
GBTrudeau

YOU DON'T LIKE BEING QUEEN FOR A YEAR, MEL?

HELL, NO...

IT DRIVES ME CRAZY! I WORK HARD AT BEING TAKEN SERIOUSLY. I'M THE MOST SQUARED AWAY SOLDIER YOU KNOW!

THIS KIND OF UNWANTED ATTENTION IS OPPRESSIVE. IT'S DISRESPECTFUL. IT COMPROMISES READINESS!

I DUNNO, THEY LOOK READY TO ME.

DUDE. BE A SISTER, OKAY?

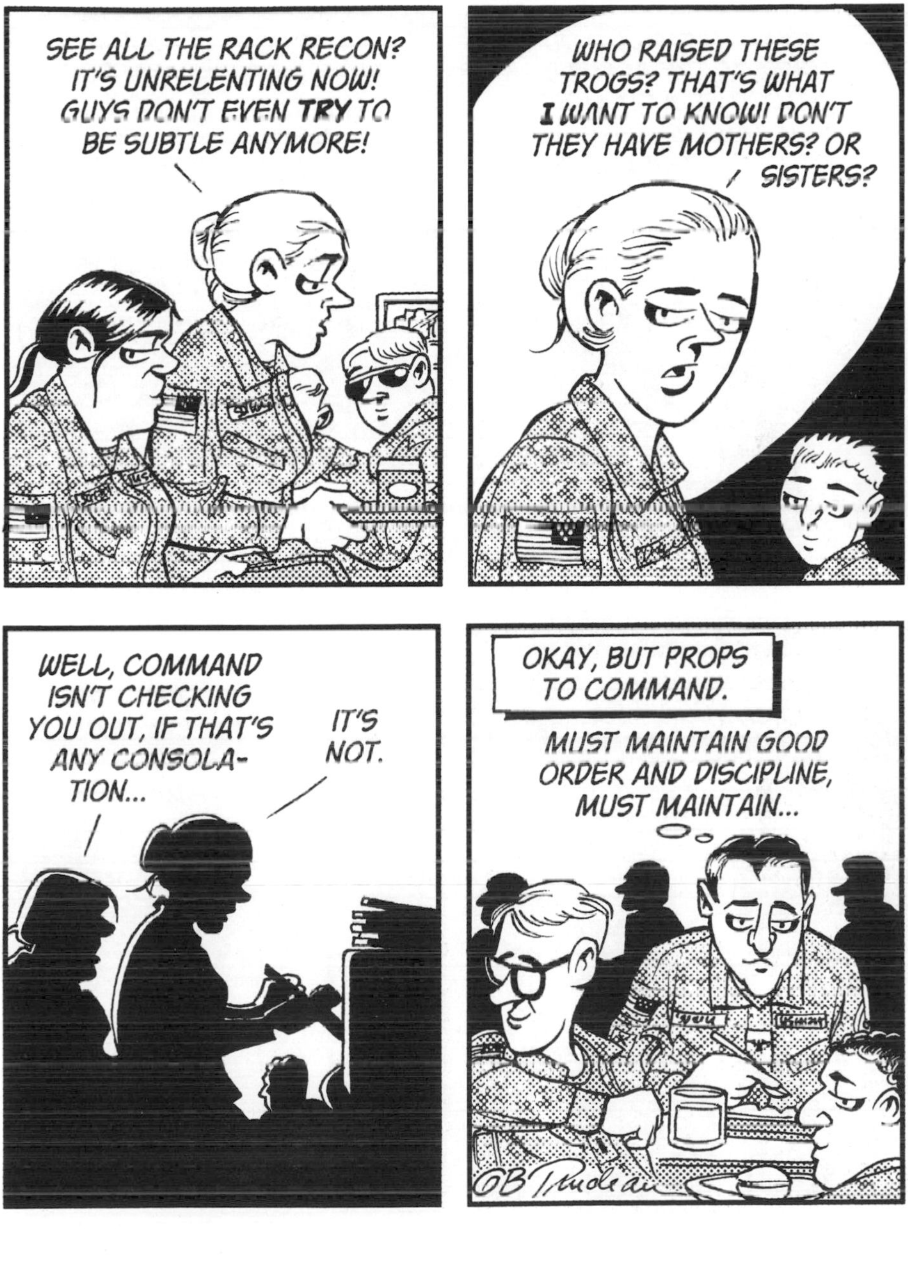
SEE ALL THE RACK RECON? IT'S UNRELENTING NOW! GUYS DON'T EVEN TRY TO BE SUBTLE ANYMORE!
WHO RAISED THESE TROGS? THAT'S WHAT I WANT TO KNOW! DON'T THEY HAVE MOTHERS? OR SISTERS?
WELL, COMMAND ISN'T CHECKING YOU OUT, IF THAT'S ANY CONSOLA-TION...
IT'S NOT.
OKAY, BUT PROPS TO COMMAND.
MUST MAINTAIN GOOD ORDER AND DISCIPLINE, MUST MAINTAIN...
©B Trudeau

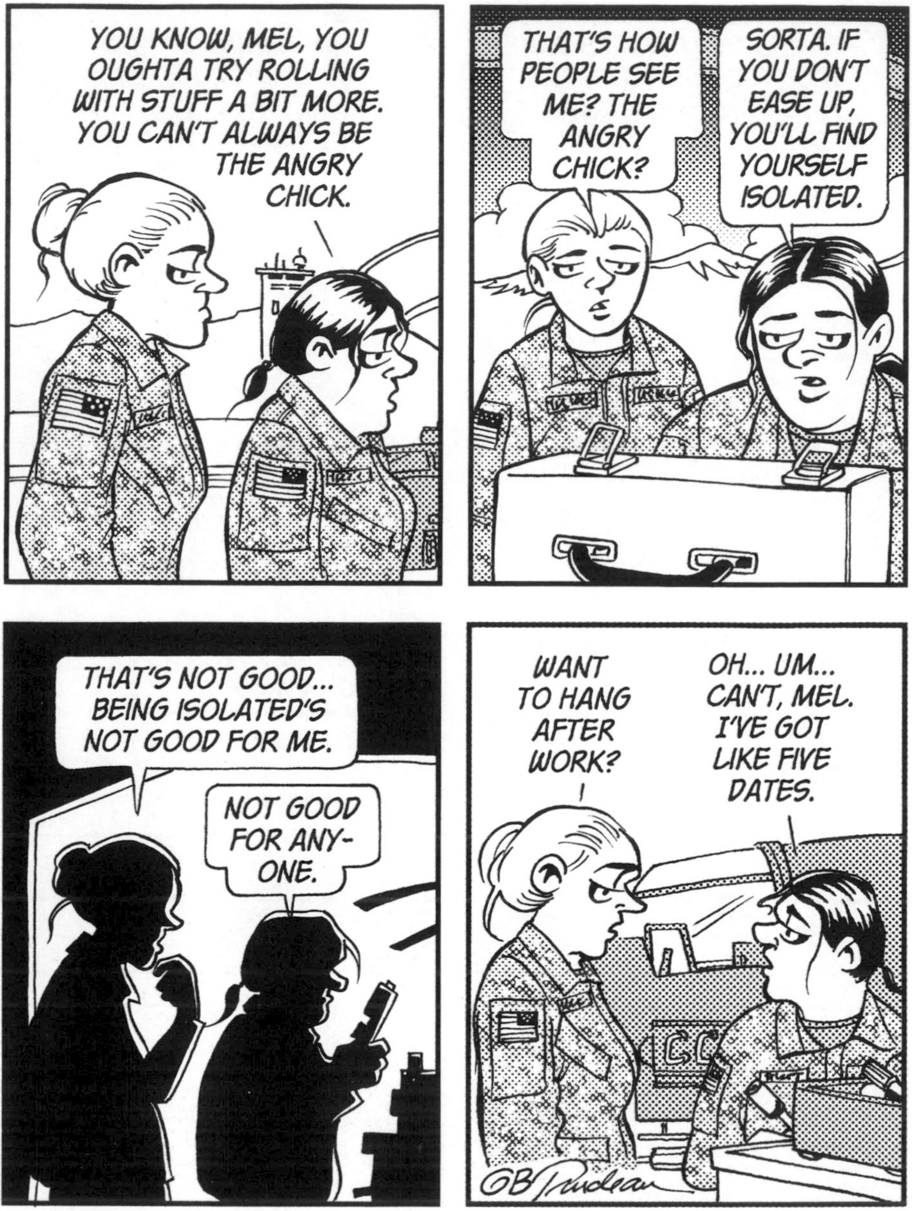
YOU KNOW, MEL, YOU OUGHTA TRY ROLLING WITH STUFF A BIT MORE. YOU CAN'T ALWAYS BE THE ANGRY CHICK.
THAT'S HOW PEOPLE SEE ME? THE ANGRY CHICK?
SORTA. IF YOU DON'T EASE UP, YOU'LL FIND YOURSELF ISOLATED.
THAT'S NOT GOOD... BEING ISOLATED'S NOT GOOD FOR ME.
NOT GOOD FOR ANY-ONE.
WANT TO HANG AFTER WORK?
OH... UM... CAN'T, MEL. I'VE GOT LIKE FIVE DATES.
GB Trudeau

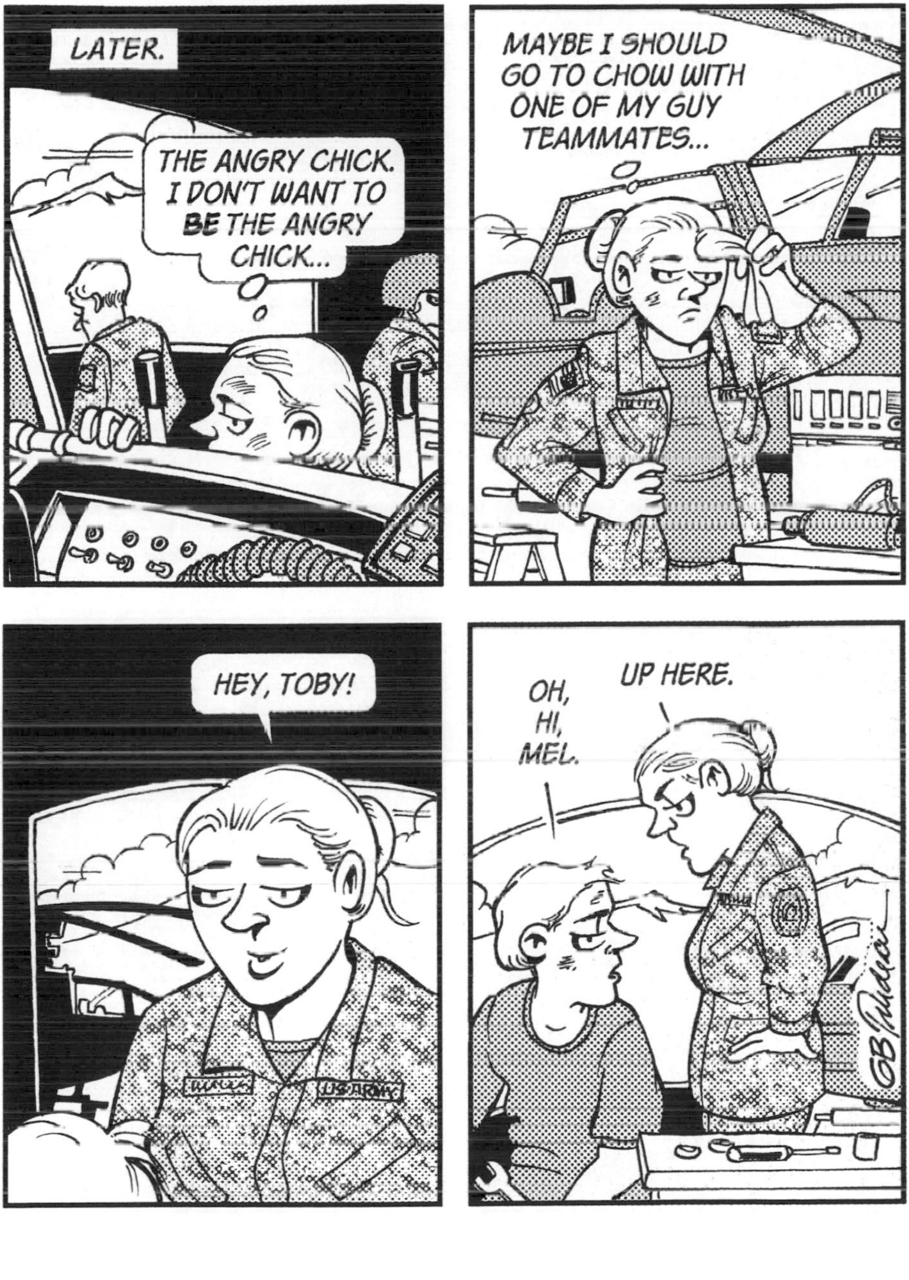
LATER.
THE ANGRY CHICK. I DON'T WANT TO BE THE ANGRY CHICK...
MAYBE I SHOULD GO TO CHOW WITH ONE OF MY GUY TEAMMATES...
HEY, TOBY!
OH, HI, MEL.
UP HERE.
US ARMY
GB Trudeau

HEY, MEL! CAPTAIN SEABROOK WANTS TO SEE YOU ASAP!
ME? SEABROOK WANTS TO SEE **ME**?
YEAH, IN HIS OFFICE... WHOA... LOOK AT YOU, GIRL!
WHAT?
DUDE. YOU JUST TURNED BEET RED. AND YOU'RE HYPERVENTILATING!
THIS ISN'T HAPPENING...
SOMEONE'S GOT A CRUSH! ♫
GB Trudeau

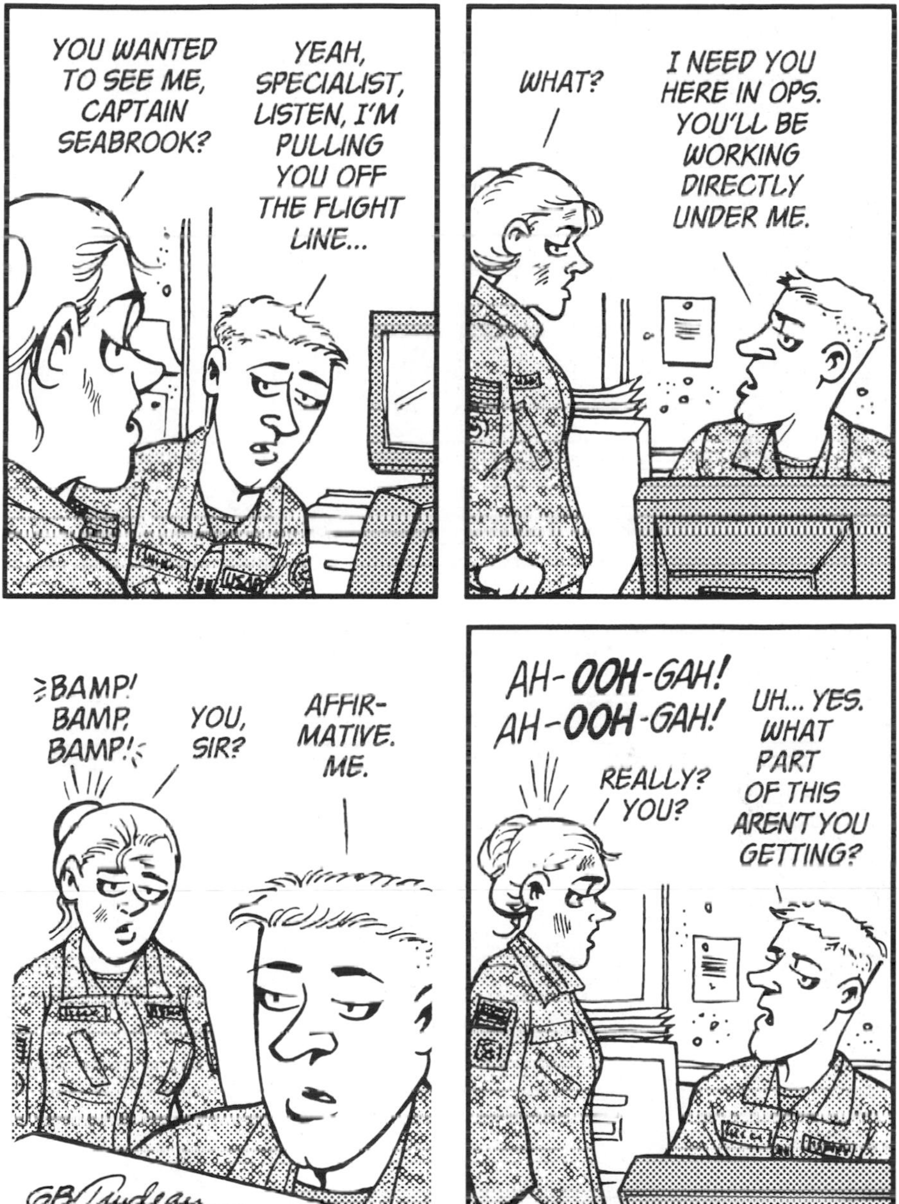

YOU WANTED TO SEE ME, CAPTAIN SEABROOK?
YEAH, SPECIALIST, LISTEN, I'M PULLING YOU OFF THE FLIGHT LINE...
WHAT?
I NEED YOU HERE IN OPS. YOU'LL BE WORKING DIRECTLY UNDER ME.
BAMP! BAMP, BAMP!
YOU, SIR?
AFFIR-MATIVE. ME.
GB Trudeau
AH-OOH-GAH! AH-OOH-GAH!
REALLY? YOU?
UH... YES. WHAT PART OF THIS AREN'T YOU GETTING?

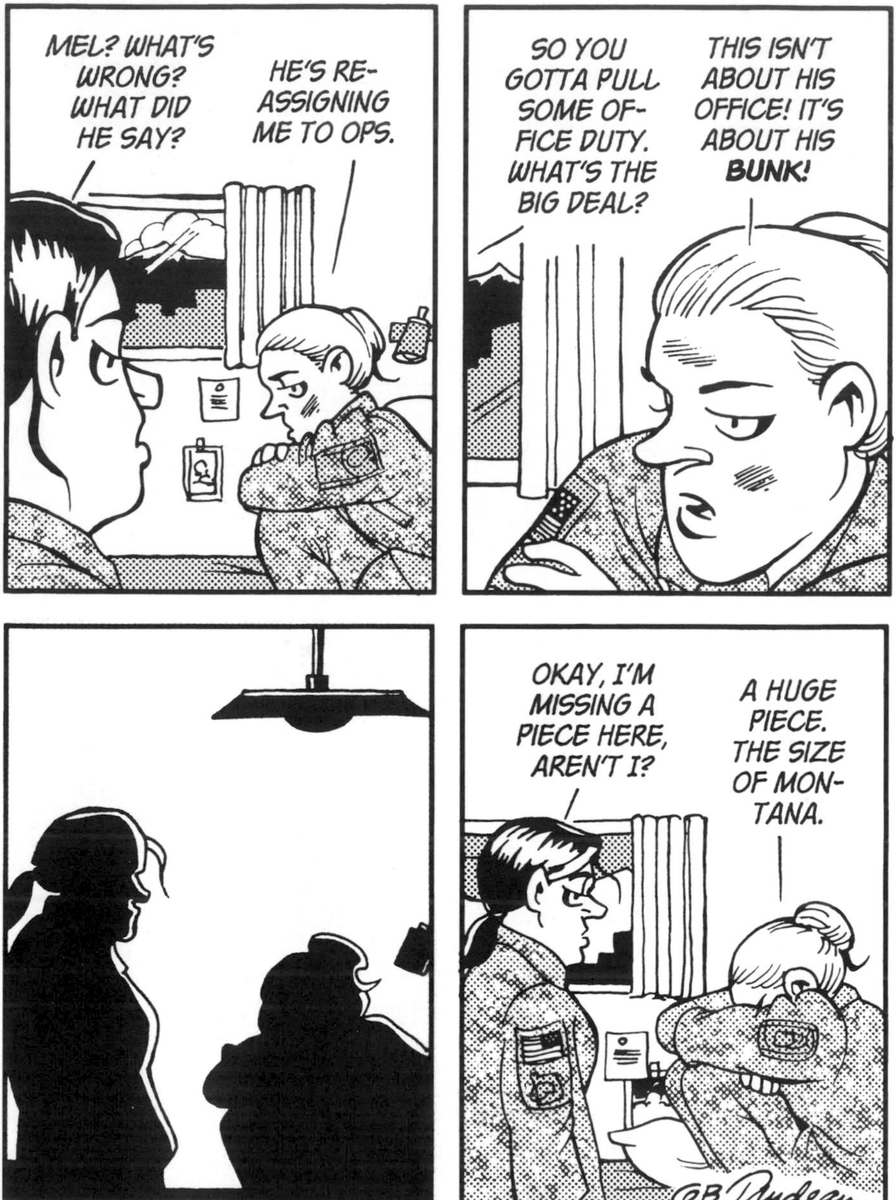
MEL? WHAT'S WRONG? WHAT DID HE SAY?
HE'S RE-ASSIGNING ME TO OPS.
SO YOU GOTTA PULL SOME OF-FICE DUTY. WHAT'S THE BIG DEAL?
THIS ISN'T ABOUT HIS OFFICE! IT'S ABOUT HIS **BUNK!**
OKAY, I'M MISSING A PIECE HERE, AREN'T I?
A HUGE PIECE. THE SIZE OF MON-TANA.
GB Trudeau

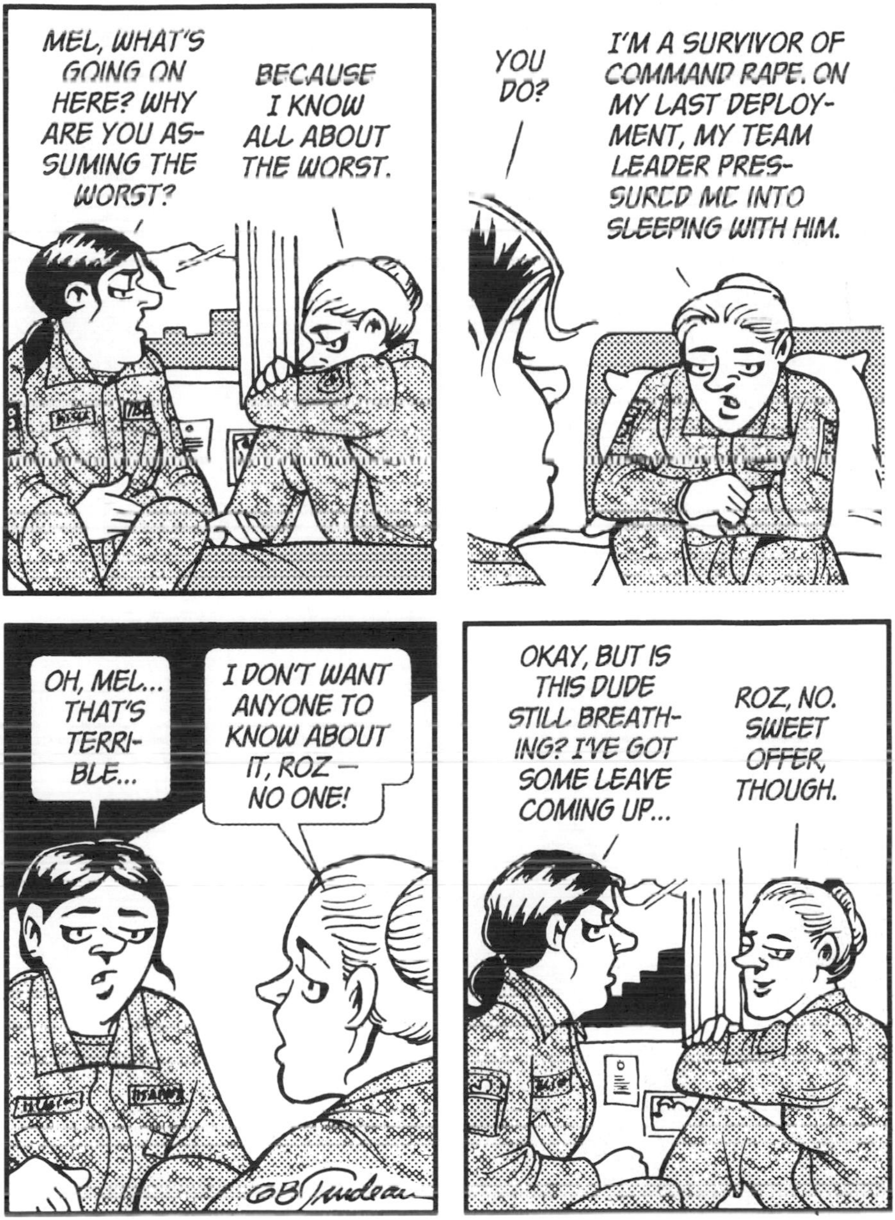
MEL, WHAT'S GOING ON HERE? WHY ARE YOU ASSUMING THE WORST?
BECAUSE I KNOW ALL ABOUT THE WORST.
YOU DO?
I'M A SURVIVOR OF COMMAND RAPE. ON MY LAST DEPLOYMENT, MY TEAM LEADER PRESSURED ME INTO SLEEPING WITH HIM.
OH, MEL... THAT'S TERRIBLE...
I DON'T WANT ANYONE TO KNOW ABOUT IT, ROZ — NO ONE!
OKAY, BUT IS THIS DUDE STILL BREATHING? I'VE GOT SOME LEAVE COMING UP...
ROZ, NO. SWEET OFFER, THOUGH.
GBTrudeau

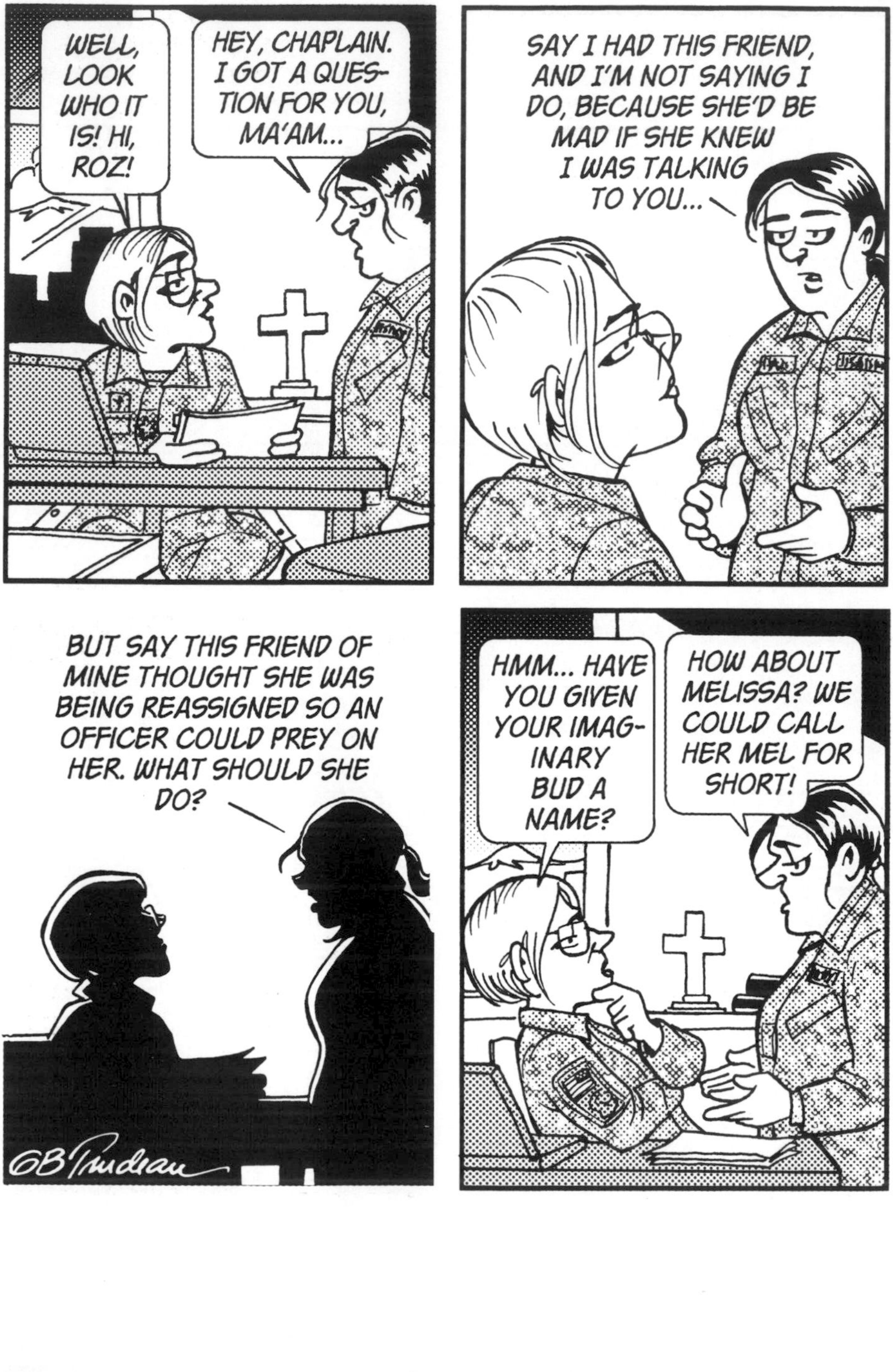
WELL, LOOK WHO IT IS! HI, ROZ!
HEY, CHAPLAIN. I GOT A QUESTION FOR YOU, MA'AM...
SAY I HAD THIS FRIEND, AND I'M NOT SAYING I DO, BECAUSE SHE'D BE MAD IF SHE KNEW I WAS TALKING TO YOU...
BUT SAY THIS FRIEND OF MINE THOUGHT SHE WAS BEING REASSIGNED SO AN OFFICER COULD PREY ON HER. WHAT SHOULD SHE DO?
HMM... HAVE YOU GIVEN YOUR IMAGINARY BUD A NAME?
HOW ABOUT MELISSA? WE COULD CALL HER MEL FOR SHORT!
GB Trudeau

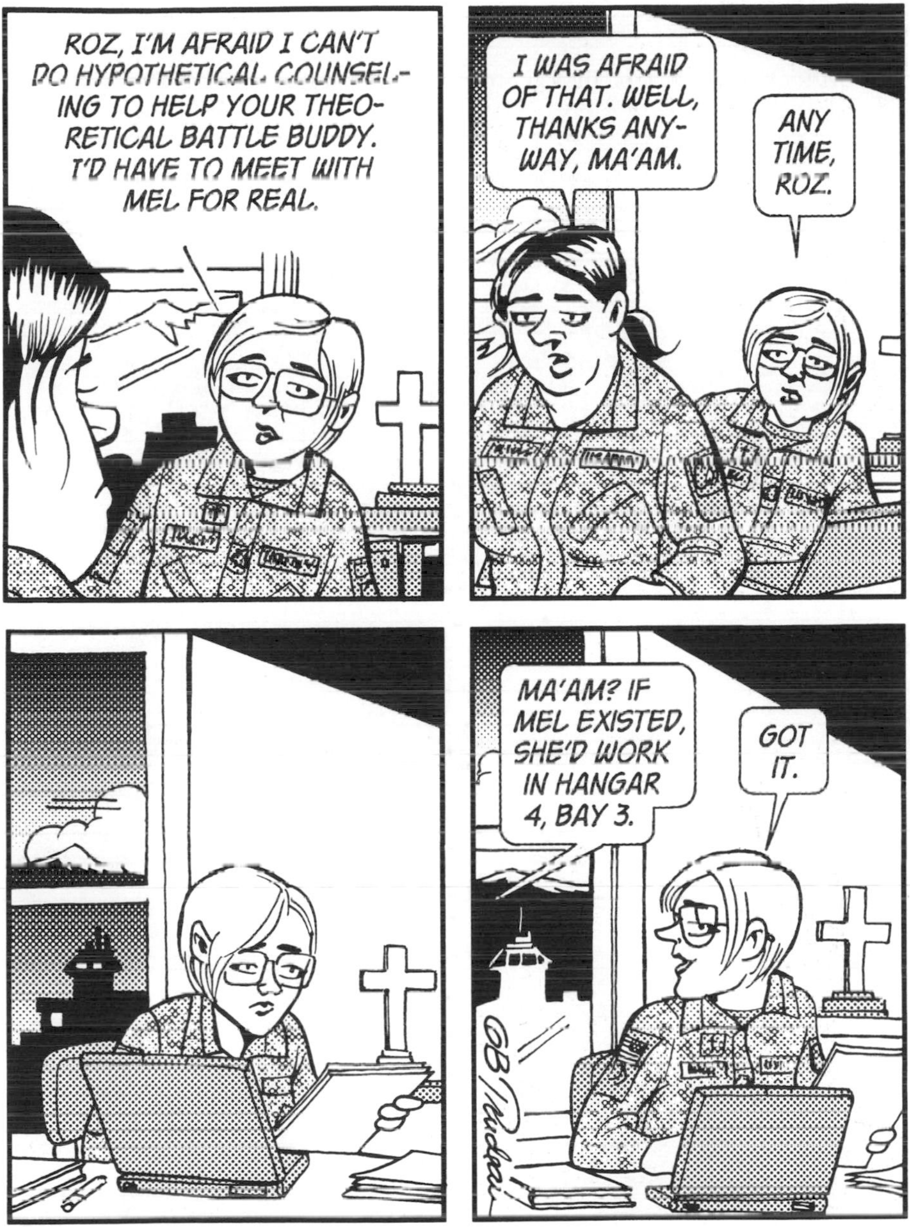
ROZ, I'M AFRAID I CAN'T DO HYPOTHETICAL COUNSEL-ING TO HELP YOUR THEO-RETICAL BATTLE BUDDY. I'D HAVE TO MEET WITH MEL FOR REAL.
I WAS AFRAID OF THAT. WELL, THANKS ANY-WAY, MA'AM.
ANY TIME, ROZ.
MA'AM? IF MEL EXISTED, SHE'D WORK IN HANGAR 4, BAY 3.
GOT IT.
GB Trudeau

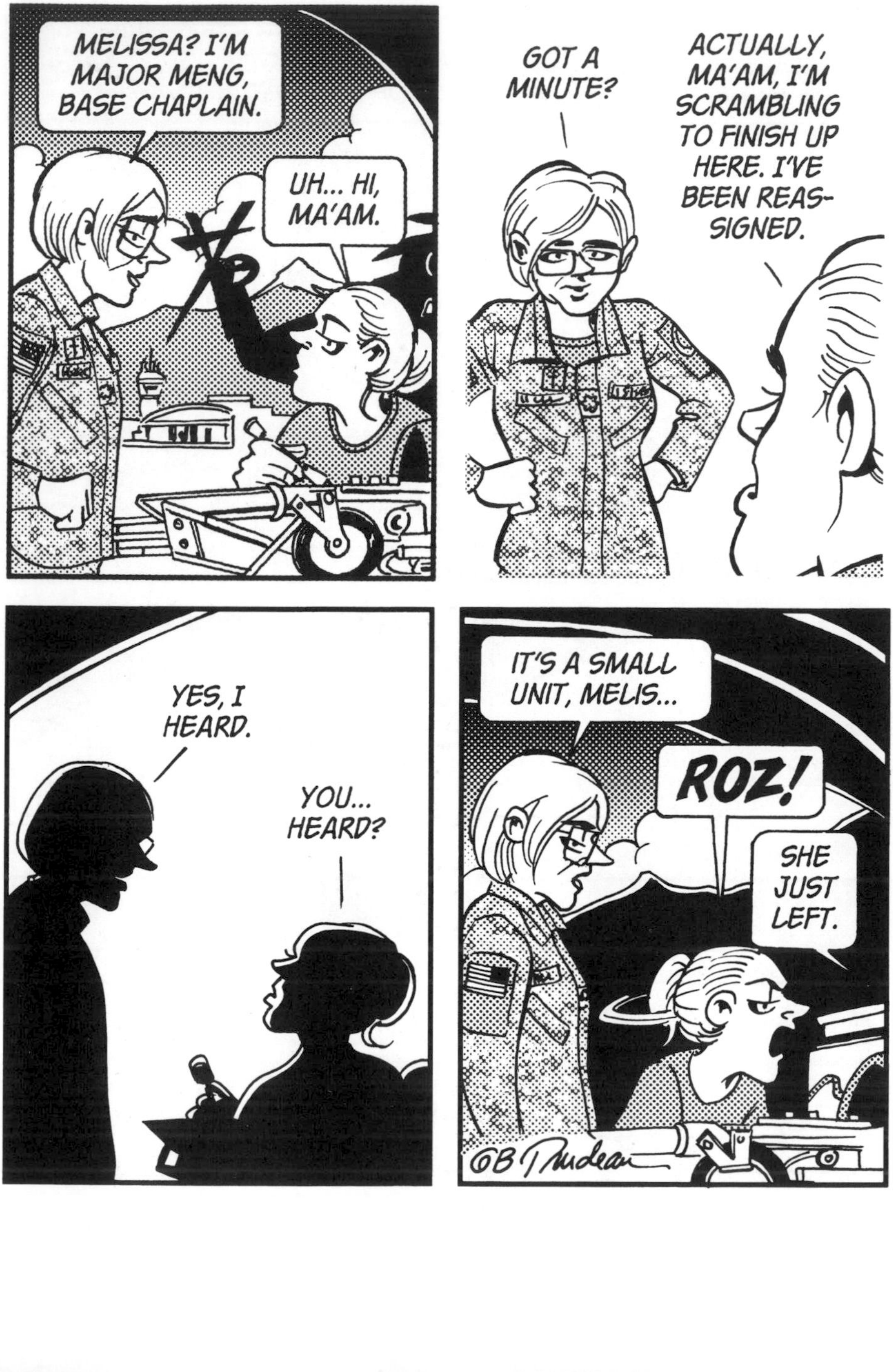
MELISSA? I'M MAJOR MENG, BASE CHAPLAIN.
UH... HI, MA'AM.
GOT A MINUTE?
ACTUALLY, MA'AM, I'M SCRAMBLING TO FINISH UP HERE. I'VE BEEN REAS-SIGNED.
YES, I HEARD.
YOU... HEARD?
IT'S A SMALL UNIT, MELIS...
ROZ!
SHE JUST LEFT.
©B Trudeau

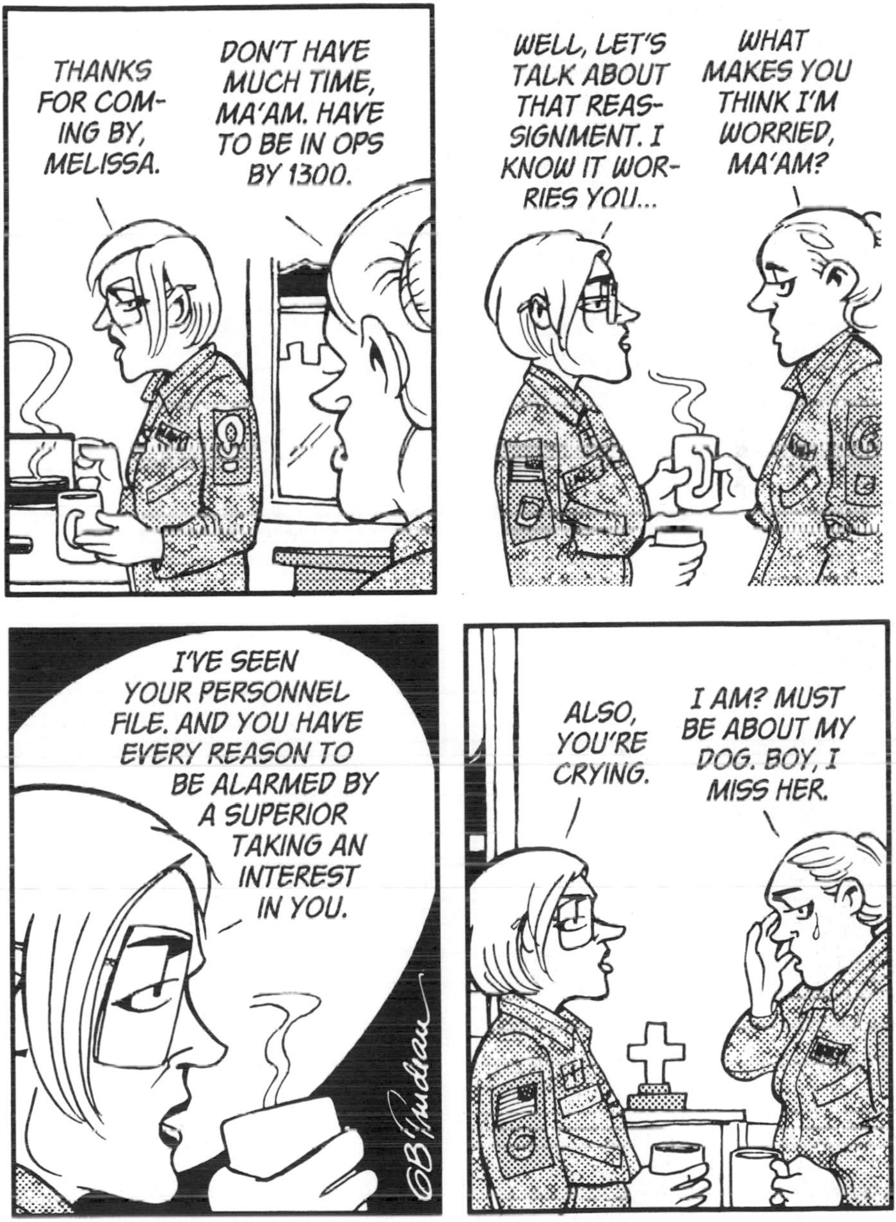
THANKS FOR COMING BY, MELISSA.
DON'T HAVE MUCH TIME, MA'AM. HAVE TO BE IN OPS BY 1300.
WELL, LET'S TALK ABOUT THAT REASSIGNMENT. I KNOW IT WORRIES YOU...
WHAT MAKES YOU THINK I'M WORRIED, MA'AM?
I'VE SEEN YOUR PERSONNEL FILE. AND YOU HAVE EVERY REASON TO BE ALARMED BY A SUPERIOR TAKING AN INTEREST IN YOU.
ALSO, YOU'RE CRYING.
I AM? MUST BE ABOUT MY DOG. BOY, I MISS HER.

MELISSA, HAS CAPTAIN SEABROOK ACTUALLY MADE ANY ADVANCES?

NO, BUT HE'S ALWAYS WATCHING ME...

AND IT MAKES **NO** SENSE PULLING ME OFF THE FLIGHT LINE! WE'RE TOTALLY OVER-EXTENDED, AND I'M THE TOP MECHANIC ON THE TEAM!

MAYBE HE'S JUST GIVING YOU MORE RE-SPONSIBILITY, TRYING TO MENTOR YOU...

MENTOR ME? THAT'S WHAT MY OLD **PERP** CALLED IT!

OH... THEN WE'LL NEED ANOTHER WORD.

DO YOU KNOW HOW MANY CREEPS WANT TO **MENTOR** ME?

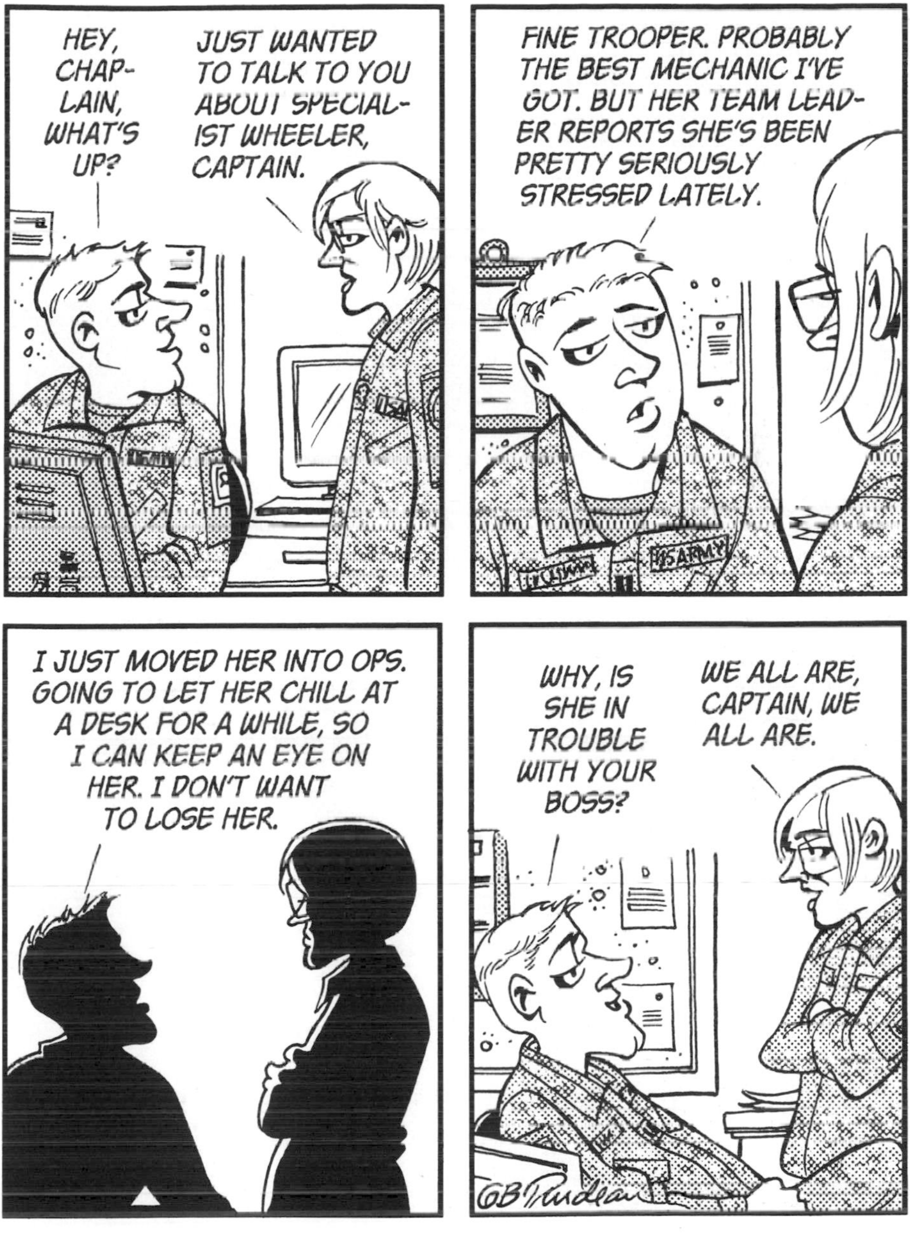

HEY, CHAP-LAIN, WHAT'S UP?
JUST WANTED TO TALK TO YOU ABOUT SPECIAL-IST WHEELER, CAPTAIN.
FINE TROOPER. PROBABLY THE BEST MECHANIC I'VE GOT. BUT HER TEAM LEAD-ER REPORTS SHE'S BEEN PRETTY SERIOUSLY STRESSED LATELY.
I JUST MOVED HER INTO OPS. GOING TO LET HER CHILL AT A DESK FOR A WHILE, SO I CAN KEEP AN EYE ON HER. I DON'T WANT TO LOSE HER.
WHY, IS SHE IN TROUBLE WITH YOUR BOSS?
WE ALL ARE, CAPTAIN, WE ALL ARE.

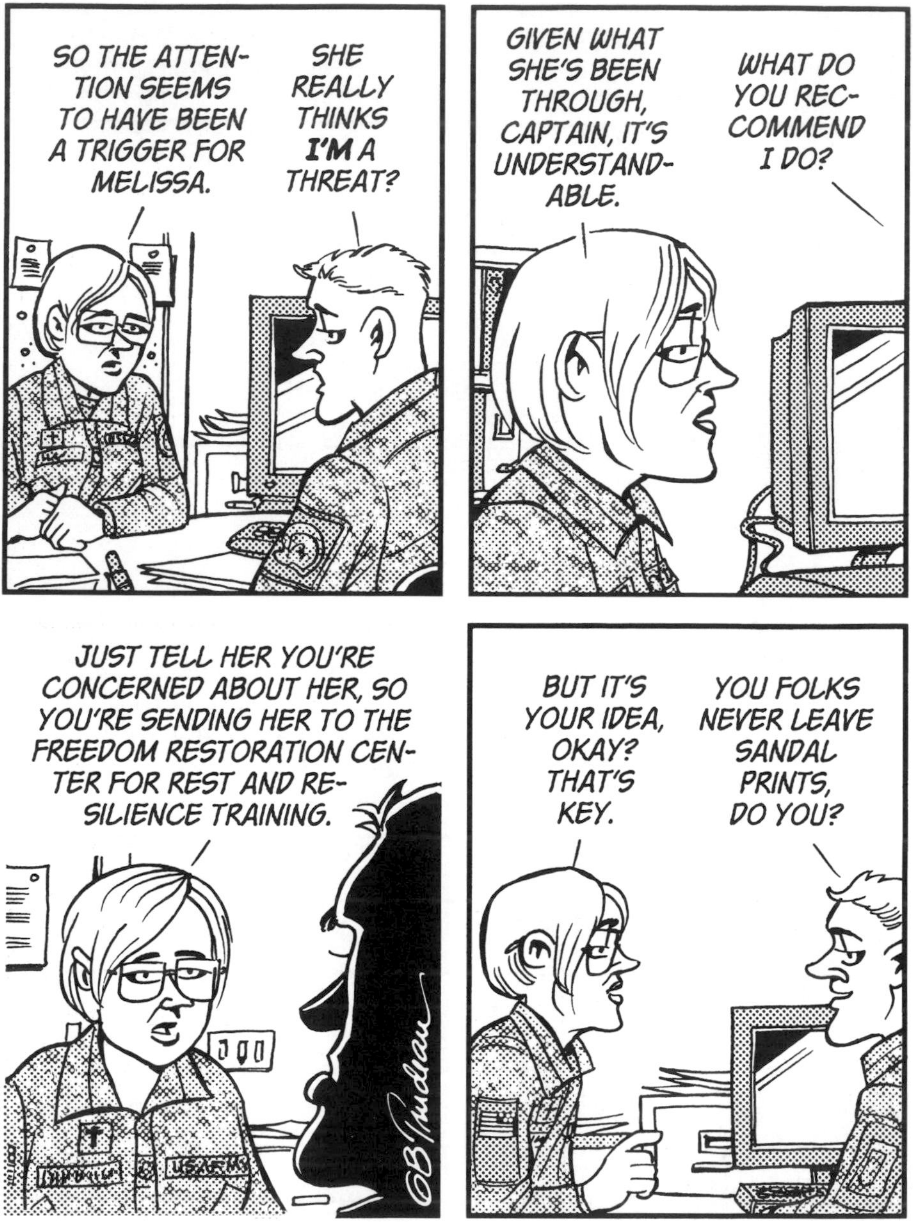
SO THE ATTENTION SEEMS TO HAVE BEEN A TRIGGER FOR MELISSA.
SHE REALLY THINKS **I'M** A THREAT?
GIVEN WHAT SHE'S BEEN THROUGH, CAPTAIN, IT'S UNDERSTANDABLE.
WHAT DO YOU RECOMMEND I DO?
JUST TELL HER YOU'RE CONCERNED ABOUT HER, SO YOU'RE SENDING HER TO THE FREEDOM RESTORATION CENTER FOR REST AND RESILIENCE TRAINING.
BUT IT'S YOUR IDEA, OKAY? THAT'S KEY.
YOU FOLKS NEVER LEAVE SANDAL PRINTS, DO YOU?
GBTrudeau

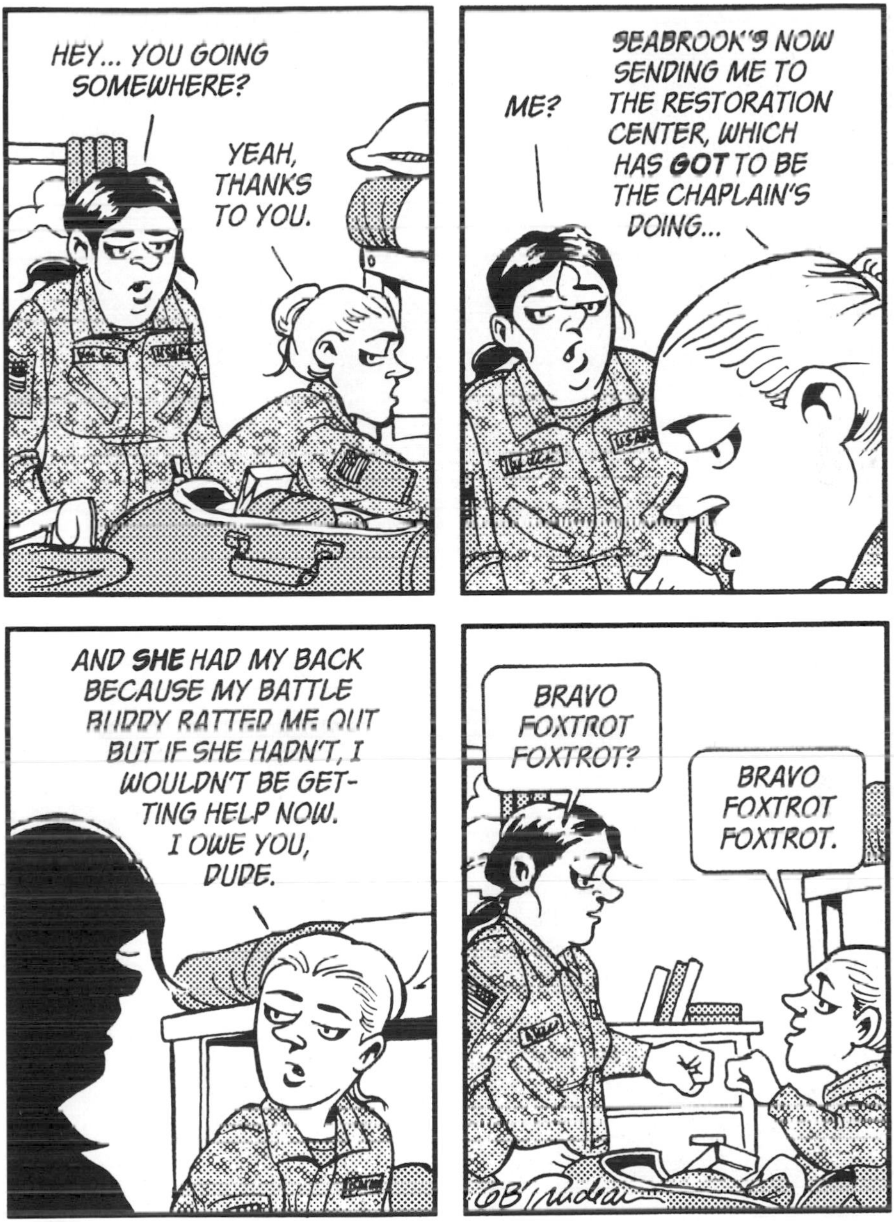
HEY... YOU GOING SOMEWHERE?
YEAH, THANKS TO YOU.
ME?
SEABROOK'S NOW SENDING ME TO THE RESTORATION CENTER, WHICH HAS **GOT** TO BE THE CHAPLAIN'S DOING...
AND **SHE** HAD MY BACK BECAUSE MY BATTLE BUDDY RATTED ME OUT BUT IF SHE HADN'T, I WOULDN'T BE GETTING HELP NOW. I OWE YOU, DUDE.
BRAVO FOXTROT FOXTROT?
BRAVO FOXTROT FOXTROT.
GB Trudeau

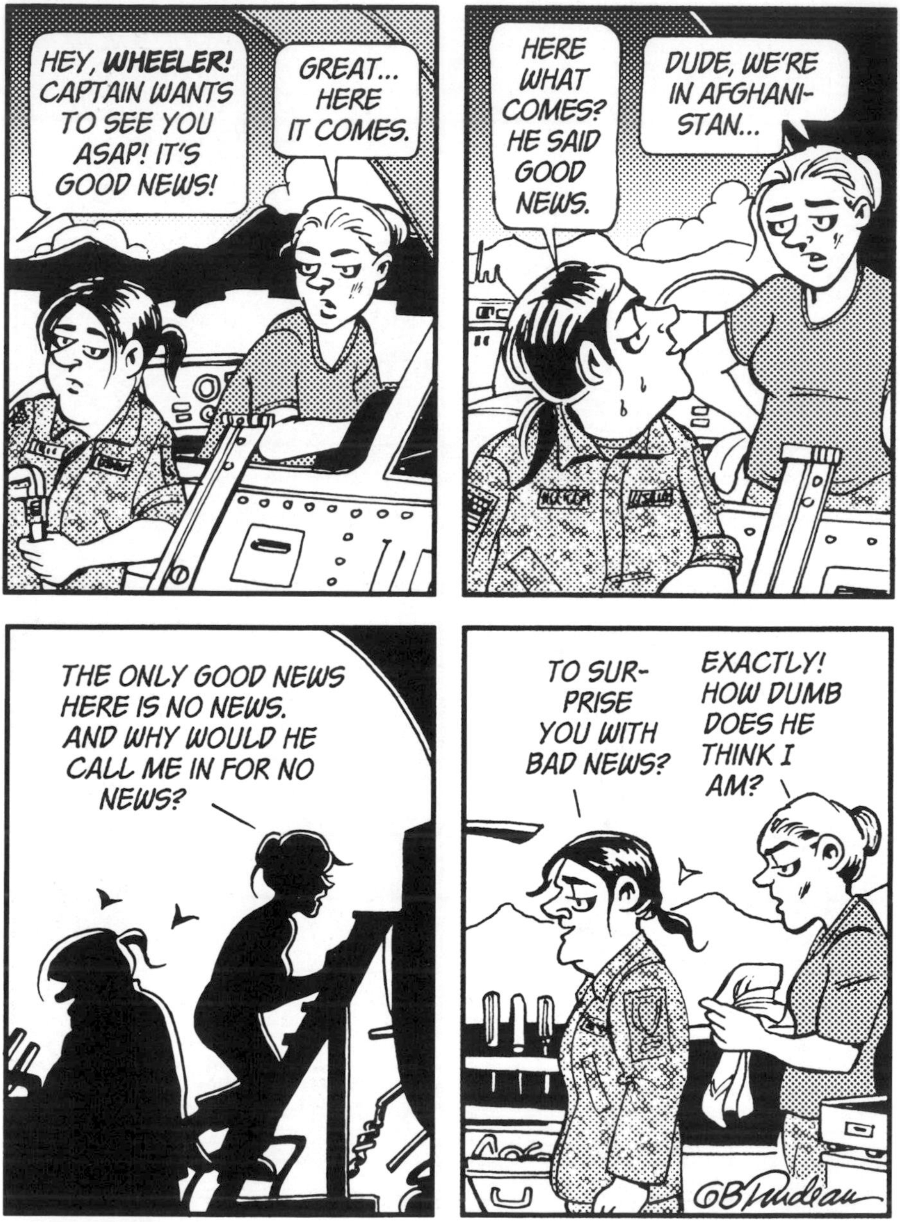
HEY, **WHEELER!** CAPTAIN WANTS TO SEE YOU ASAP! IT'S GOOD NEWS!
GREAT... HERE IT COMES.
HERE WHAT COMES? HE SAID GOOD NEWS.
DUDE, WE'RE IN AFGHANI-STAN...
THE ONLY GOOD NEWS HERE IS NO NEWS. AND WHY WOULD HE CALL ME IN FOR NO NEWS?
TO SUR-PRISE YOU WITH BAD NEWS?
EXACTLY! HOW DUMB DOES HE THINK I AM?
GBTrudeau

YOU'RE SMILING! IT IS GOOD NEWS!
I'M... I'M BEING PROMOTED, E-5.
YOU? A SERGEANT? GET OUT! WHEN?
RIGHT AWAY. 1500 TODAY.
I DON'T BELIEVE IT! THIS IS SO GREAT! DO YOU KNOW WHAT THIS MEANS, DUDE?
WHAT'S THAT?
I NOW HAVE A BUD WITH JUICE! I'M WIRED IN, MEL!
WAY TO GO, GIRL.

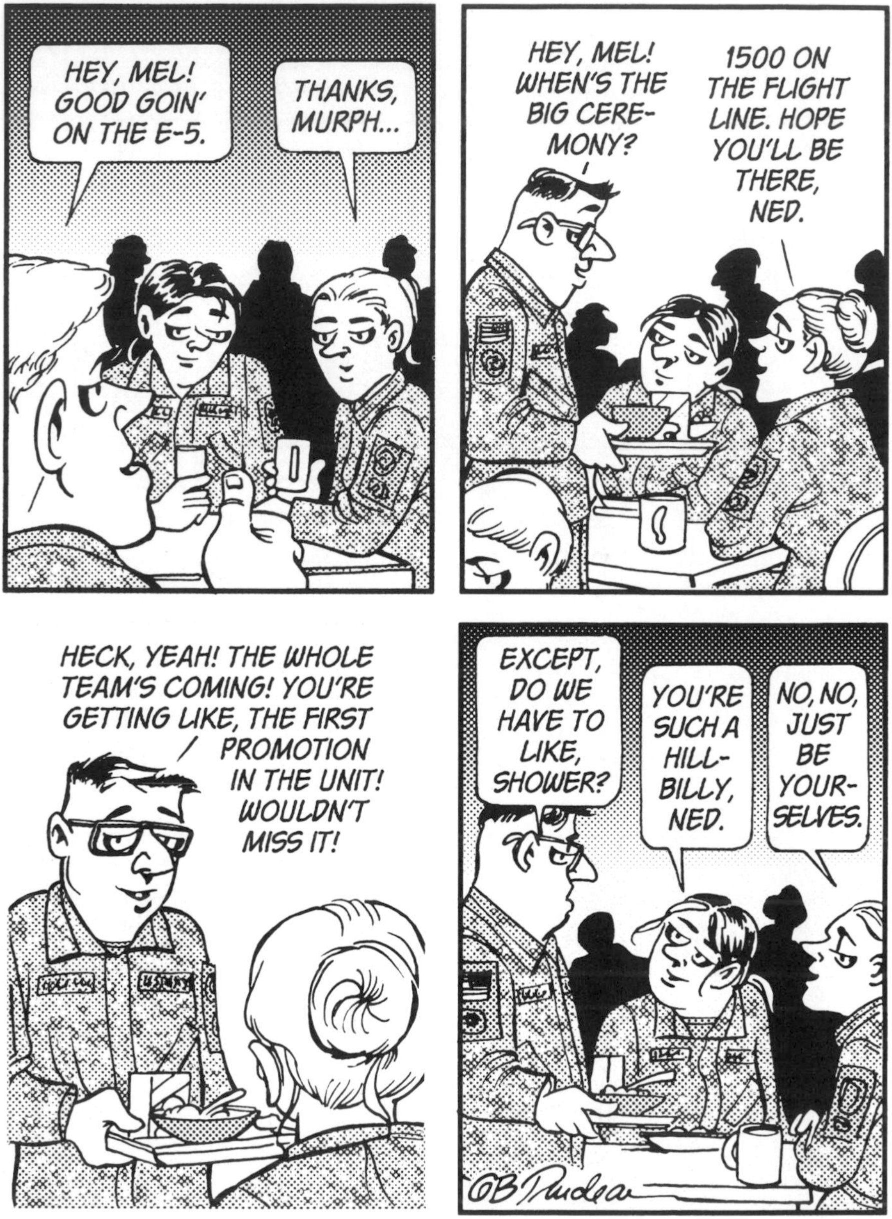
HEY, MEL! GOOD GOIN' ON THE E-5.
THANKS, MURPH...
HEY, MEL! WHEN'S THE BIG CERE-MONY?
1500 ON THE FLIGHT LINE. HOPE YOU'LL BE THERE, NED.
HECK, YEAH! THE WHOLE TEAM'S COMING! YOU'RE GETTING LIKE, THE FIRST PROMOTION IN THE UNIT! WOULDN'T MISS IT!
EXCEPT, DO WE HAVE TO LIKE, SHOWER?
YOU'RE SUCH A HILL-BILLY, NED.
NO, NO, JUST BE YOUR-SELVES.
GB Trudeau

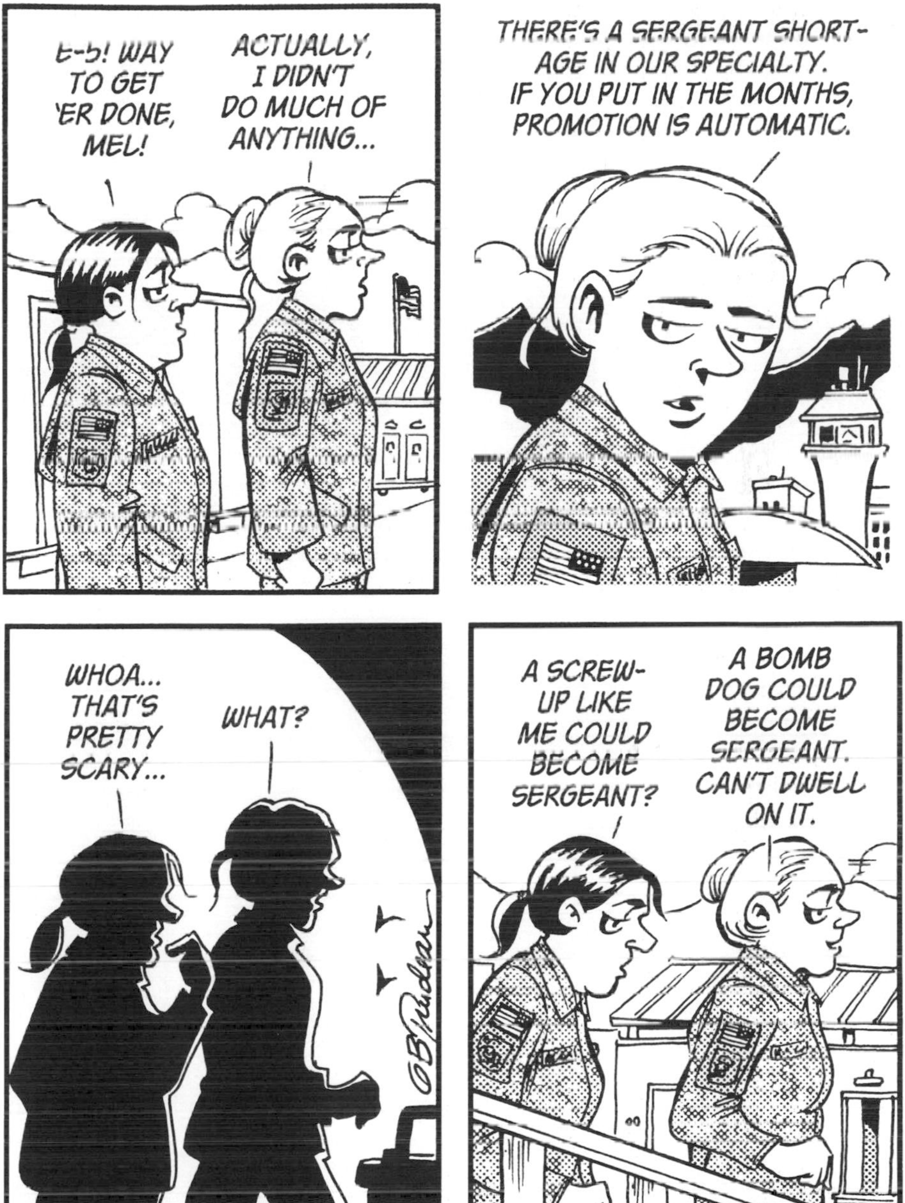
E-5! WAY TO GET 'ER DONE, MEL!
ACTUALLY, I DIDN'T DO MUCH OF ANYTHING...
THERE'S A SERGEANT SHORTAGE IN OUR SPECIALTY. IF YOU PUT IN THE MONTHS, PROMOTION IS AUTOMATIC.
WHOA... THAT'S PRETTY SCARY...
WHAT?
A SCREW-UP LIKE ME COULD BECOME SERGEANT?
A BOMB DOG COULD BECOME SERGEANT. CAN'T DWELL ON IT.

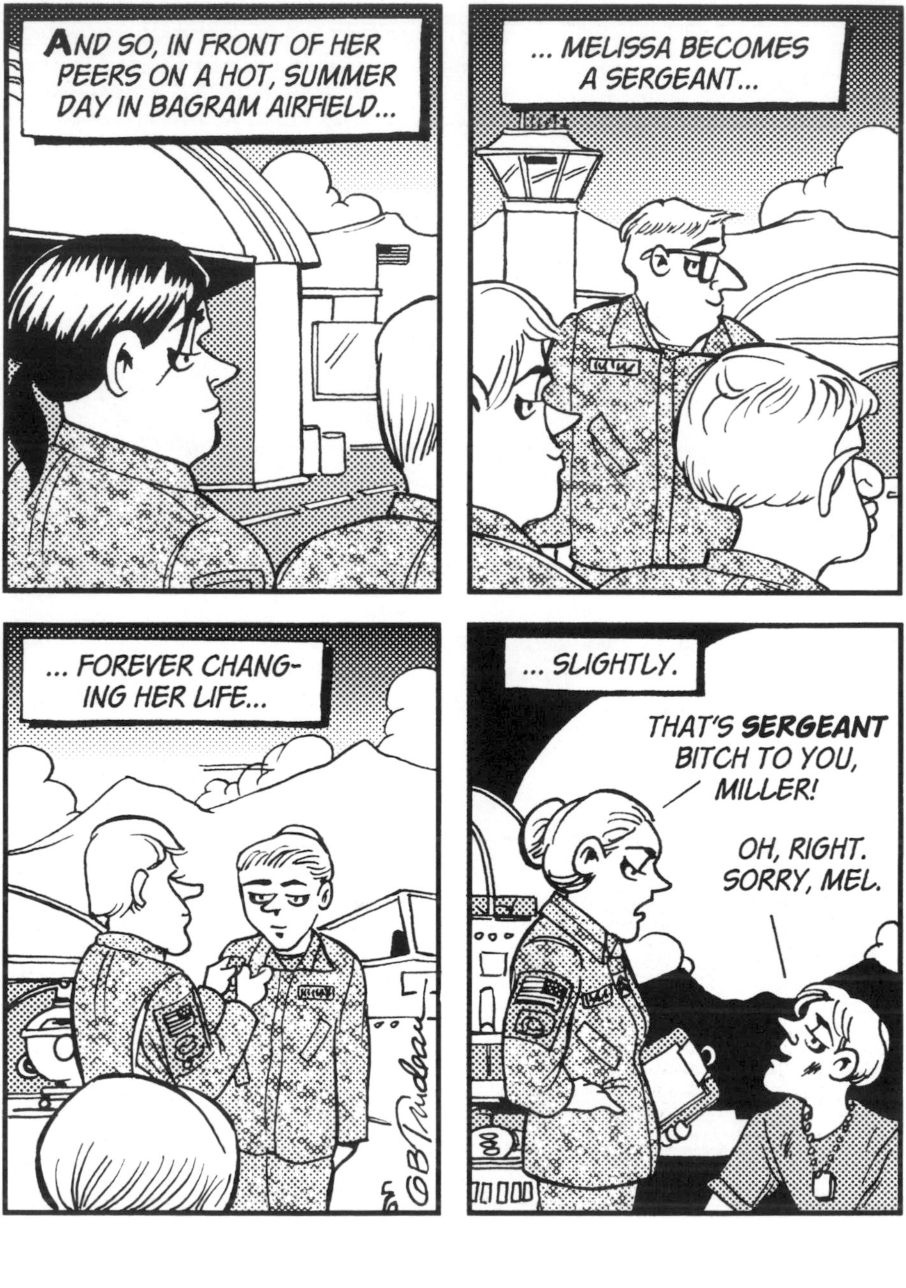
AND SO, IN FRONT OF HER PEERS ON A HOT, SUMMER DAY IN BAGRAM AIRFIELD...
... MELISSA BECOMES A SERGEANT...
... FOREVER CHANGING HER LIFE...
... SLIGHTLY.
THAT'S **SERGEANT** BITCH TO YOU, MILLER!
OH, RIGHT. SORRY, MEL.

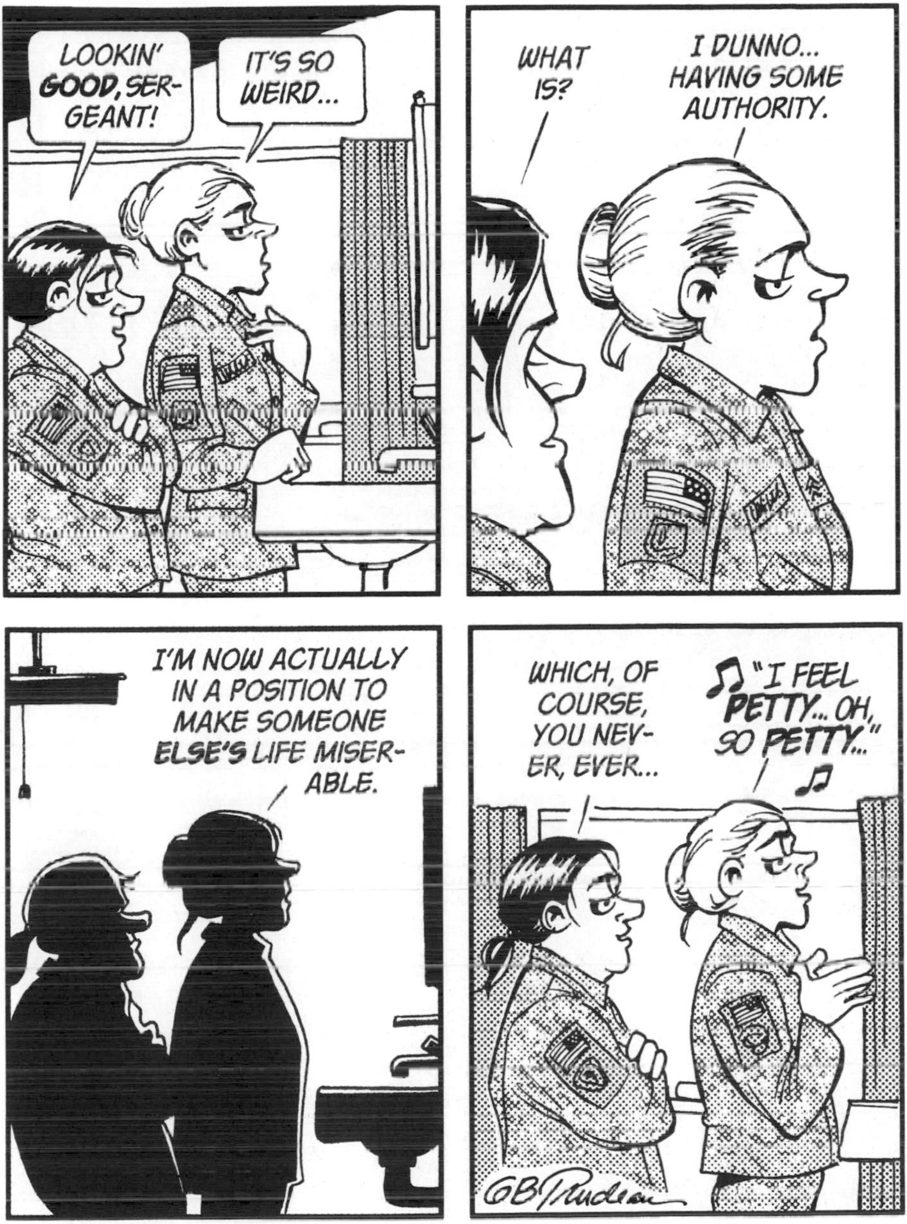

LOOKIN' **GOOD,** SER-GEANT!
IT'S SO WEIRD...
WHAT IS?
I DUNNO... HAVING SOME AUTHORITY.
I'M NOW ACTUALLY IN A POSITION TO MAKE SOMEONE **ELSE'S** LIFE MISER-ABLE.
WHICH, OF COURSE, YOU NEV-ER, EVER...
♫ "I FEEL **PETTY**... OH, SO **PETTY**..." ♫
GB Trudeau

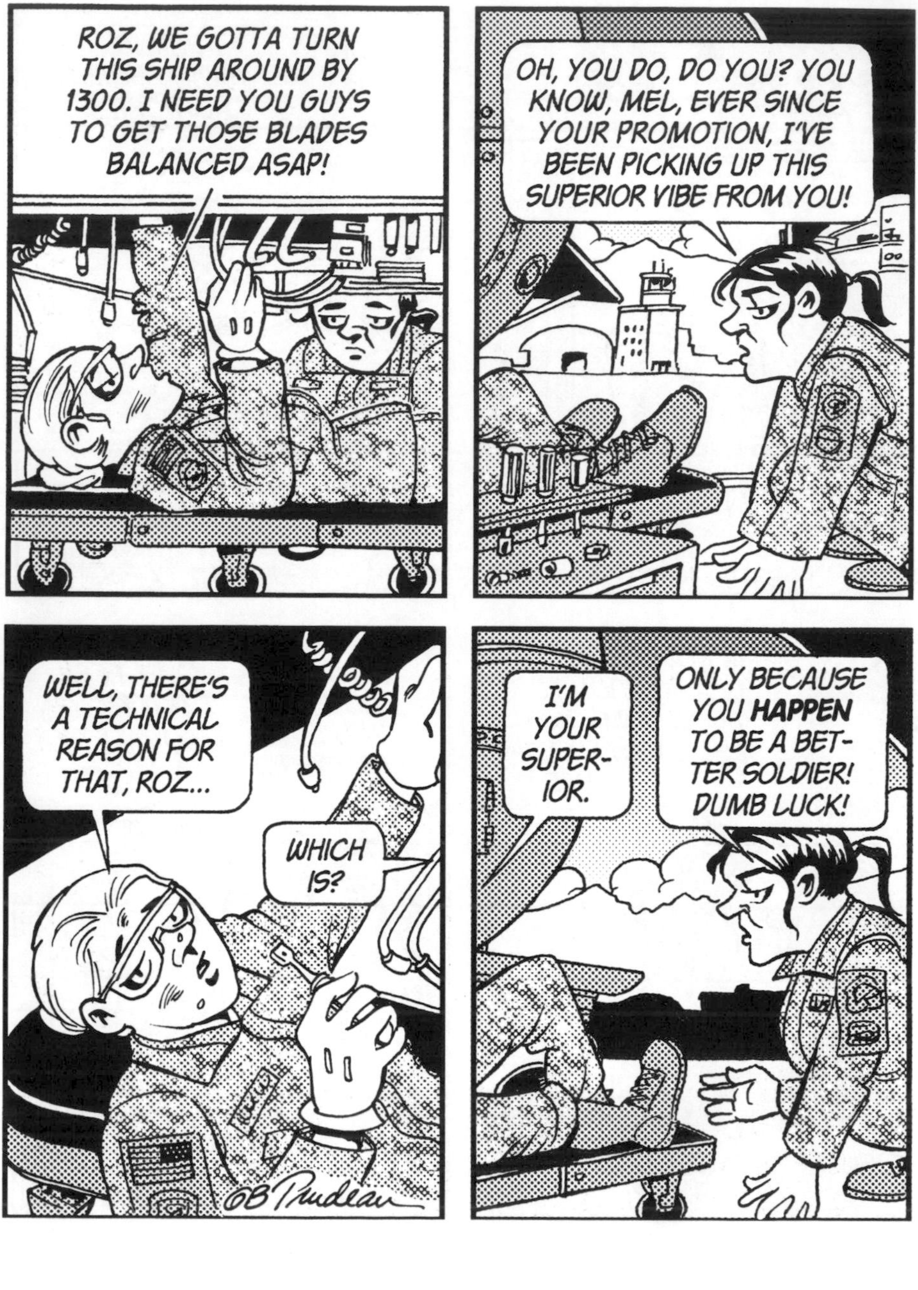
ROZ, WE GOTTA TURN THIS SHIP AROUND BY 1300. I NEED YOU GUYS TO GET THOSE BLADES BALANCED ASAP!
OH, YOU DO, DO YOU? YOU KNOW, MEL, EVER SINCE YOUR PROMOTION, I'VE BEEN PICKING UP THIS SUPERIOR VIBE FROM YOU!
WELL, THERE'S A TECHNICAL REASON FOR THAT, ROZ...
WHICH IS?
I'M YOUR SUPER-IOR.
ONLY BECAUSE YOU **HAPPEN** TO BE A BET-TER SOLDIER! DUMB LUCK!
©B Trudeau

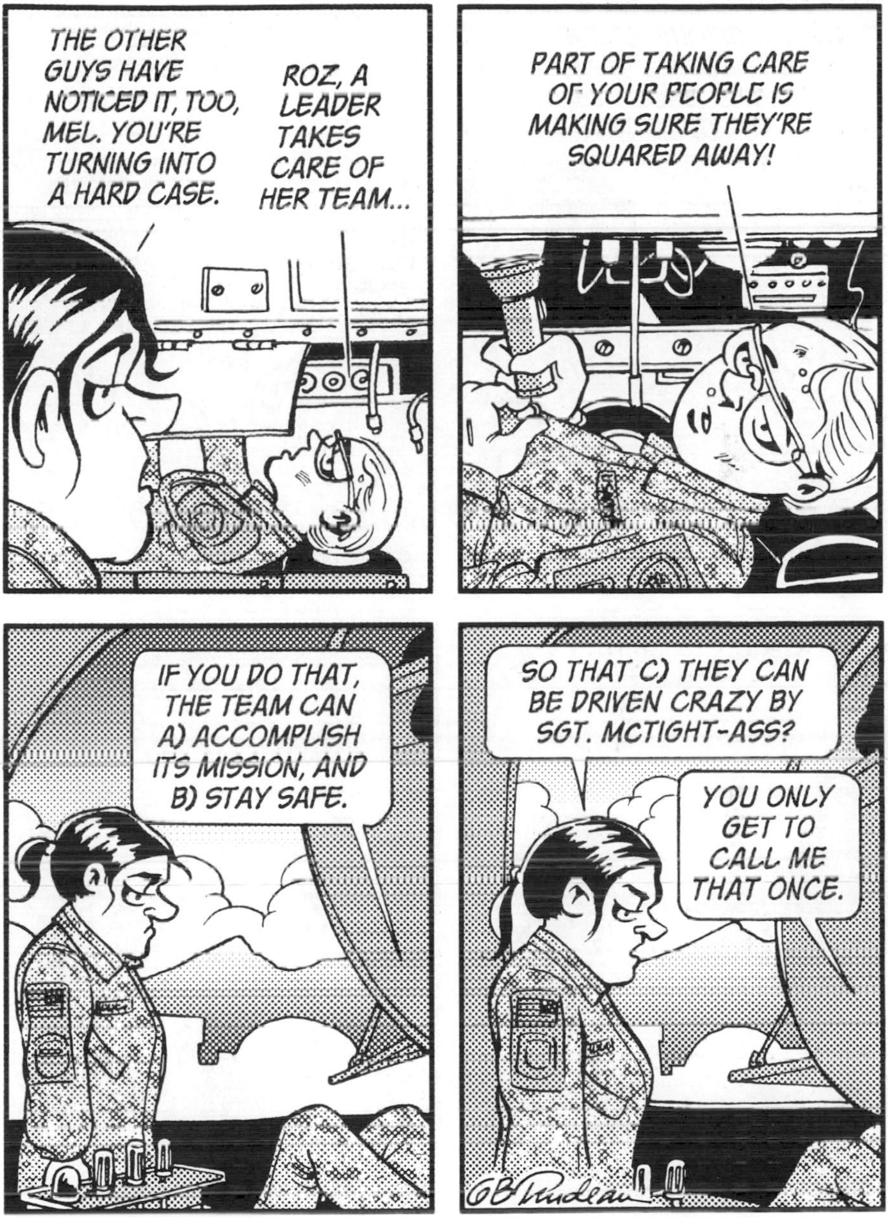
THE OTHER GUYS HAVE NOTICED IT, TOO, MEL. YOU'RE TURNING INTO A HARD CASE.
ROZ, A LEADER TAKES CARE OF HER TEAM...
PART OF TAKING CARE OF YOUR PEOPLE IS MAKING SURE THEY'RE SQUARED AWAY!
IF YOU DO THAT, THE TEAM CAN A) ACCOMPLISH ITS MISSION, AND B) STAY SAFE.
SO THAT C) THEY CAN BE DRIVEN CRAZY BY SGT. MCTIGHT-ASS?
YOU ONLY GET TO CALL ME THAT ONCE.
GB Trudeau

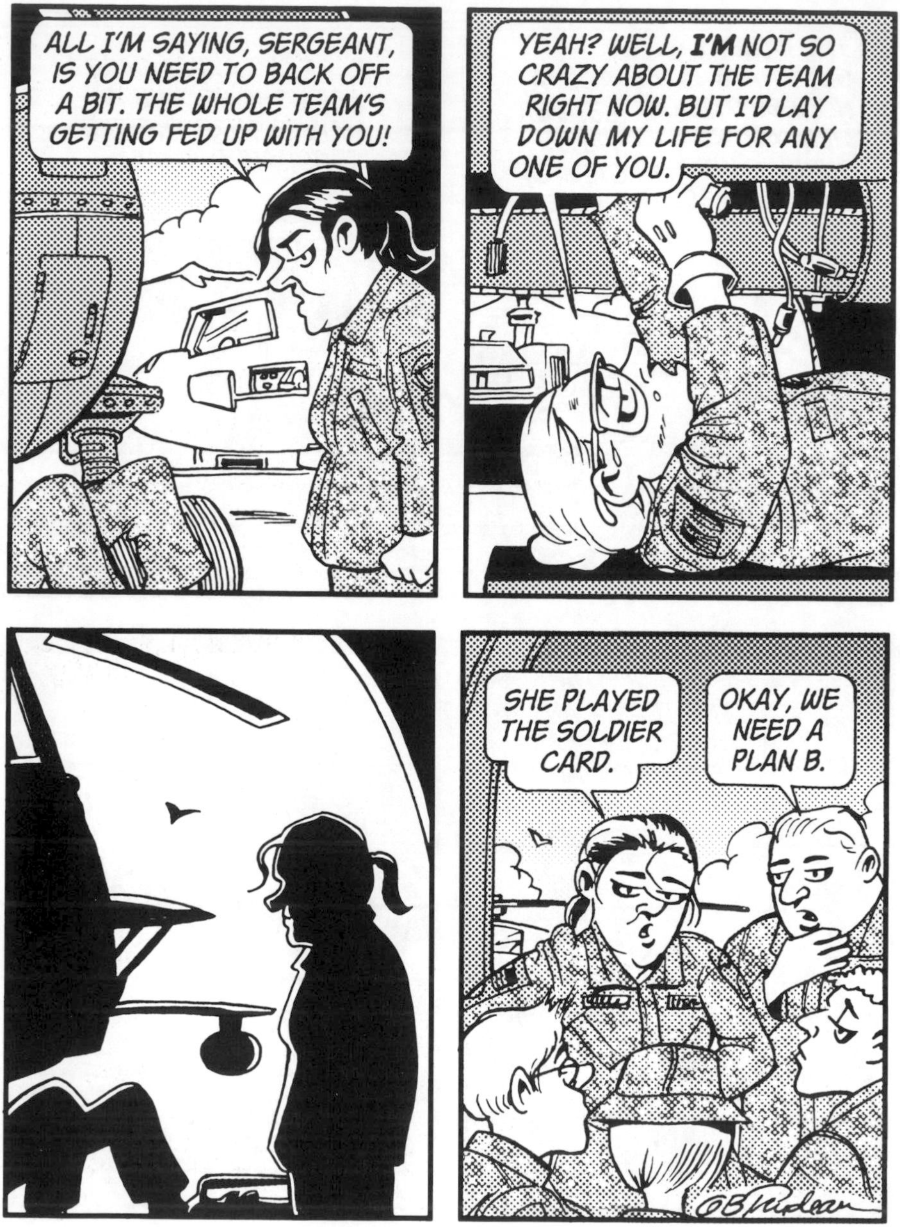
ALL I'M SAYING, SERGEANT, IS YOU NEED TO BACK OFF A BIT. THE WHOLE TEAM'S GETTING FED UP WITH YOU!
YEAH? WELL, **I'M** NOT SO CRAZY ABOUT THE TEAM RIGHT NOW. BUT I'D LAY DOWN MY LIFE FOR ANY ONE OF YOU.
SHE PLAYED THE SOLDIER CARD.
OKAY, WE NEED A PLAN B.

CHAPLAIN? GOT A MOMENT?
OF COURSE, MELISSA — COME ON IN! HOW'S THE NCO LIFE?
IT'S CHALLENGING. I'M NOT GETTING A LOT OF BUY-IN FROM MY TEAMMATES.
WHY NOT?
NOT SURE, MA'AM. IT COULD BE THE INCREASED TEMPO OF THE OPS. OR MAYBE IT'S JUST MY LEADERSHIP STYLE.
WHICH IS WHAT?
MY WAY OR MY WAY.
SO YOU DO GIVE THEM A CHOICE?
GB Trudeau

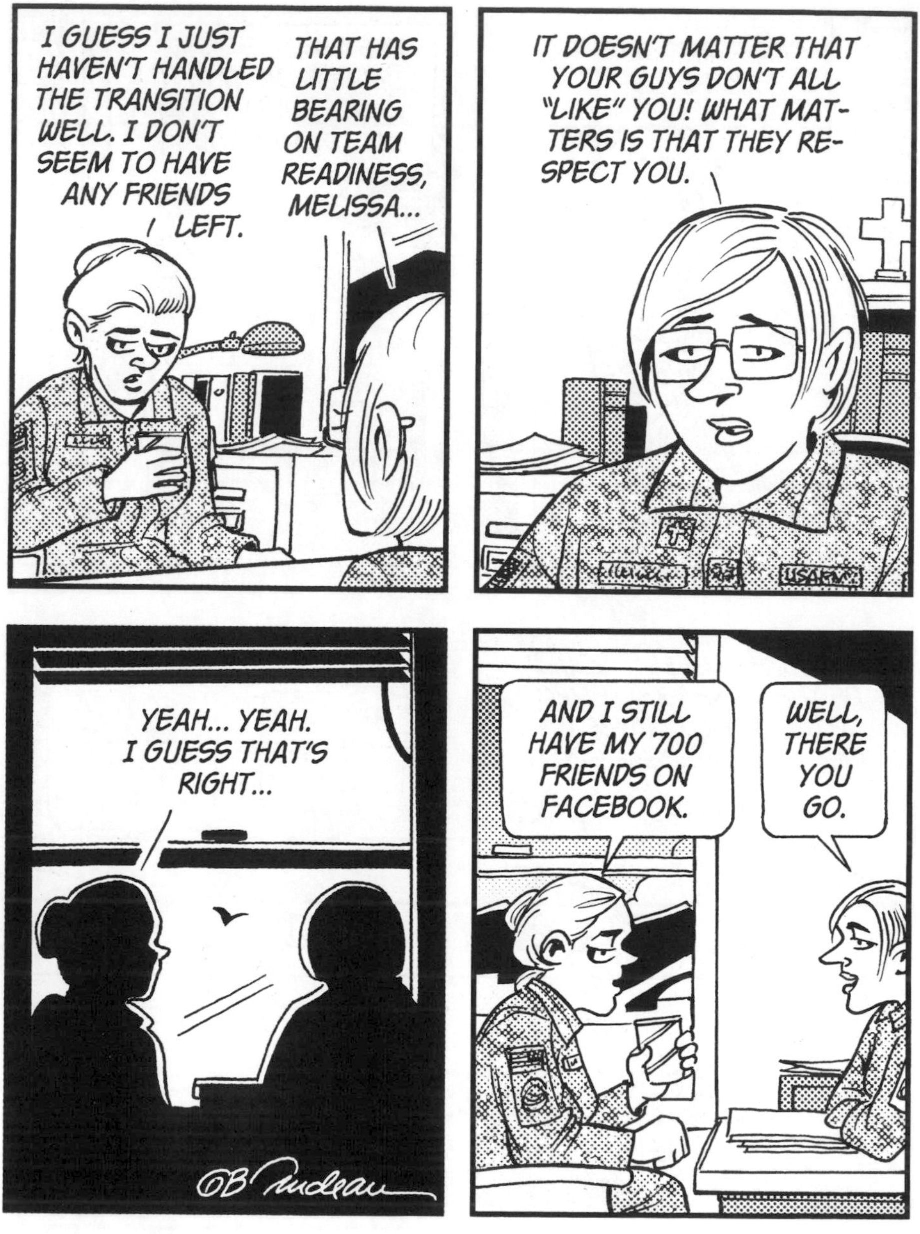
I GUESS I JUST HAVEN'T HANDLED THE TRANSITION WELL. I DON'T SEEM TO HAVE ANY FRIENDS LEFT.
THAT HAS LITTLE BEARING ON TEAM READINESS, MELISSA...
IT DOESN'T MATTER THAT YOUR GUYS DON'T ALL "LIKE" YOU! WHAT MATTERS IS THAT THEY RESPECT YOU.
YEAH... YEAH. I GUESS THAT'S RIGHT...
AND I STILL HAVE MY 700 FRIENDS ON FACEBOOK.
WELL, THERE YOU GO.

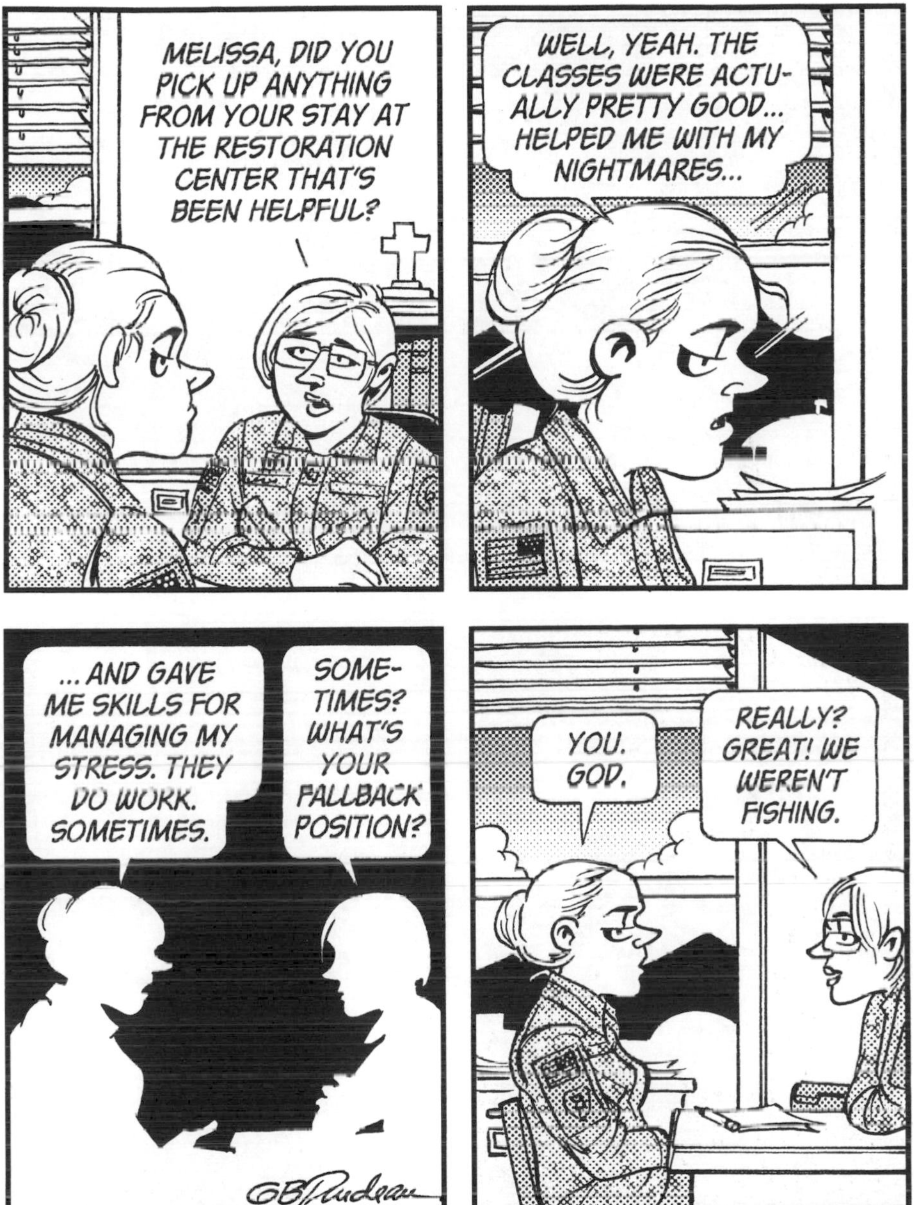
MELISSA, DID YOU PICK UP ANYTHING FROM YOUR STAY AT THE RESTORATION CENTER THAT'S BEEN HELPFUL?
WELL, YEAH. THE CLASSES WERE ACTU-ALLY PRETTY GOOD... HELPED ME WITH MY NIGHTMARES...
... AND GAVE ME SKILLS FOR MANAGING MY STRESS. THEY DO WORK. SOMETIMES.
SOME-TIMES? WHAT'S YOUR FALLBACK POSITION?
YOU. GOD.
REALLY? GREAT! WE WEREN'T FISHING.
GBTrudeau

ALL ACROSS AFGHANISTAN...
RAP RAP RAP RAP!
... FROM HERAT TO KANDAHAR...
WHOOM!
... HELMAND TO KABUL...
BAP BAPPA BAP!
... IT'S GAME ON!
"BLACK OPS" IS IN!
ZOMBIES? REALLY? REALLY?
LIGHT 'EM UP, DUDE!
BAP BAP BAP!
©B Trudeau

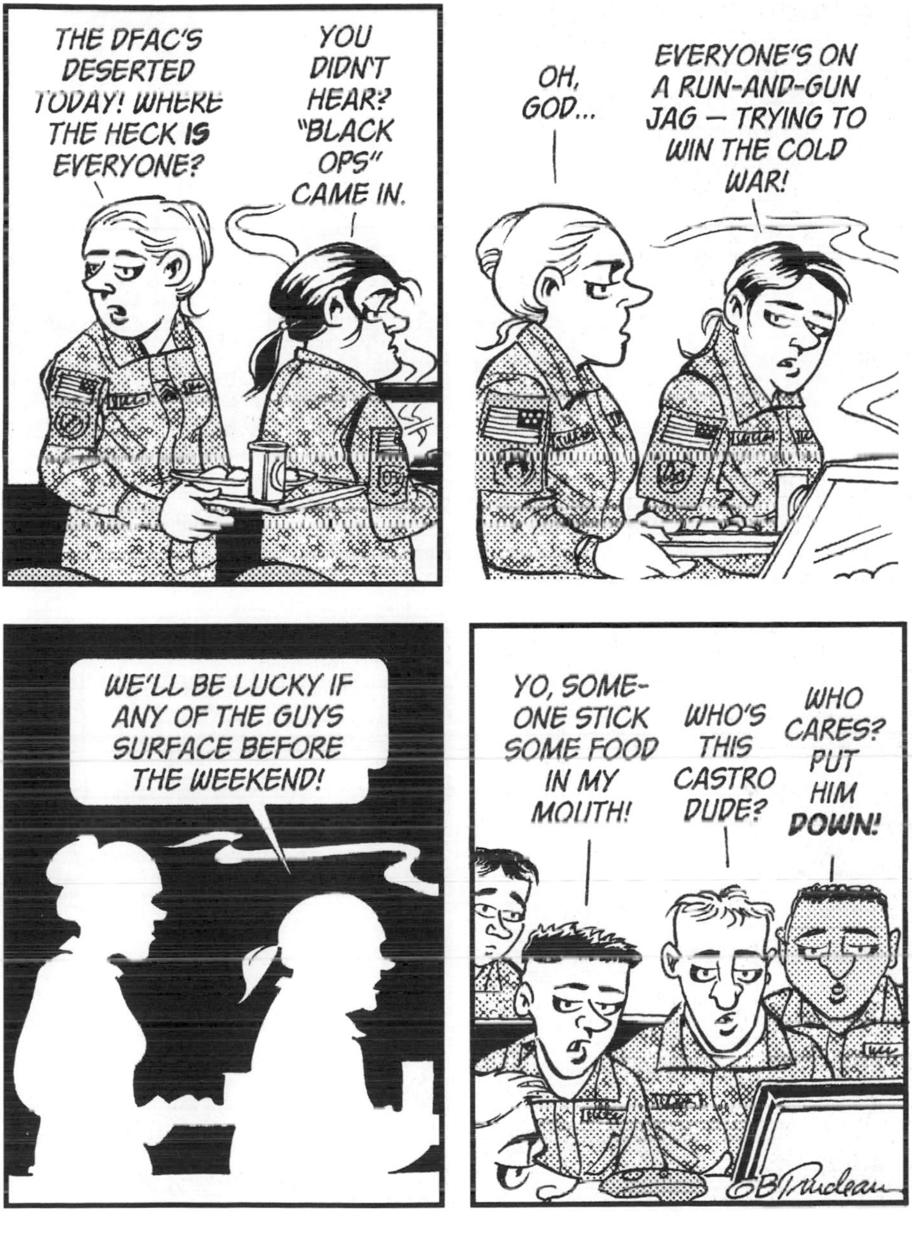
THE DFAC'S DESERTED TODAY! WHERE THE HECK IS EVERYONE?
YOU DIDN'T HEAR? "BLACK OPS" CAME IN.
OH, GOD...
EVERYONE'S ON A RUN-AND-GUN JAG — TRYING TO WIN THE COLD WAR!
WE'LL BE LUCKY IF ANY OF THE GUYS SURFACE BEFORE THE WEEKEND!
YO, SOME-ONE STICK SOME FOOD IN MY MOUTH!
WHO'S THIS CASTRO DUDE?
WHO CARES? PUT HIM DOWN!
GBTrudeau

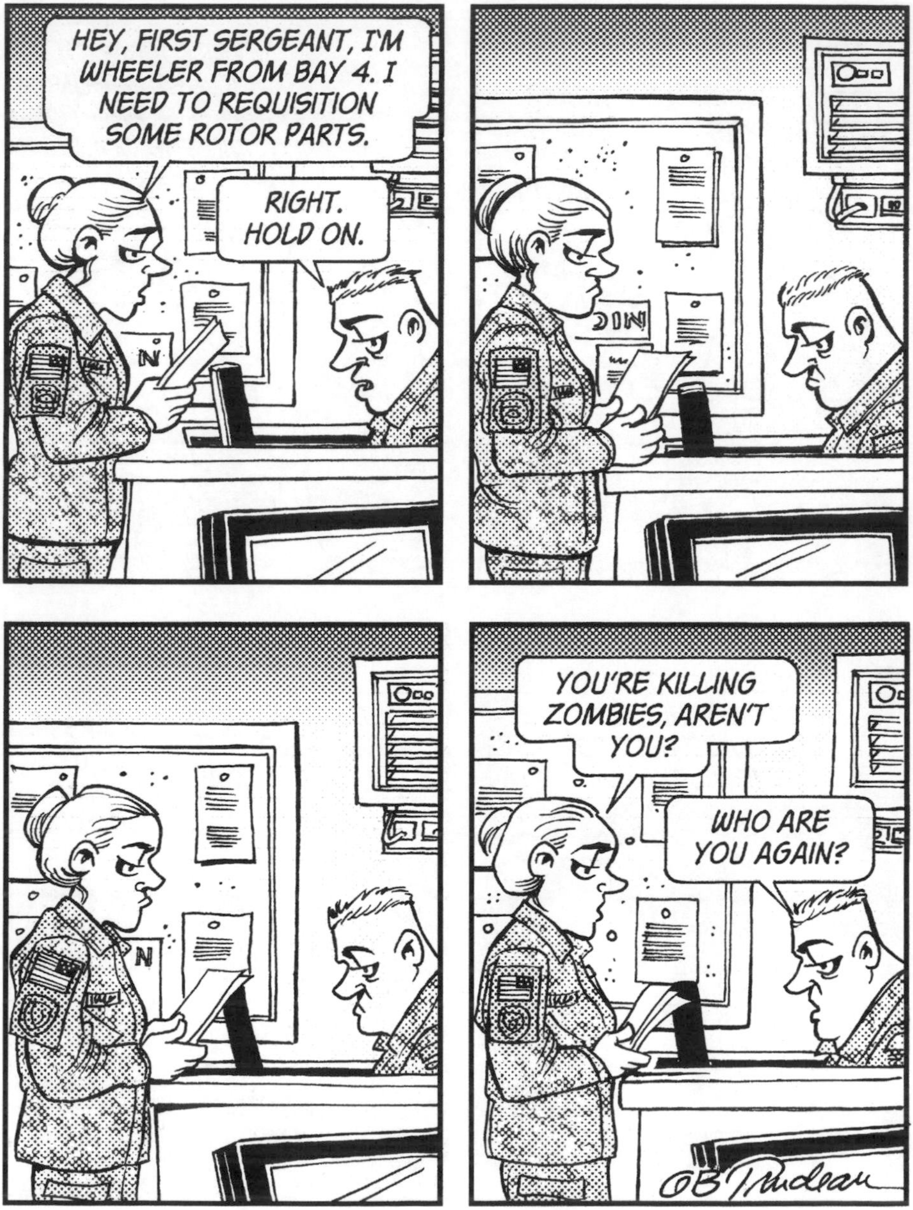
HEY, FIRST SERGEANT, I'M WHEELER FROM BAY 4. I NEED TO REQUISITION SOME ROTOR PARTS.
RIGHT. HOLD ON.
YOU'RE KILLING ZOMBIES, AREN'T YOU?
WHO ARE YOU AGAIN?
©B Trudeau

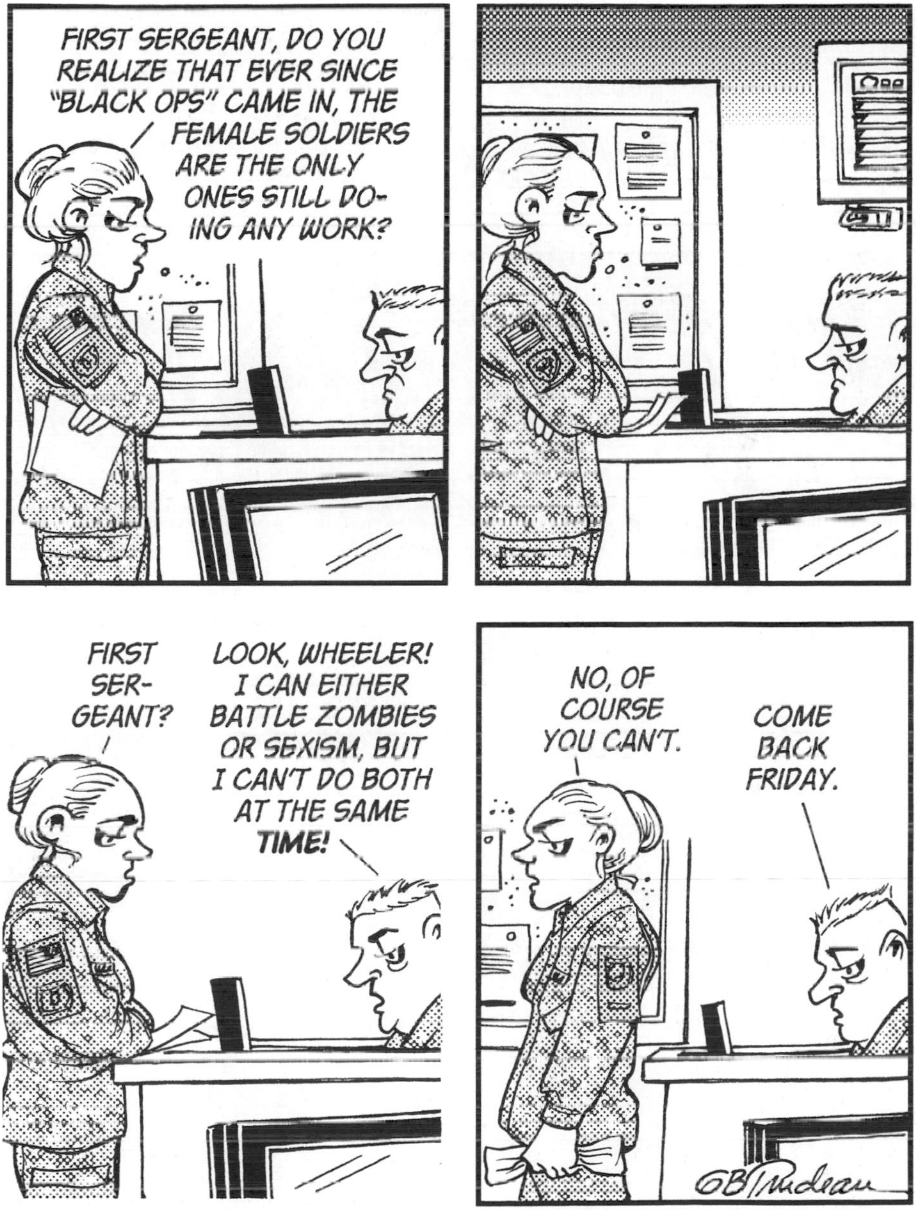
FIRST SERGEANT, DO YOU REALIZE THAT EVER SINCE "BLACK OPS" CAME IN, THE FEMALE SOLDIERS ARE THE ONLY ONES STILL DOING ANY WORK?
FIRST SERGEANT?
LOOK, WHEELER! I CAN EITHER BATTLE ZOMBIES OR SEXISM, BUT I CAN'T DO BOTH AT THE SAME TIME!
NO, OF COURSE YOU CAN'T.
COME BACK FRIDAY.
GBTrudeau

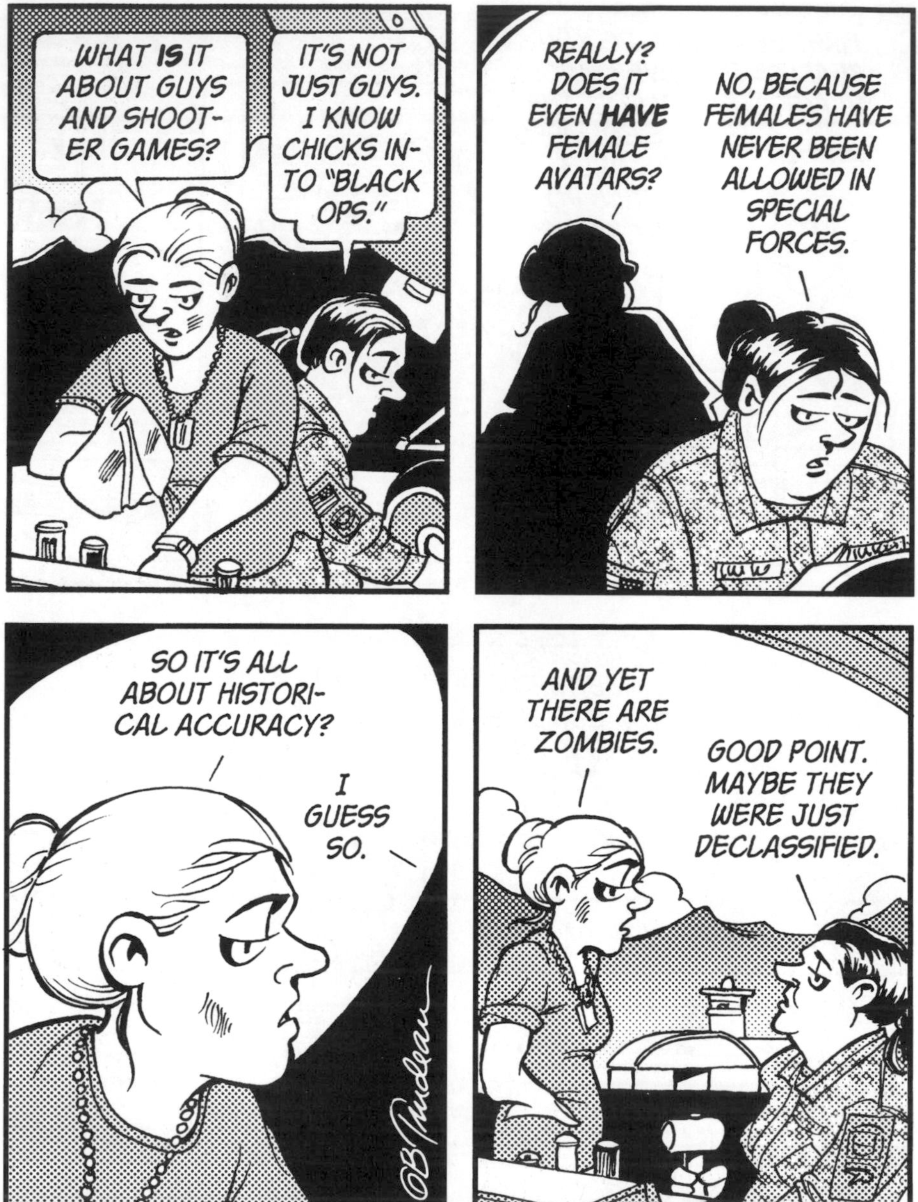
WHAT **IS** IT ABOUT GUYS AND SHOOTER GAMES?
IT'S NOT JUST GUYS. I KNOW CHICKS INTO "BLACK OPS."
REALLY? DOES IT EVEN **HAVE** FEMALE AVATARS?
NO, BECAUSE FEMALES HAVE NEVER BEEN ALLOWED IN SPECIAL FORCES.
SO IT'S ALL ABOUT HISTORICAL ACCURACY?
I GUESS SO.
AND YET THERE ARE ZOMBIES.
GOOD POINT. MAYBE THEY WERE JUST DECLASSIFIED.

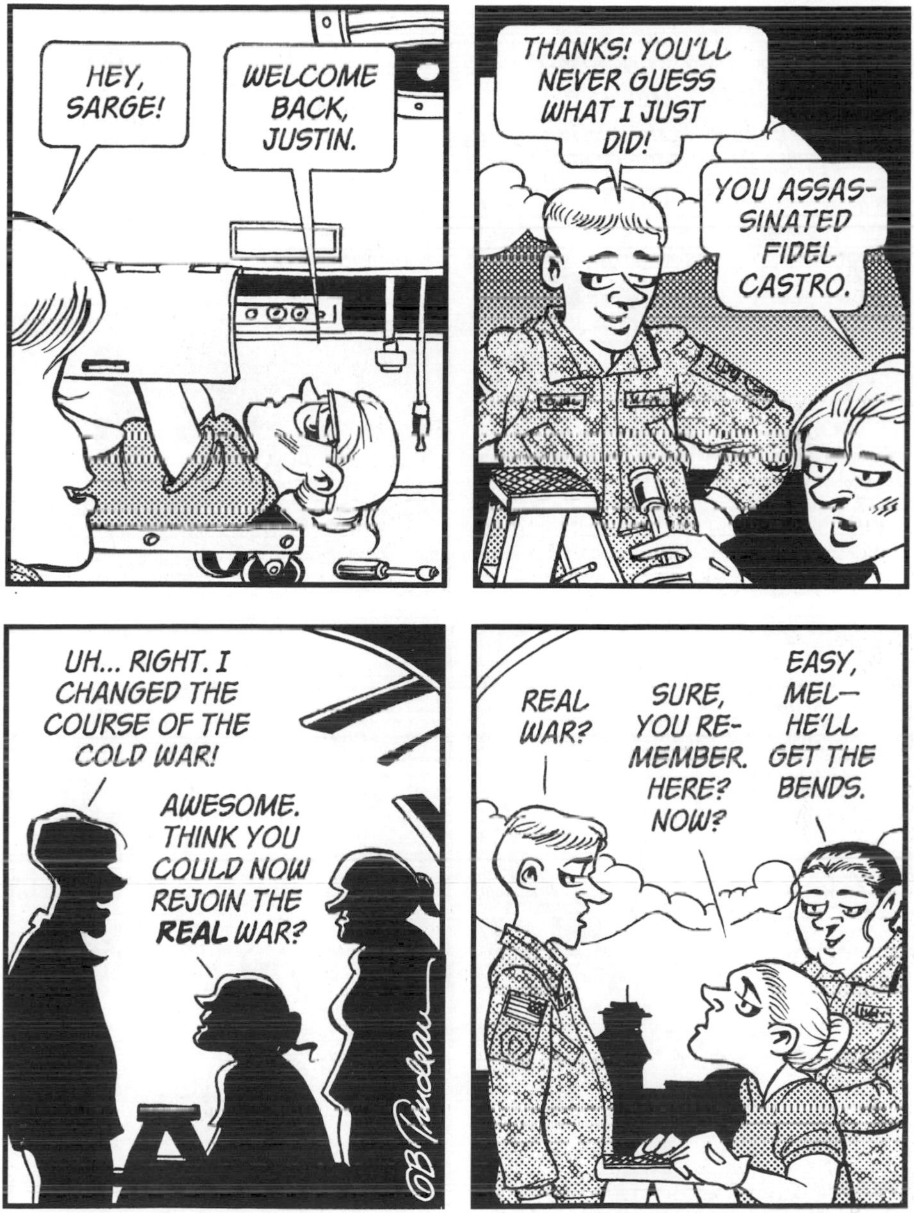
HEY, SARGE!
WELCOME BACK, JUSTIN.
THANKS! YOU'LL NEVER GUESS WHAT I JUST DID!
YOU ASSAS-SINATED FIDEL CASTRO.
UH... RIGHT. I CHANGED THE COURSE OF THE COLD WAR!
AWESOME. THINK YOU COULD NOW REJOIN THE **REAL** WAR?
©B Trudeau
REAL WAR?
SURE, YOU RE-MEMBER. HERE? NOW?
EASY, MEL— HE'LL GET THE BENDS.

OKAY, SO YOU DIDN'T ASK, AND IT MAY NOT COME AS A TOTAL SUR-PRISE, BUT HERE GOES: I'M GAY.
WHAT?
THAT SOUNDS SO WEIRD. I CAN'T BELIEVE I'M ALLOWED TO TELL YOU THAT NOW...
YOU'RE GAY? REALLY?
REALLY. HOLD ON, I GOT A CALL...
BUT YOU **CAN'T** BE...
HI, MOM! I JUST TOLD MY SERGEANT I'M GAY!
YOU'RE WHAT?
GB Trudeau

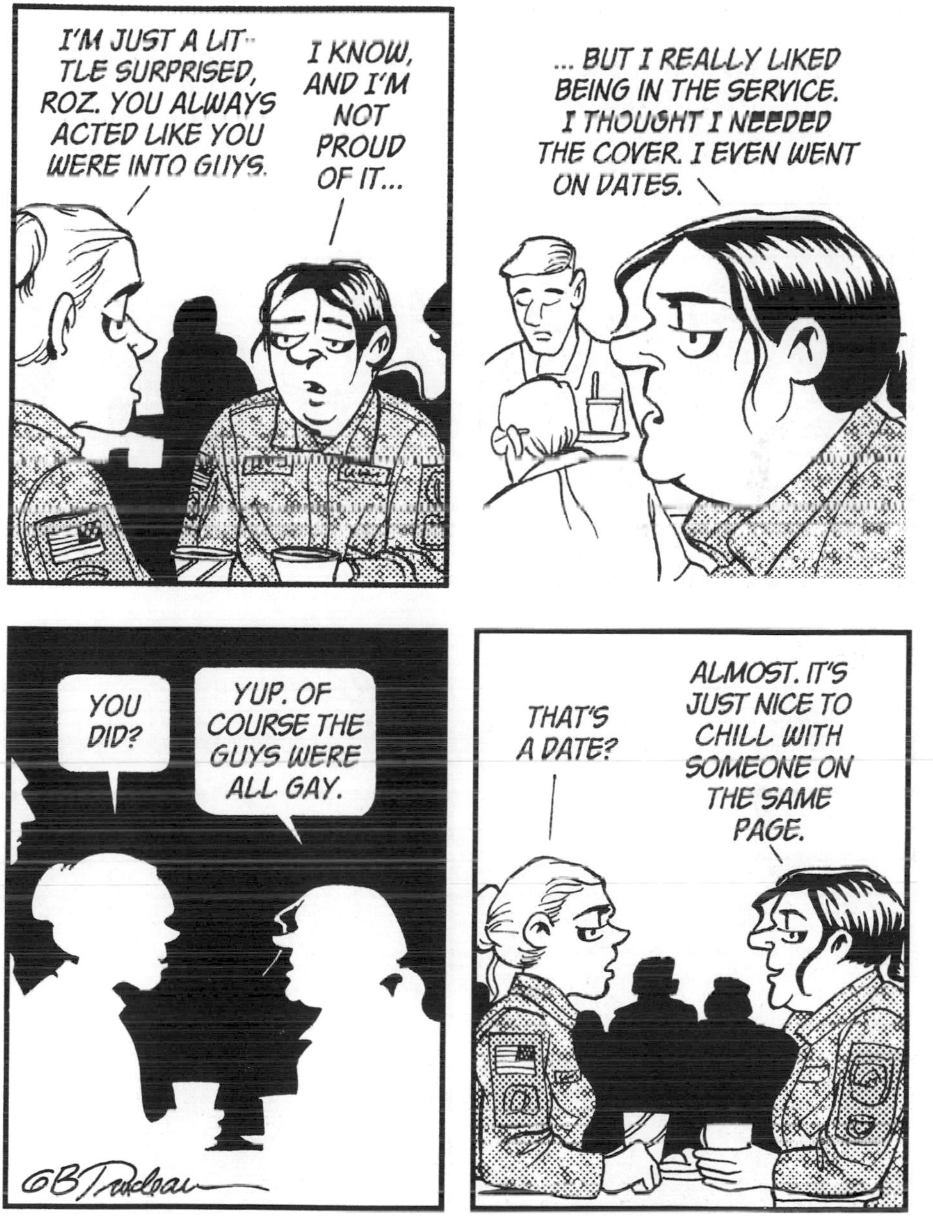
I'M JUST A LIT-TLE SURPRISED, ROZ. YOU ALWAYS ACTED LIKE YOU WERE INTO GUYS.
I KNOW, AND I'M NOT PROUD OF IT...
... BUT I REALLY LIKED BEING IN THE SERVICE. I THOUGHT I NEEDED THE COVER. I EVEN WENT ON DATES.
YOU DID?
YUP. OF COURSE THE GUYS WERE ALL GAY.
THAT'S A DATE?
ALMOST. IT'S JUST NICE TO CHILL WITH SOMEONE ON THE SAME PAGE.

SO YOU THINK YOU'LL TELL ANYONE ELSE, ROZ?
WHY WOULDN'T I TELL ANYONE ELSE?
I DON'T KNOW, SOME ON THE TEAM MIGHT NOT RESPOND WELL?
HEY, GUYS! CHECK IT OUT – I'M GAY!
NO KID-DING!
AND LIFE GOES ON.
AMAZING.
GB Trudeau

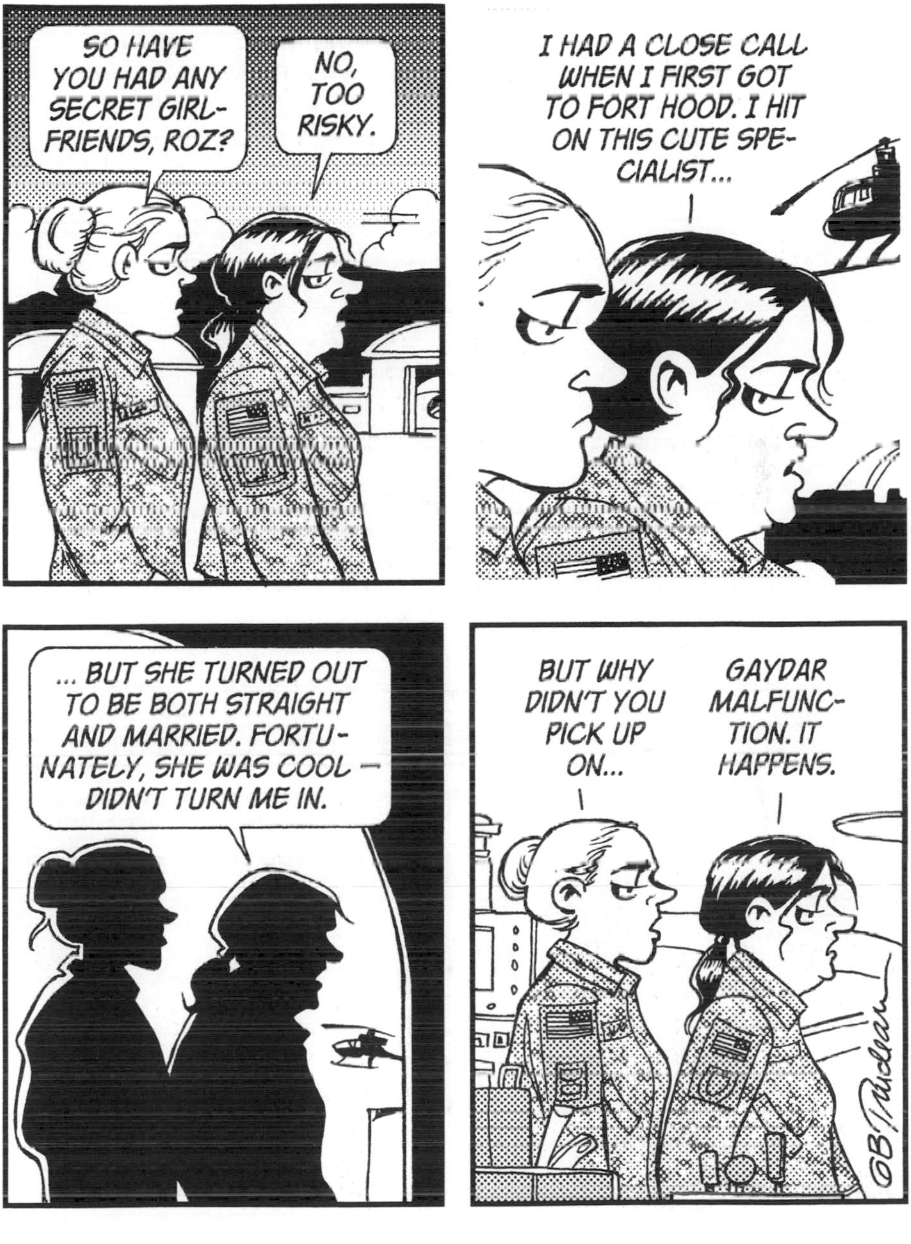
SO HAVE YOU HAD ANY SECRET GIRL-FRIENDS, ROZ?
NO, TOO RISKY.
I HAD A CLOSE CALL WHEN I FIRST GOT TO FORT HOOD. I HIT ON THIS CUTE SPE-CIALIST...
... BUT SHE TURNED OUT TO BE BOTH STRAIGHT AND MARRIED. FORTU-NATELY, SHE WAS COOL — DIDN'T TURN ME IN.
BUT WHY DIDN'T YOU PICK UP ON...
GAYDAR MALFUNC-TION. IT HAPPENS.
©B. Trudeau

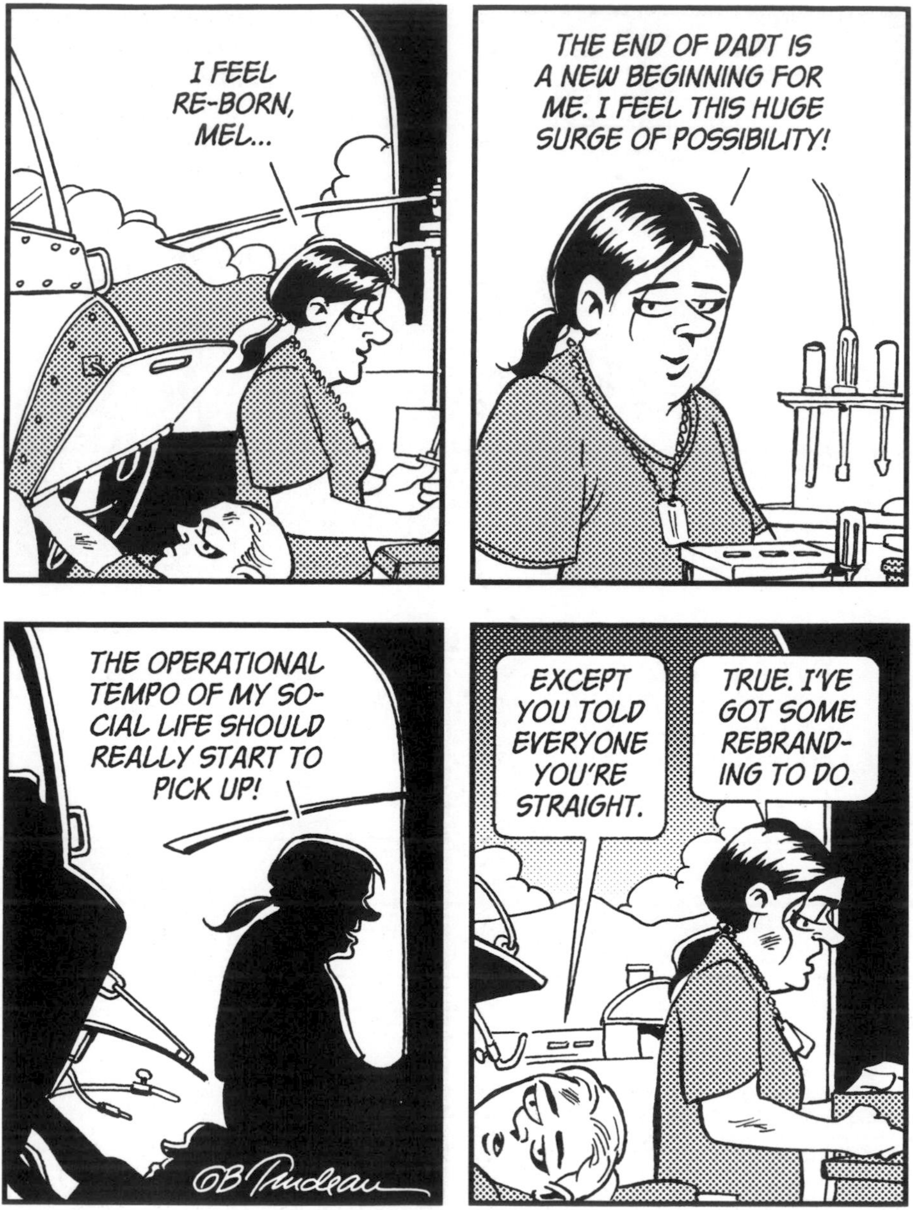
I FEEL RE-BORN, MEL...
THE END OF DADT IS A NEW BEGINNING FOR ME. I FEEL THIS HUGE SURGE OF POSSIBILITY!
THE OPERATIONAL TEMPO OF MY SO-CIAL LIFE SHOULD REALLY START TO PICK UP!
EXCEPT YOU TOLD EVERYONE YOU'RE STRAIGHT.
TRUE. I'VE GOT SOME REBRAND-ING TO DO.
©B Trudeau

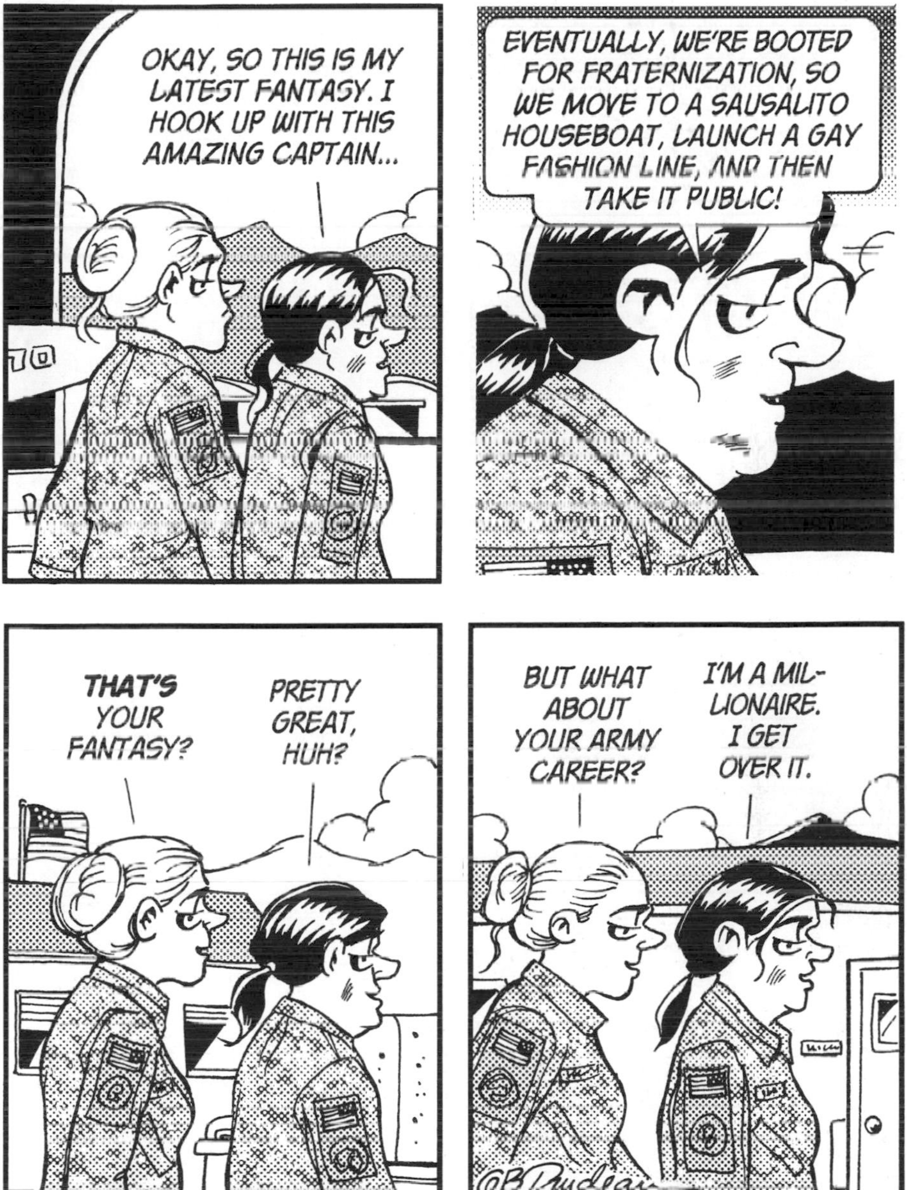
OKAY, SO THIS IS MY LATEST FANTASY. I HOOK UP WITH THIS AMAZING CAPTAIN...
EVENTUALLY, WE'RE BOOTED FOR FRATERNIZATION, SO WE MOVE TO A SAUSALITO HOUSEBOAT, LAUNCH A GAY FASHION LINE, AND THEN TAKE IT PUBLIC!
THAT'S YOUR FANTASY?
PRETTY GREAT, HUH?
BUT WHAT ABOUT YOUR ARMY CAREER?
I'M A MIL-LIONAIRE. I GET OVER IT.
©B. Trudeau

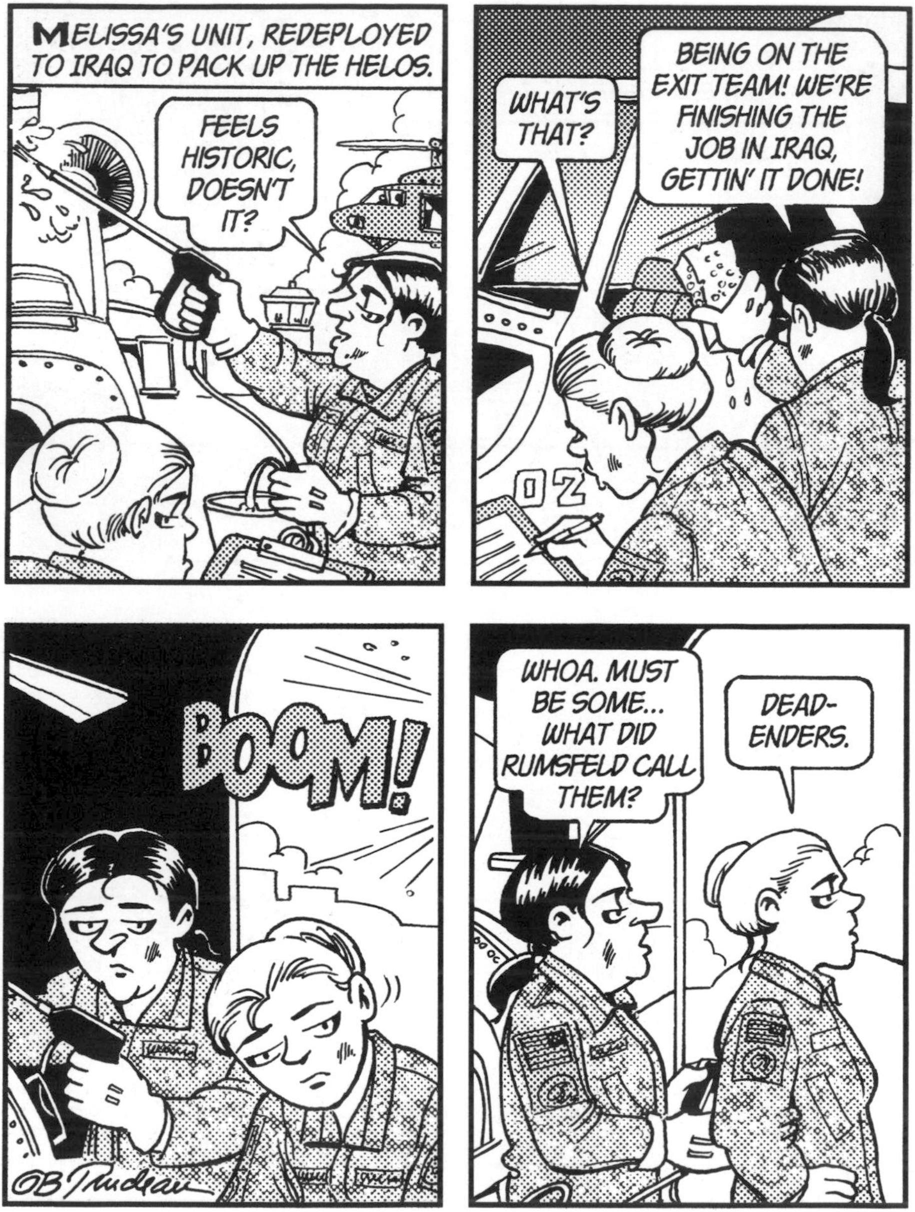
MELISSA'S UNIT, REDEPLOYED TO IRAQ TO PACK UP THE HELOS.
FEELS HISTORIC, DOESN'T IT?
WHAT'S THAT?
BEING ON THE EXIT TEAM! WE'RE FINISHING THE JOB IN IRAQ, GETTIN' IT DONE!
02
BOOM!
WHOA. MUST BE SOME... WHAT DID RUMSFELD CALL THEM?
DEAD-ENDERS.

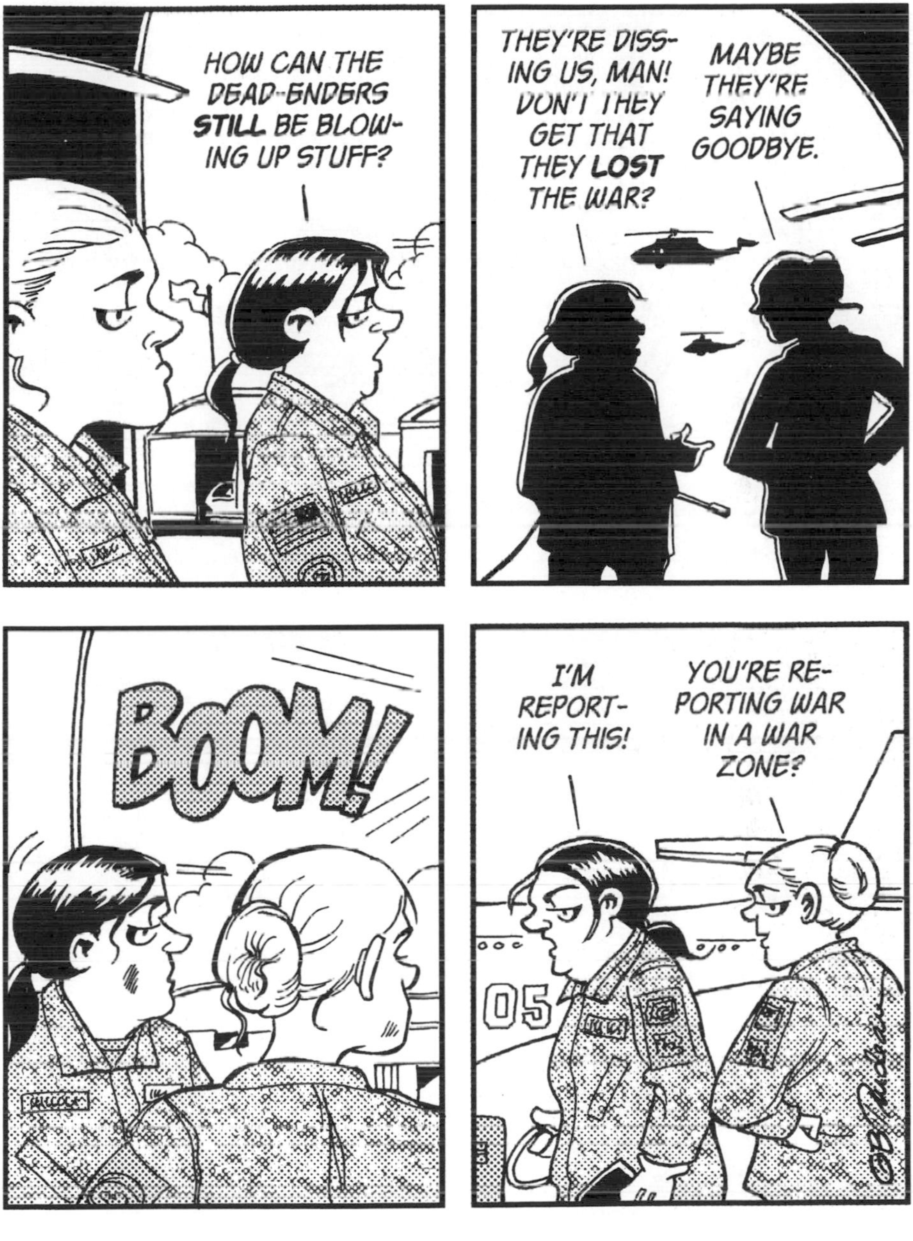
HOW CAN THE DEAD-ENDERS **STILL** BE BLOWING UP STUFF?
THEY'RE DISSING US, MAN! DON'T THEY GET THAT THEY **LOST** THE WAR?
MAYBE THEY'RE SAYING GOODBYE.
BOOM!
I'M REPORTING THIS!
YOU'RE REPORTING WAR IN A WAR ZONE?
05

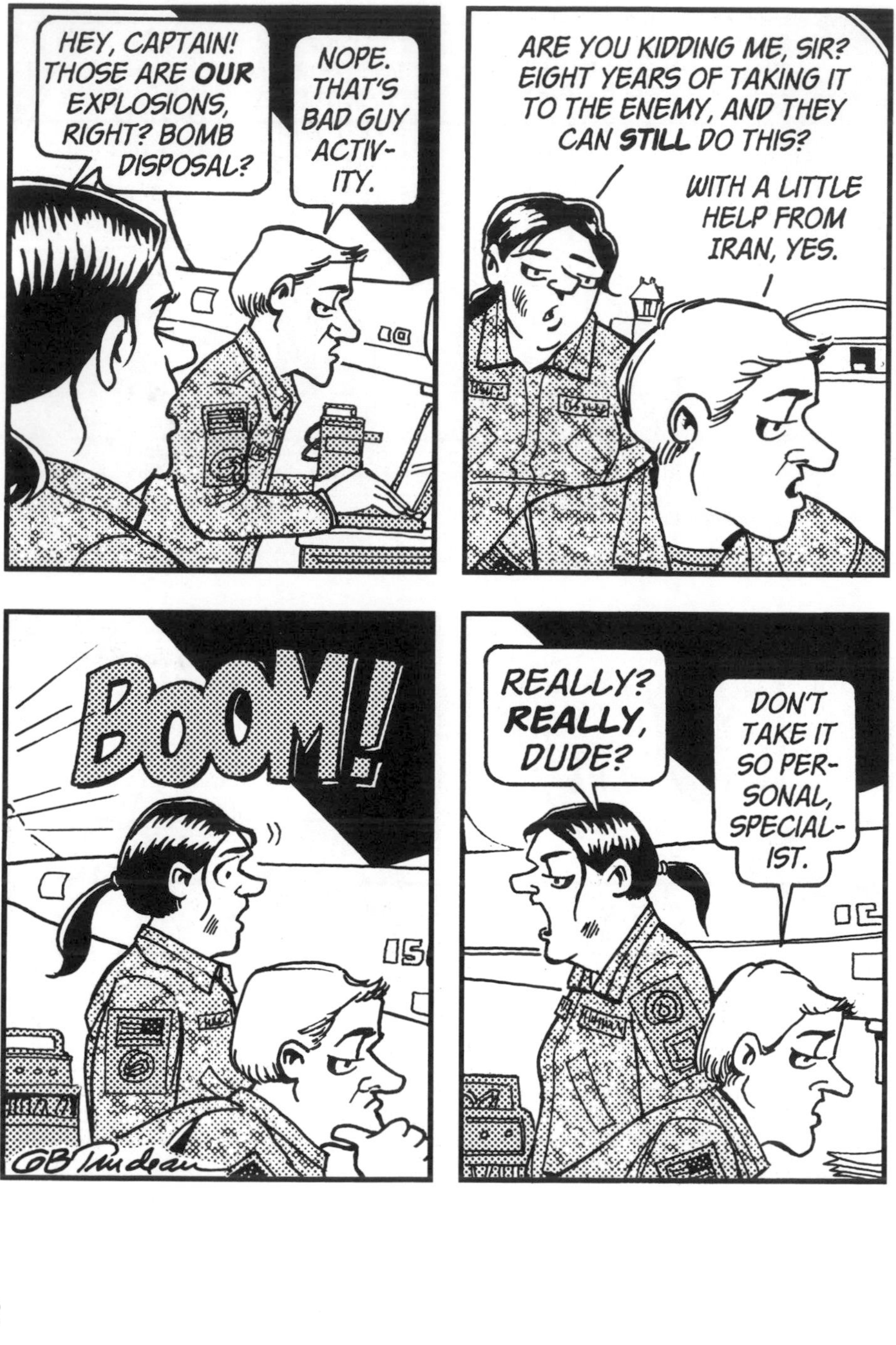
HEY, CAPTAIN! THOSE ARE **OUR** EXPLOSIONS, RIGHT? BOMB DISPOSAL?
NOPE. THAT'S BAD GUY ACTIV-ITY.
ARE YOU KIDDING ME, SIR? EIGHT YEARS OF TAKING IT TO THE ENEMY, AND THEY CAN **STILL** DO THIS?
WITH A LITTLE HELP FROM IRAN, YES.
BOOM!
REALLY? **REALLY**, DUDE?
DON'T TAKE IT SO PER-SONAL, SPECIAL-IST.
GBTrudeau

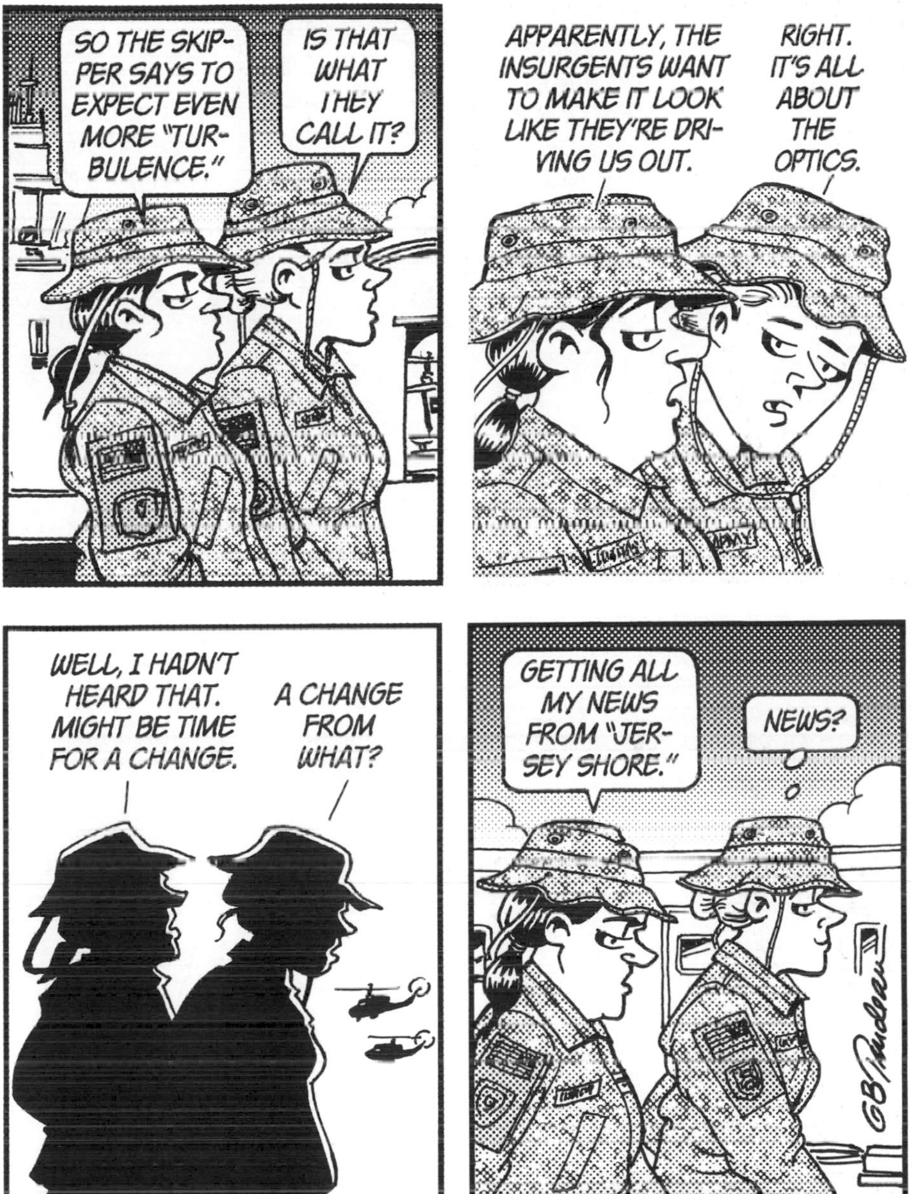
SO THE SKIPPER SAYS TO EXPECT EVEN MORE "TURBULENCE."
IS THAT WHAT THEY CALL IT?
APPARENTLY, THE INSURGENTS WANT TO MAKE IT LOOK LIKE THEY'RE DRIVING US OUT.
RIGHT. IT'S ALL ABOUT THE OPTICS.
WELL, I HADN'T HEARD THAT. MIGHT BE TIME FOR A CHANGE.
A CHANGE FROM WHAT?
GETTING ALL MY NEWS FROM "JERSEY SHORE."
NEWS?
GB Trudeau

WOW... LOOK AT HOW EMPTY THIS PLACE IS!
YEAH, THEY'RE DRAWING DOWN QUICK-LY NOW.
HOW LONG WILL **WE** BE HERE?
AS LONG AS IT TAKES TO GET ALL THE HELOS CLEANED AND LOADED UP.
I HATE SEEING THOSE AWESOME BIRDS TRUSSED IN SHRINKWRAP! IT MAKES ME FEEL LIKE... LIKE...
LIKE WHAT?
LIKE SNEAK-ING ON THE FLATBEDS AND SETTING THEM FREE!
FLY, LITTLE GUNSHIPS, FLY AWAY!
GB Trudeau

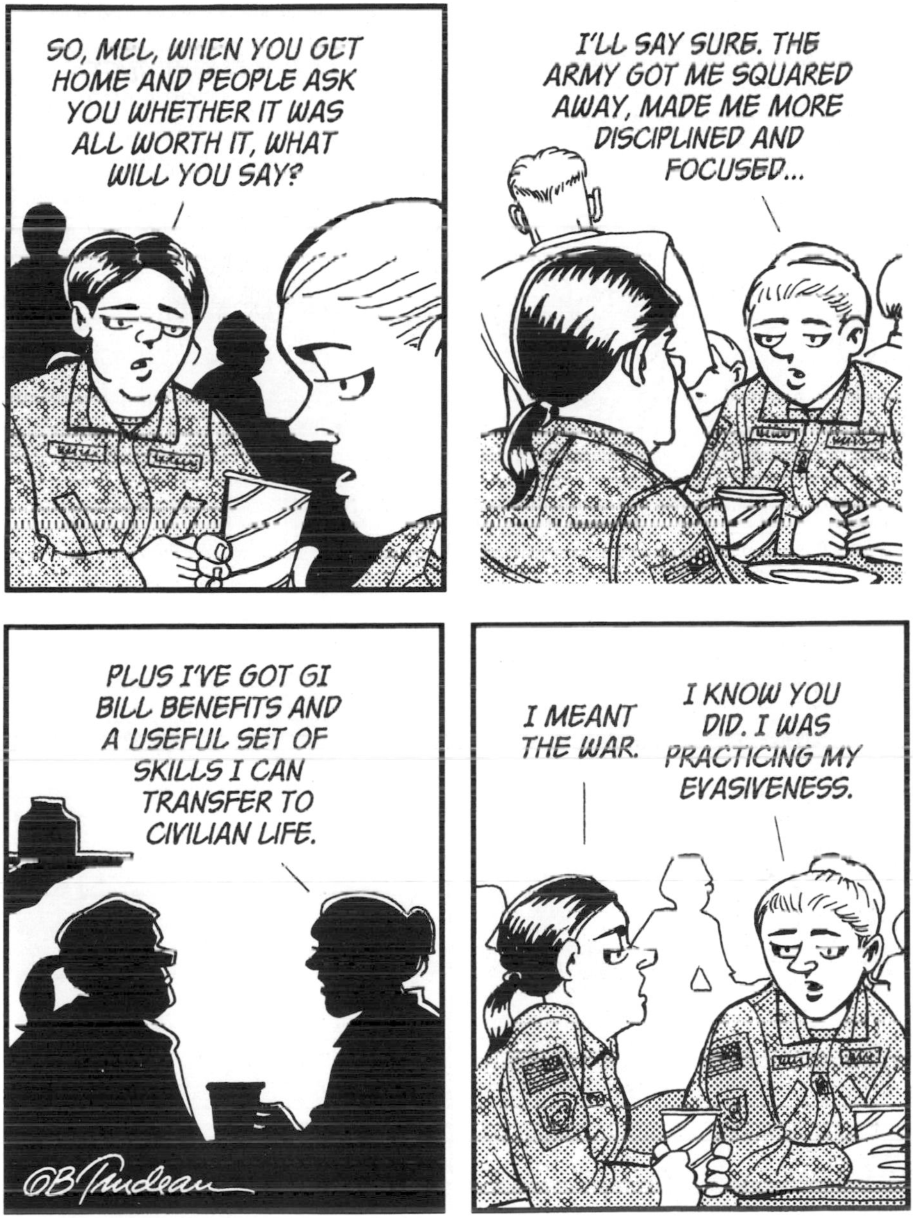
SO, MEL, WHEN YOU GET HOME AND PEOPLE ASK YOU WHETHER IT WAS ALL WORTH IT, WHAT WILL YOU SAY?
I'LL SAY SURE. THE ARMY GOT ME SQUARED AWAY, MADE ME MORE DISCIPLINED AND FOCUSED...
PLUS I'VE GOT GI BILL BENEFITS AND A USEFUL SET OF SKILLS I CAN TRANSFER TO CIVILIAN LIFE.
©B Trudeau
I MEANT THE WAR.
I KNOW YOU DID. I WAS PRACTICING MY EVASIVENESS.

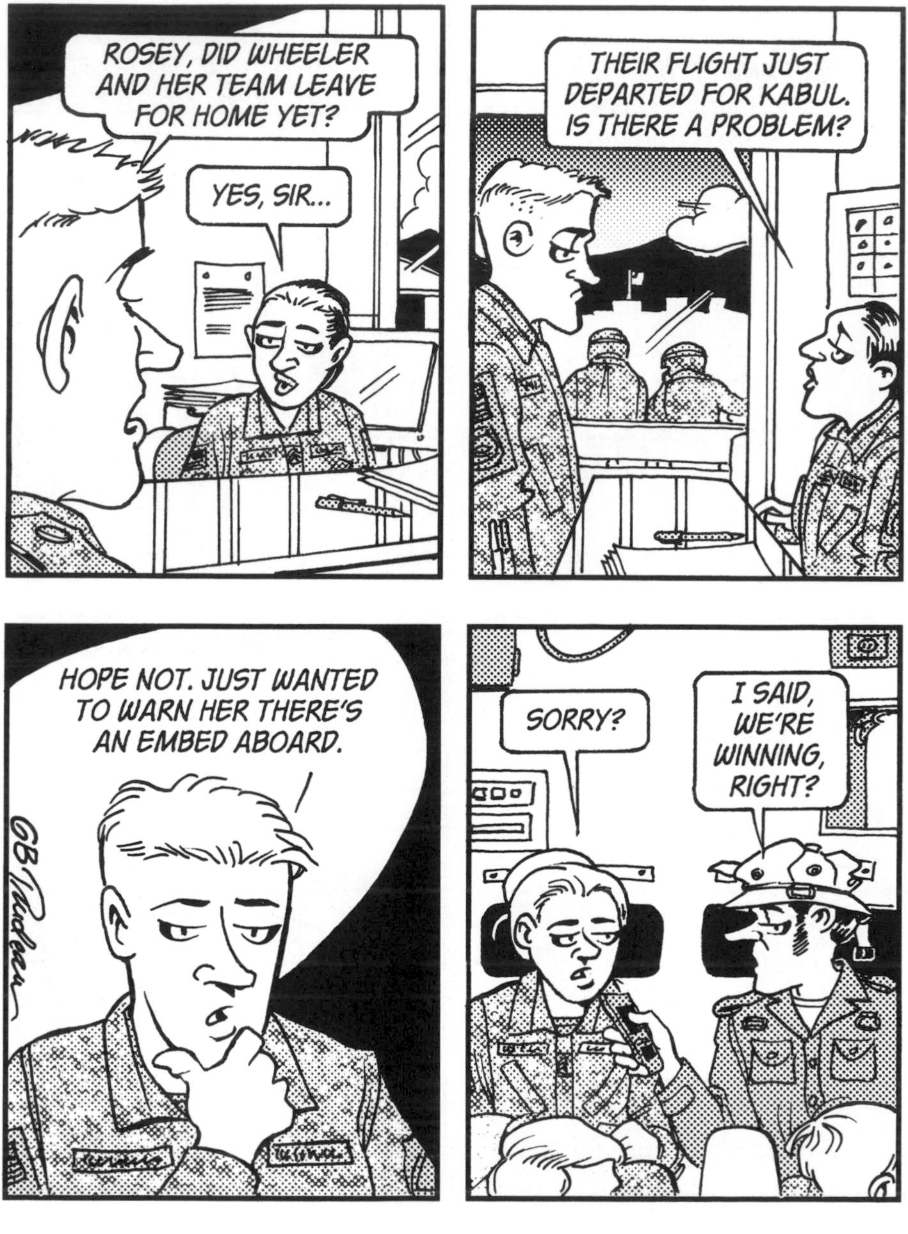
ROSEY, DID WHEELER AND HER TEAM LEAVE FOR HOME YET?
YES, SIR...
THEIR FLIGHT JUST DEPARTED FOR KABUL. IS THERE A PROBLEM?
HOPE NOT. JUST WANTED TO WARN HER THERE'S AN EMBED ABOARD.
GB Trudeau
SORRY?
I SAID, WE'RE WINNING, RIGHT?

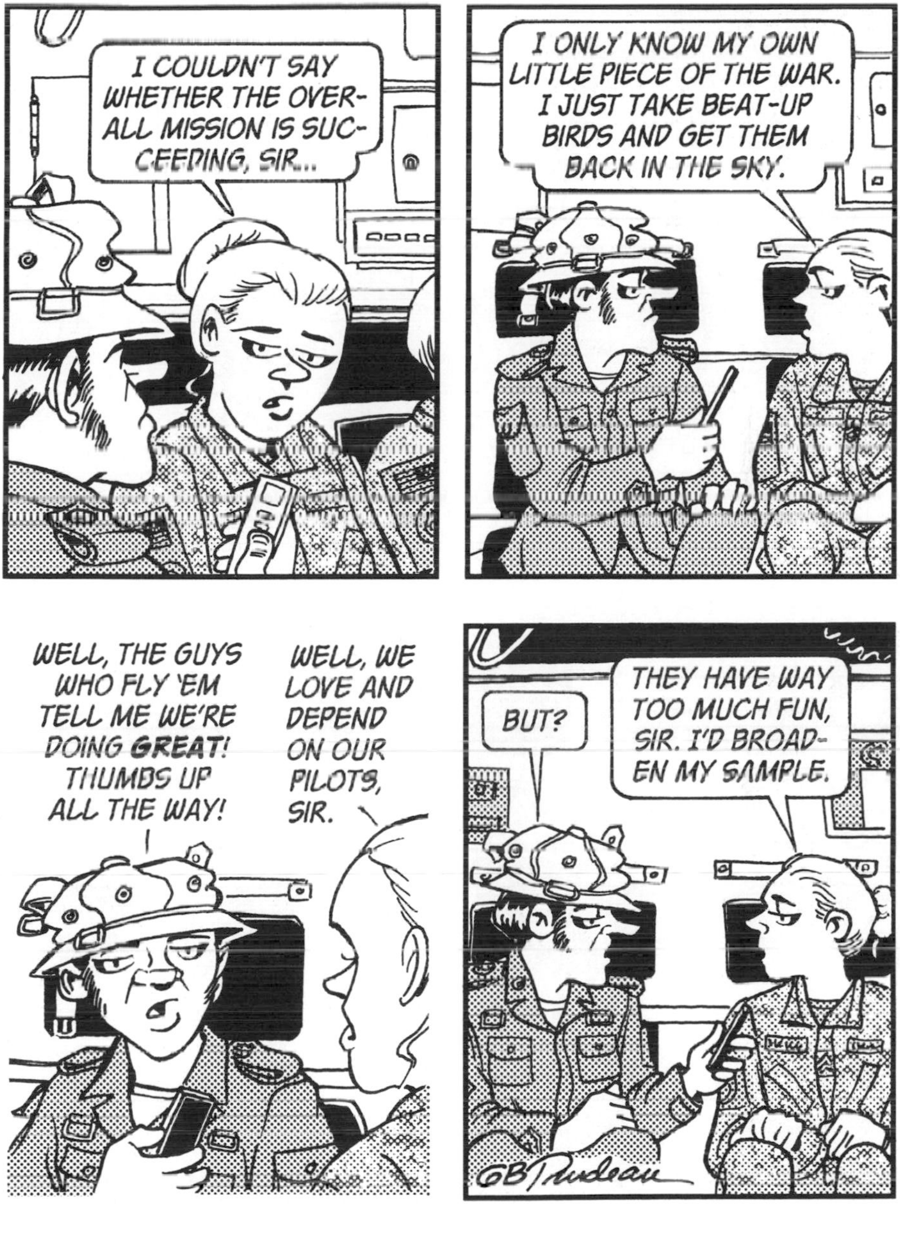

I COULDN'T SAY WHETHER THE OVER-ALL MISSION IS SUC-CEEDING, SIR...
I ONLY KNOW MY OWN LITTLE PIECE OF THE WAR. I JUST TAKE BEAT-UP BIRDS AND GET THEM BACK IN THE SKY.
WELL, THE GUYS WHO FLY 'EM TELL ME WE'RE DOING **GREAT**! THUMBS UP ALL THE WAY!
WELL, WE LOVE AND DEPEND ON OUR PILOTS, SIR.
BUT?
THEY HAVE WAY TOO MUCH FUN, SIR. I'D BROAD-EN MY SAMPLE.
GBTrudeau

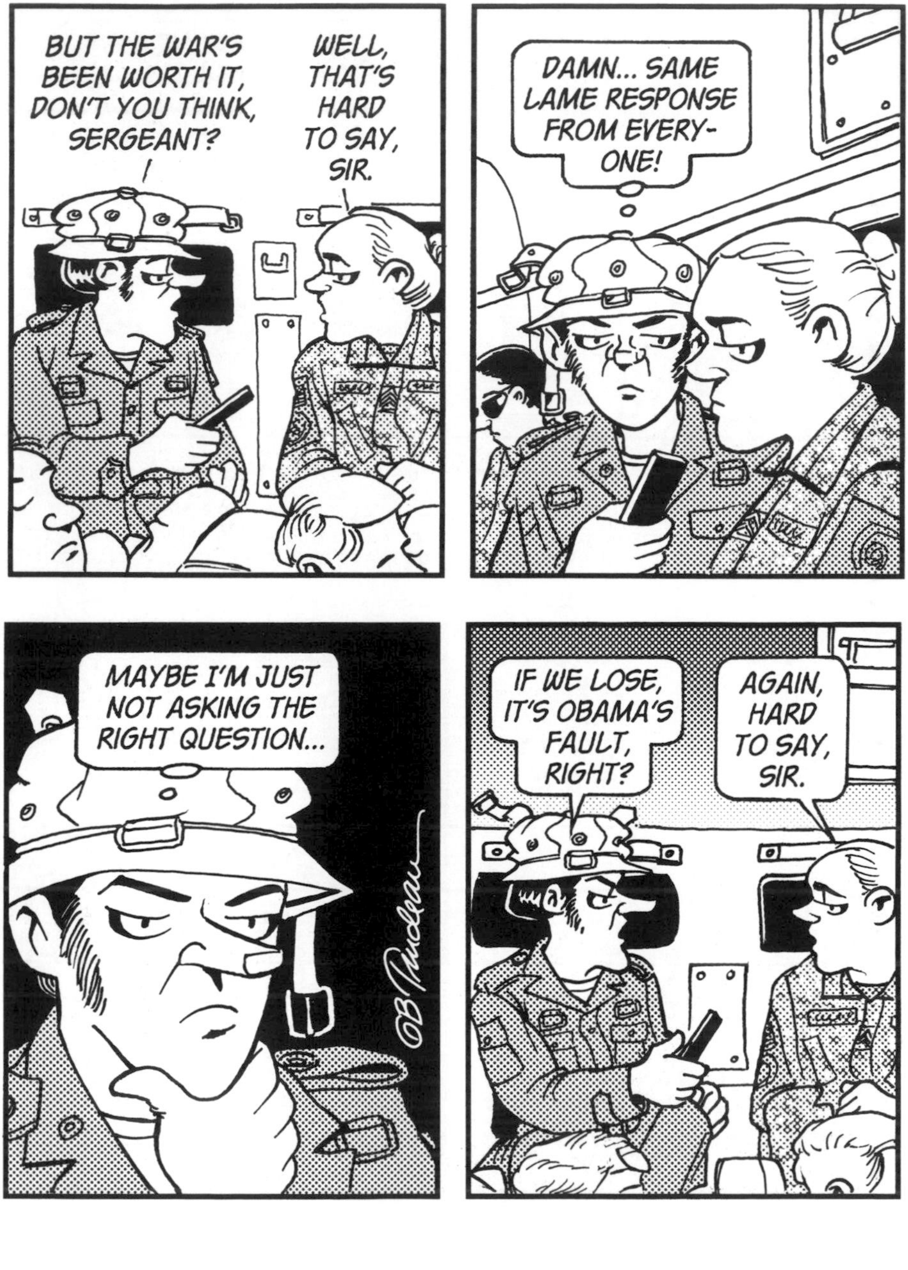
BUT THE WAR'S BEEN WORTH IT, DON'T YOU THINK, SERGEANT?
WELL, THAT'S HARD TO SAY, SIR.
DAMN... SAME LAME RESPONSE FROM EVERY-ONE!
MAYBE I'M JUST NOT ASKING THE RIGHT QUESTION...
©B Trudeau
IF WE LOSE, IT'S OBAMA'S FAULT, RIGHT?
AGAIN, HARD TO SAY, SIR.

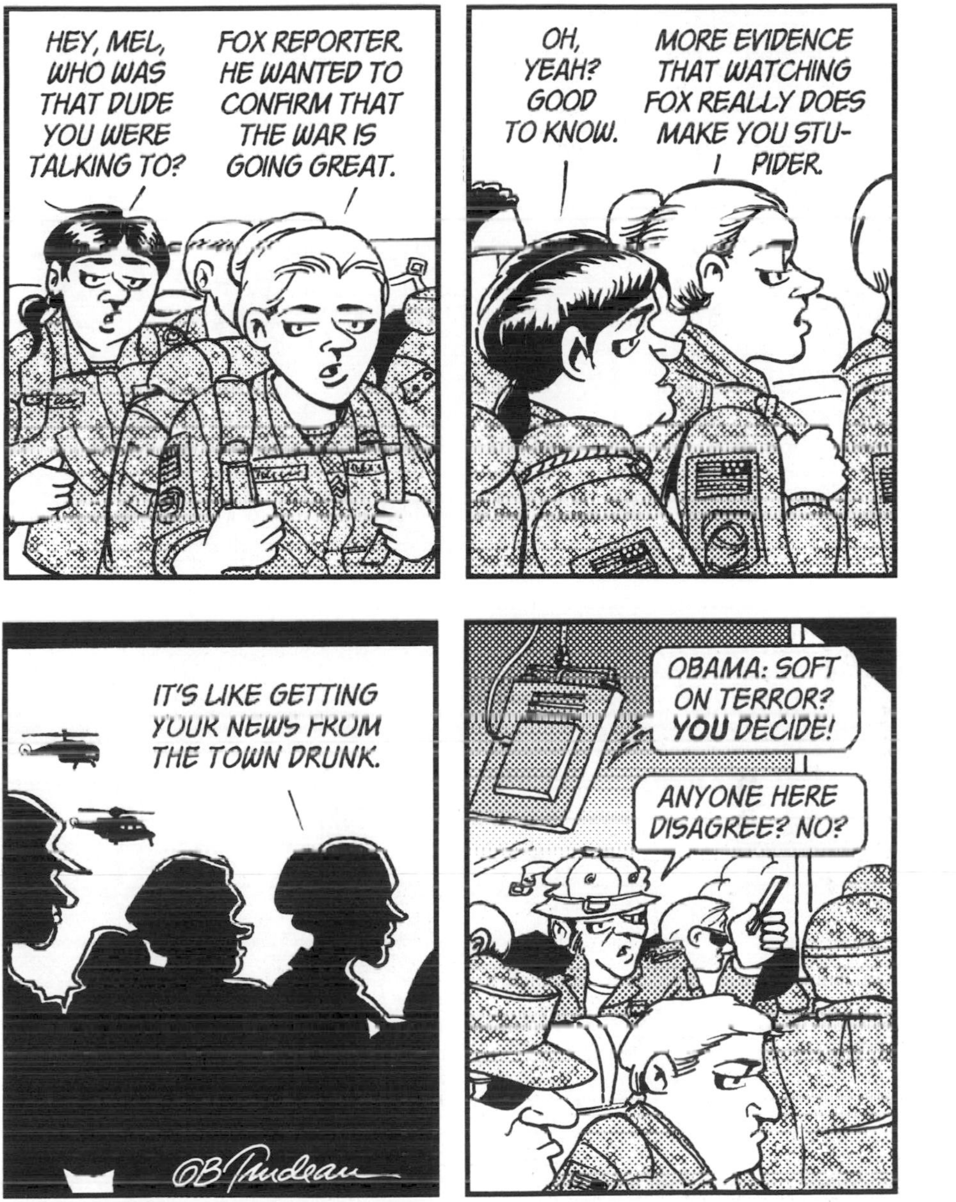
HEY, MEL, WHO WAS THAT DUDE YOU WERE TALKING TO?
FOX REPORTER. HE WANTED TO CONFIRM THAT THE WAR IS GOING GREAT.
OH, YEAH? GOOD TO KNOW.
MORE EVIDENCE THAT WATCHING FOX REALLY DOES MAKE YOU STU- PIDER.
IT'S LIKE GETTING YOUR NEWS FROM THE TOWN DRUNK.
©B Trudeau
OBAMA: SOFT ON TERROR? YOU DECIDE!
ANYONE HERE DISAGREE? NO?

NOT GETTING WHAT I NEED...
THINK, MAN! WHAT WOULD GERALDO DO?
HEY... ARE YOU THAT REPORTER WHO WAS TWEET-ING ON PATROL?
WHY, YES. YES, I AM, SON.
WHAT WERE YOU **THINK-ING**, DUDE? A CELL GIVES AWAY POSITION! YOU COULD HAVE GOTTEN THE WHOLE **TEAM** BLOWN UP!
YOU'RE LIKE FREAKIN' GERALDO, MAN!
OH... THANKS.
GB Trudeau

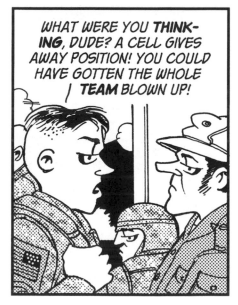

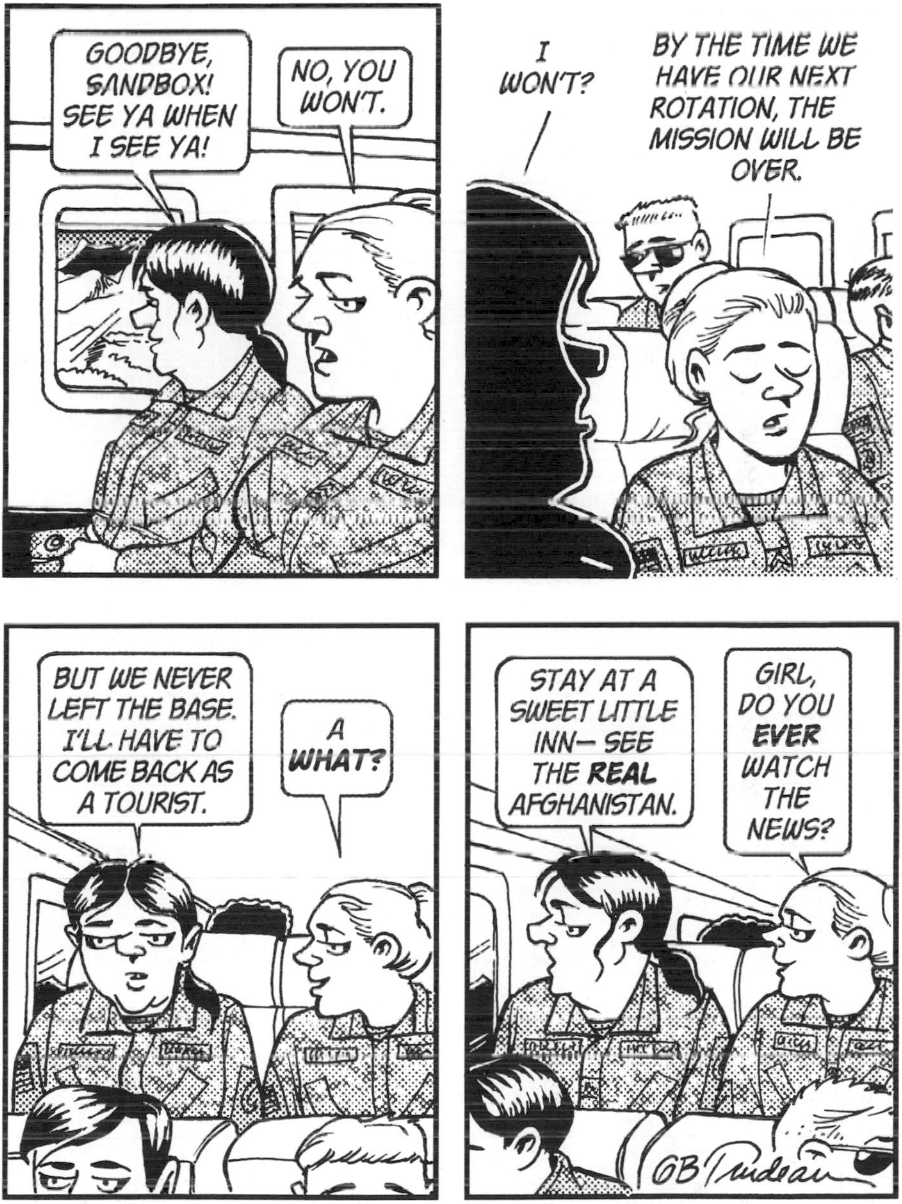
GOODBYE, SANDBOX! SEE YA WHEN I SEE YA!
NO, YOU WON'T.
I WON'T?
BY THE TIME WE HAVE OUR NEXT ROTATION, THE MISSION WILL BE OVER.
BUT WE NEVER LEFT THE BASE. I'LL HAVE TO COME BACK AS A TOURIST.
A **WHAT?**
STAY AT A SWEET LITTLE INN— SEE THE **REAL** AFGHANISTAN.
GIRL, DO YOU **EVER** WATCH THE NEWS?
GB Trudeau

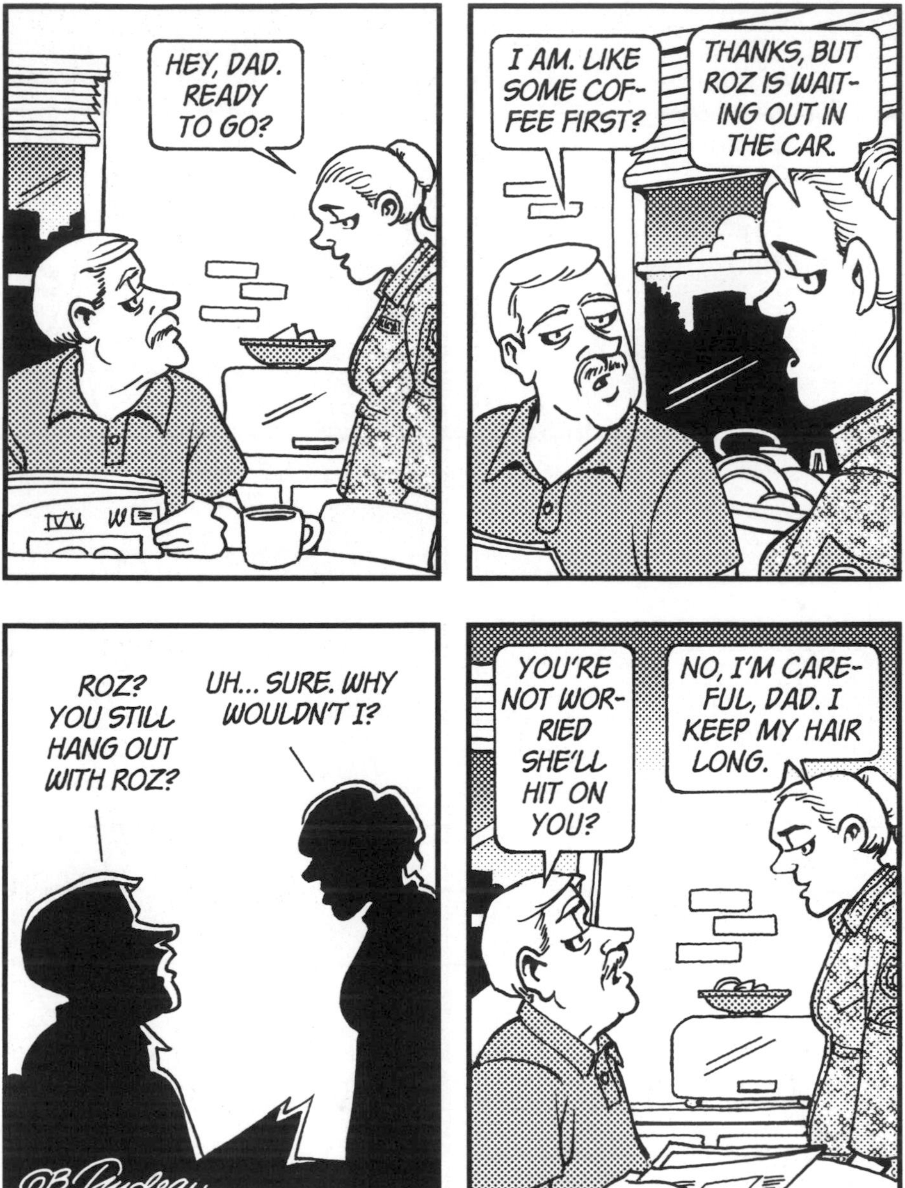
HEY, DAD. READY TO GO?
I AM. LIKE SOME COF-FEE FIRST?
THANKS, BUT ROZ IS WAIT-ING OUT IN THE CAR.
ROZ? YOU STILL HANG OUT WITH ROZ?
UH... SURE. WHY WOULDN'T I?
YOU'RE NOT WOR-RIED SHE'LL HIT ON YOU?
NO, I'M CARE-FUL, DAD. I KEEP MY HAIR LONG.
GB Trudeau

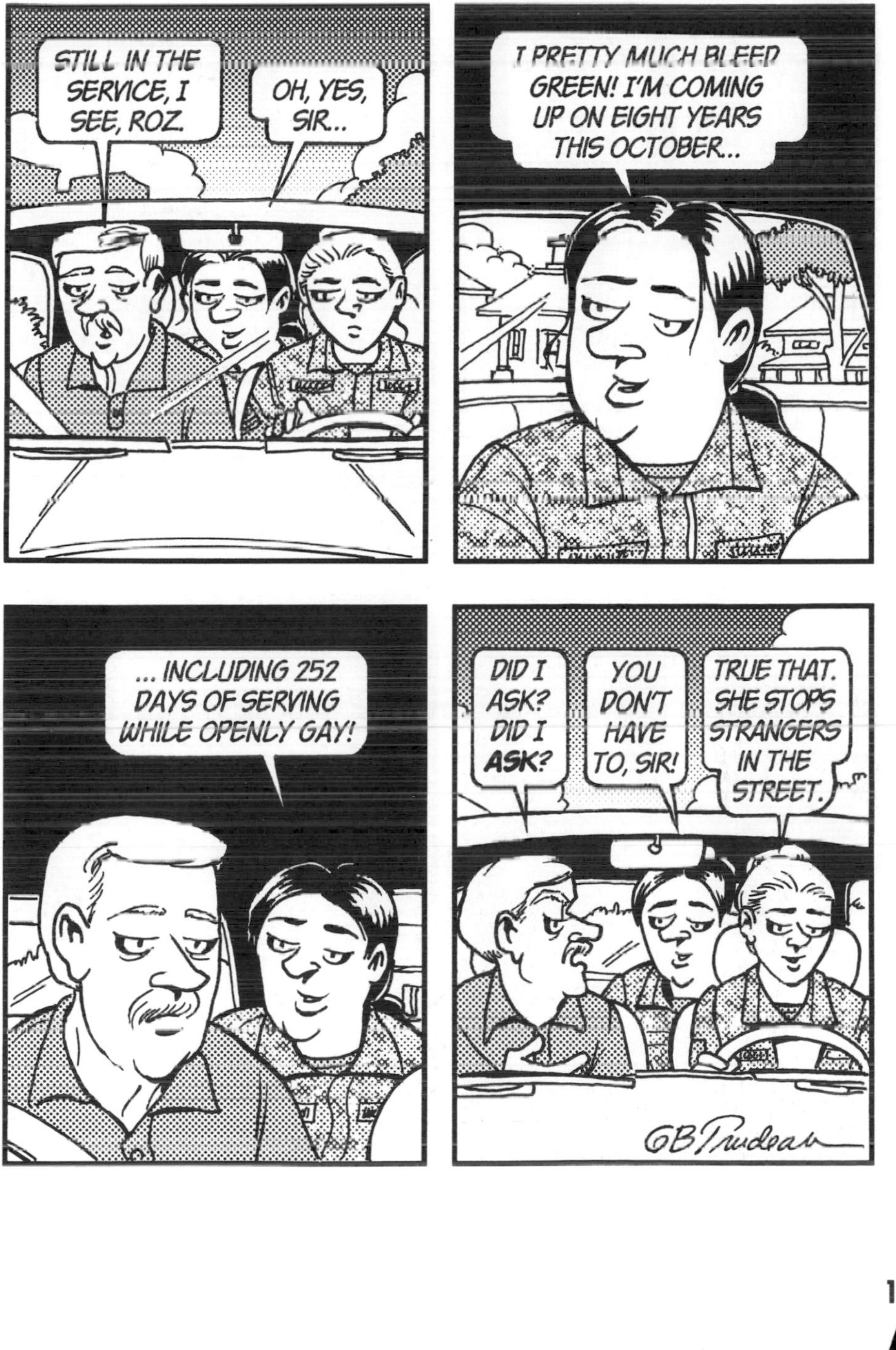
STILL IN THE SERVICE, I SEE, ROZ.
OH, YES, SIR...
I PRETTY MUCH BLEED GREEN! I'M COMING UP ON EIGHT YEARS THIS OCTOBER...
... INCLUDING 252 DAYS OF SERVING WHILE OPENLY GAY!
DID I ASK? DID I **ASK**?
YOU DON'T HAVE TO, SIR!
TRUE THAT. SHE STOPS STRANGERS IN THE STREET.
GBTrudeau

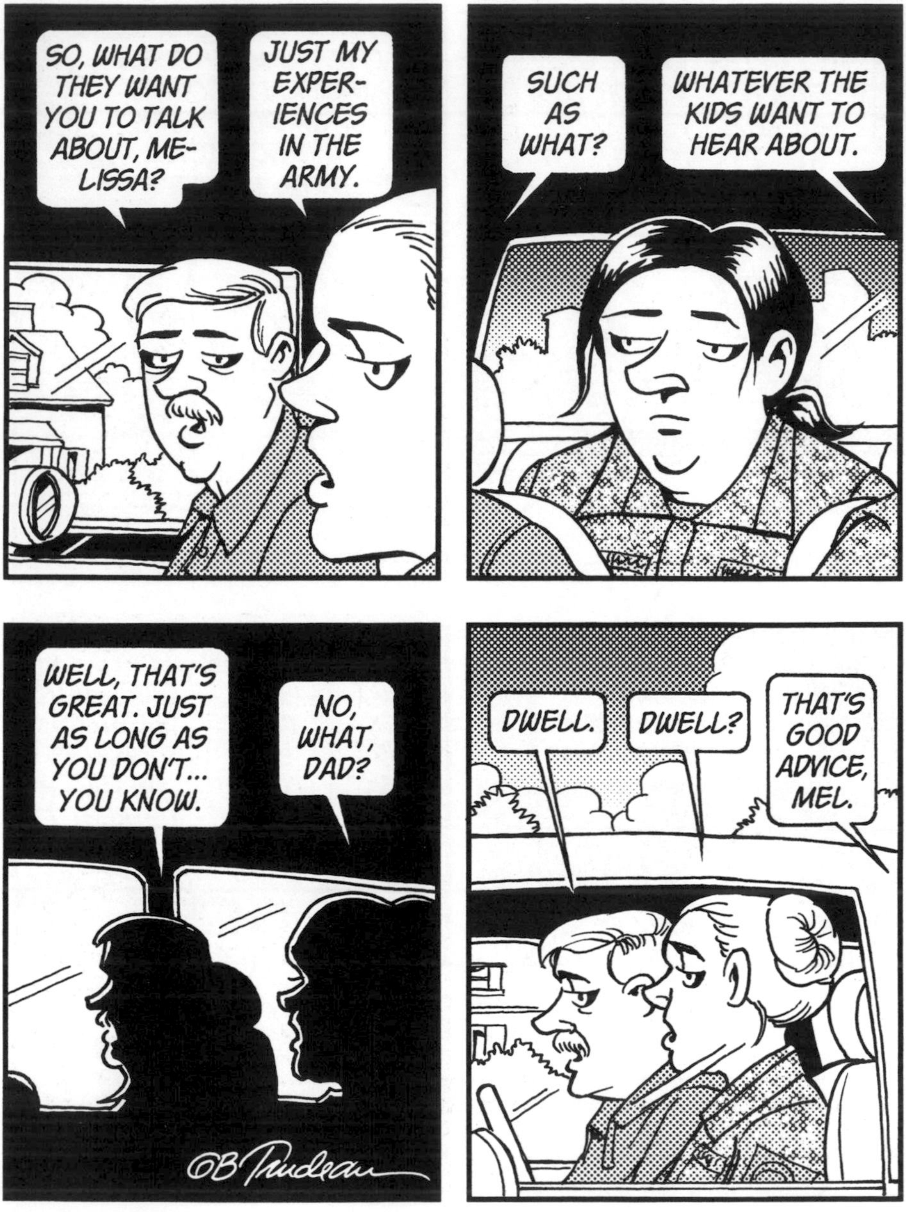
SO, WHAT DO THEY WANT YOU TO TALK ABOUT, ME-LISSA?
JUST MY EXPER-IENCES IN THE ARMY.
SUCH AS WHAT?
WHATEVER THE KIDS WANT TO HEAR ABOUT.
WELL, THAT'S GREAT. JUST AS LONG AS YOU DON'T... YOU KNOW.
NO, WHAT, DAD?
©B Trudeau
DWELL.
DWELL?
THAT'S GOOD ADVICE, MEL.

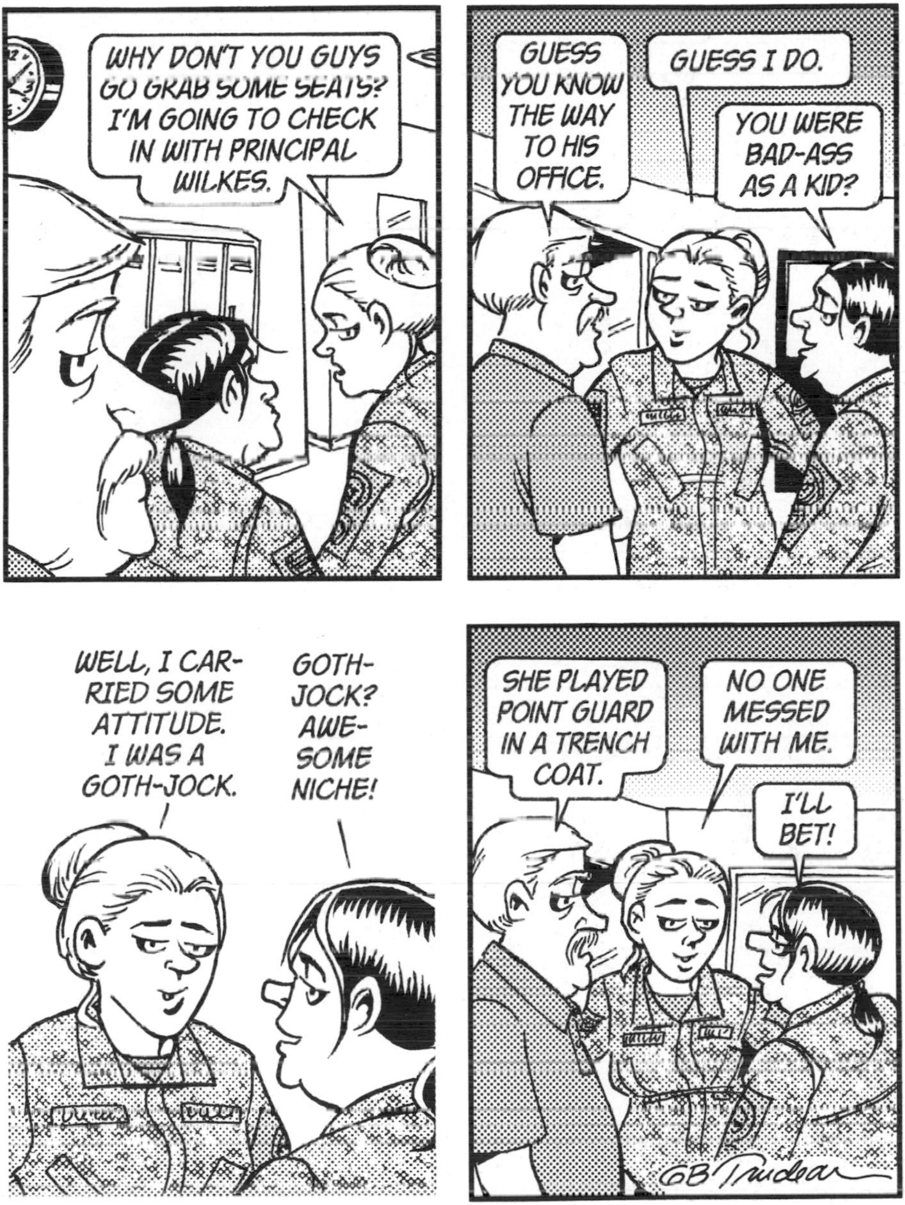
WHY DON'T YOU GUYS GO GRAB SOME SEATS? I'M GOING TO CHECK IN WITH PRINCIPAL WILKES.
GUESS YOU KNOW THE WAY TO HIS OFFICE.
GUESS I DO.
YOU WERE BAD-ASS AS A KID?
WELL, I CARRIED SOME ATTITUDE. I WAS A GOTH-JOCK.
GOTH-JOCK? AWESOME NICHE!
SHE PLAYED POINT GUARD IN A TRENCH COAT.
NO ONE MESSED WITH ME.
I'LL BET!
GB Trudeau

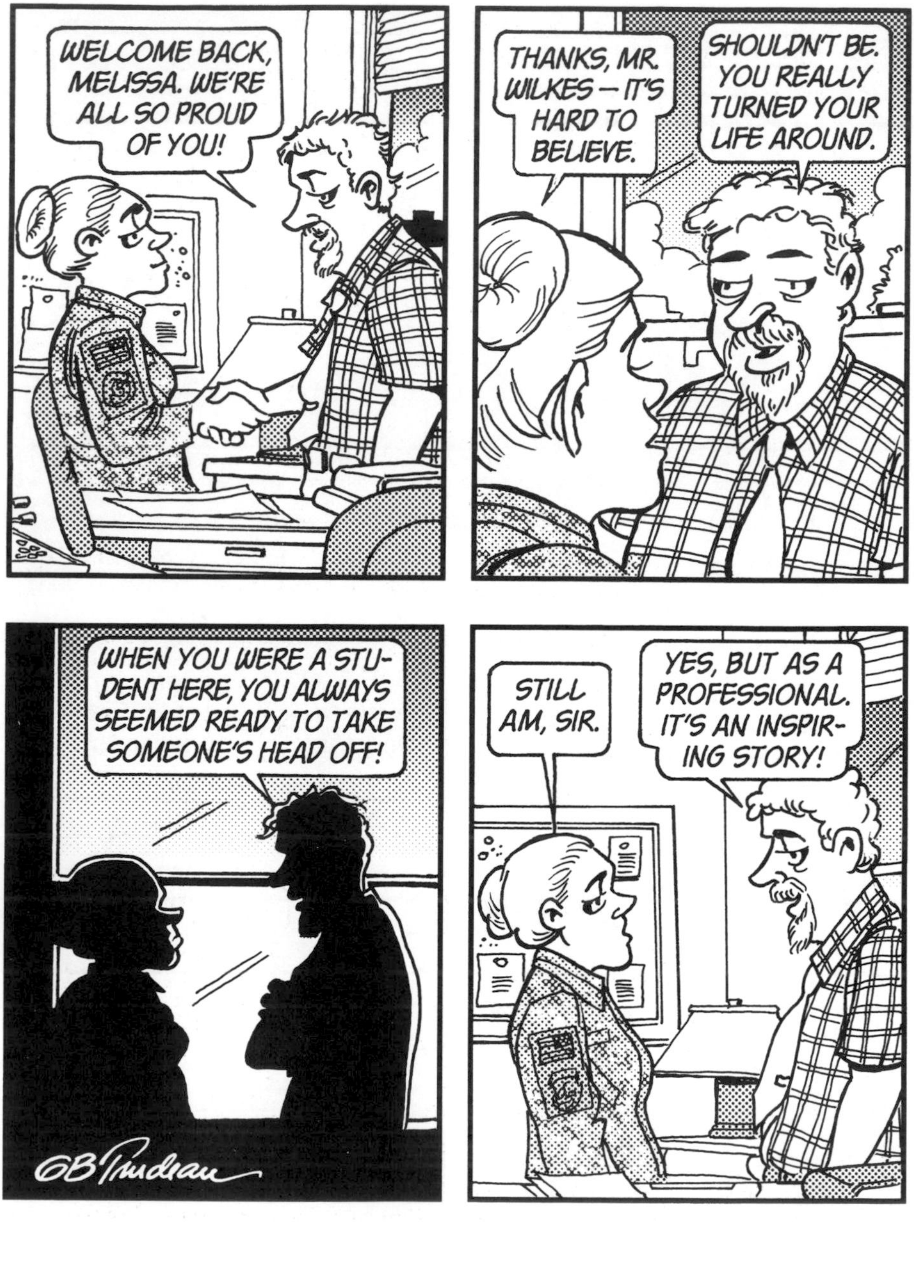
WELCOME BACK, MELISSA. WE'RE ALL SO PROUD OF YOU!
THANKS, MR. WILKES — IT'S HARD TO BELIEVE.
SHOULDN'T BE. YOU REALLY TURNED YOUR LIFE AROUND.
WHEN YOU WERE A STUDENT HERE, YOU ALWAYS SEEMED READY TO TAKE SOMEONE'S HEAD OFF!
GB Trudeau
STILL AM, SIR.
YES, BUT AS A PROFESSIONAL. IT'S AN INSPIRING STORY!

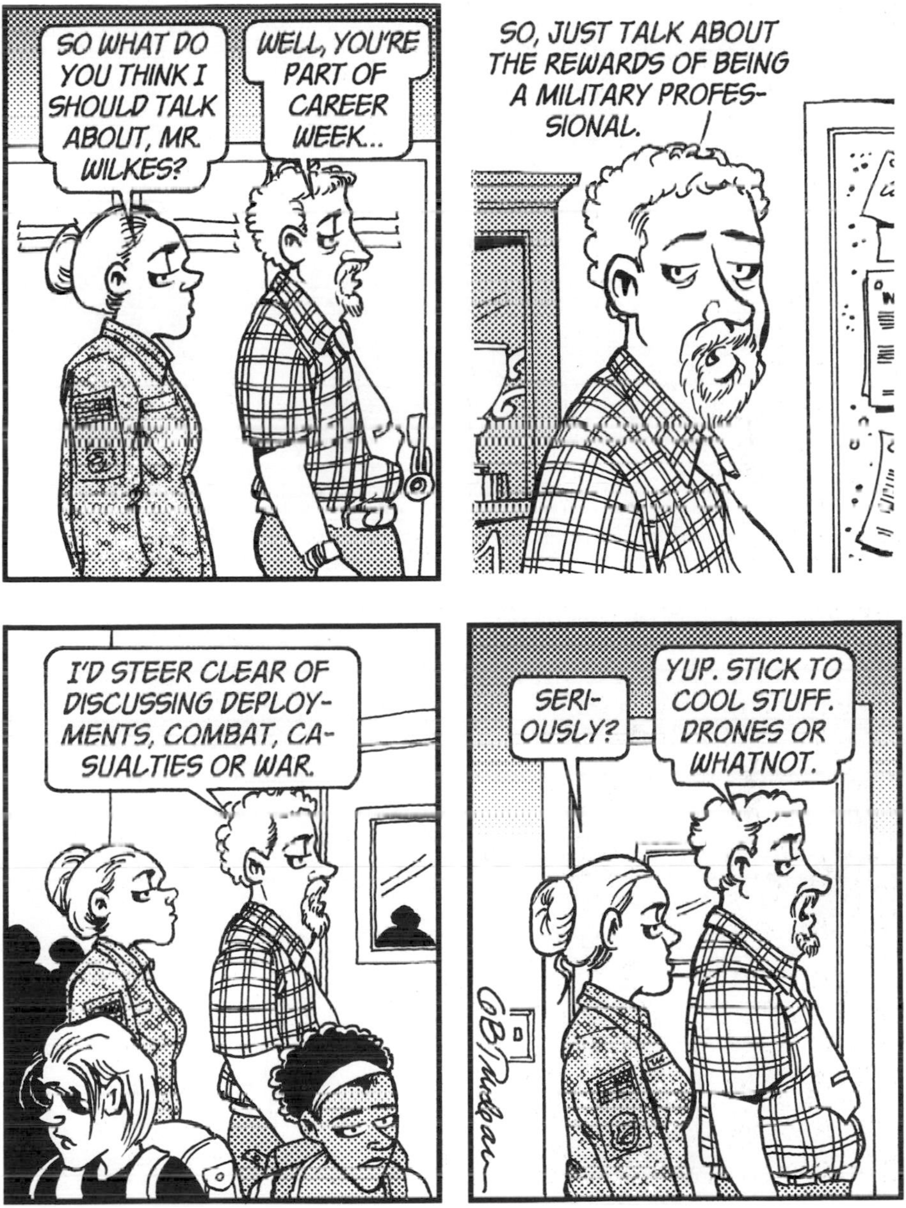
SO WHAT DO YOU THINK I SHOULD TALK ABOUT, MR. WILKES?
WELL, YOU'RE PART OF CAREER WEEK...
SO, JUST TALK ABOUT THE REWARDS OF BEING A MILITARY PROFES-SIONAL.
I'D STEER CLEAR OF DISCUSSING DEPLOY-MENTS, COMBAT, CA-SUALTIES OR WAR.
SERI-OUSLY?
YUP. STICK TO COOL STUFF. DRONES OR WHATNOT.

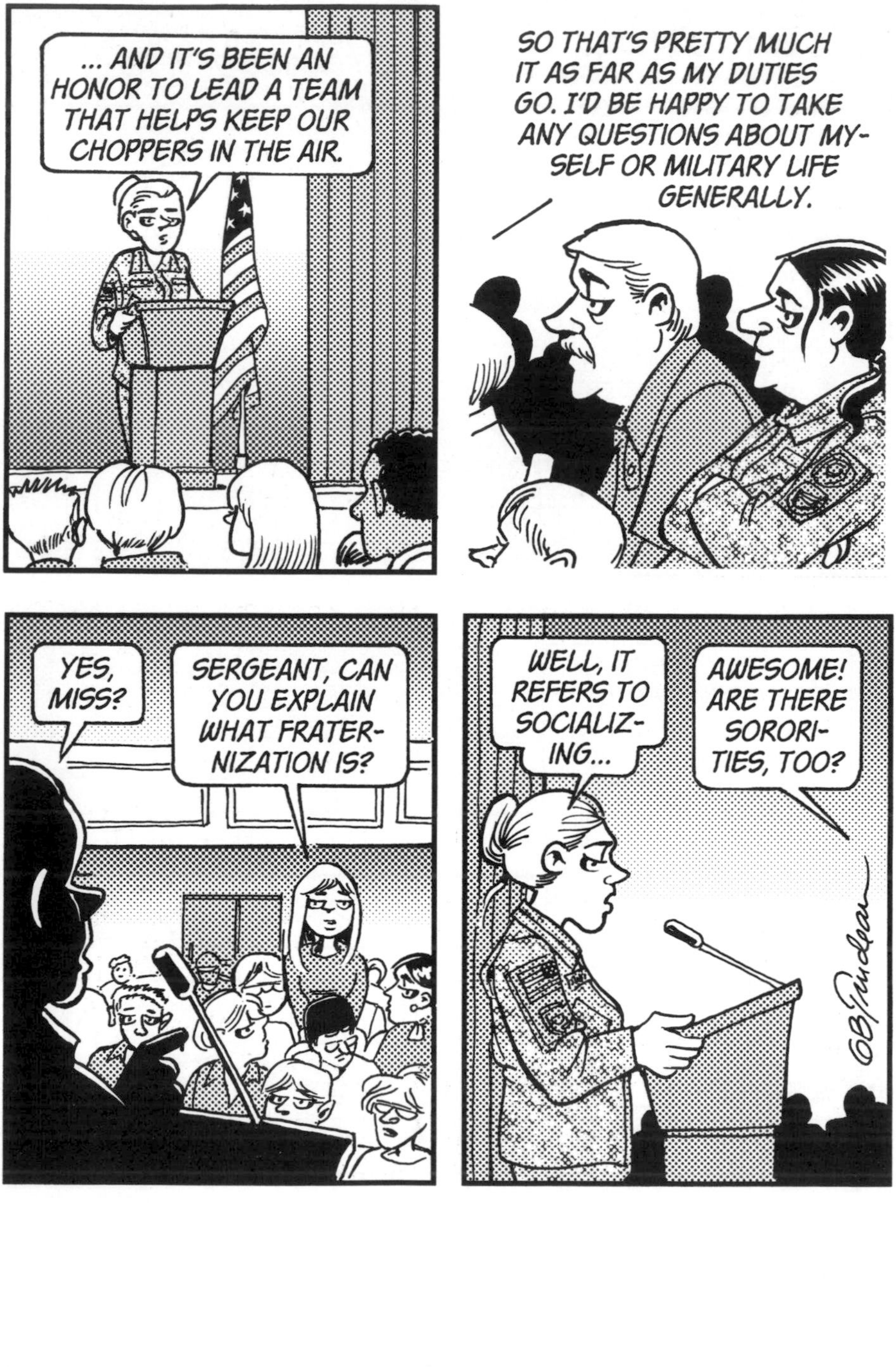
... AND IT'S BEEN AN HONOR TO LEAD A TEAM THAT HELPS KEEP OUR CHOPPERS IN THE AIR.
SO THAT'S PRETTY MUCH IT AS FAR AS MY DUTIES GO. I'D BE HAPPY TO TAKE ANY QUESTIONS ABOUT MYSELF OR MILITARY LIFE GENERALLY.
YES, MISS?
SERGEANT, CAN YOU EXPLAIN WHAT FRATERNIZATION IS?
WELL, IT REFERS TO SOCIALIZING...
AWESOME! ARE THERE SORORITIES, TOO?
GB Trudeau

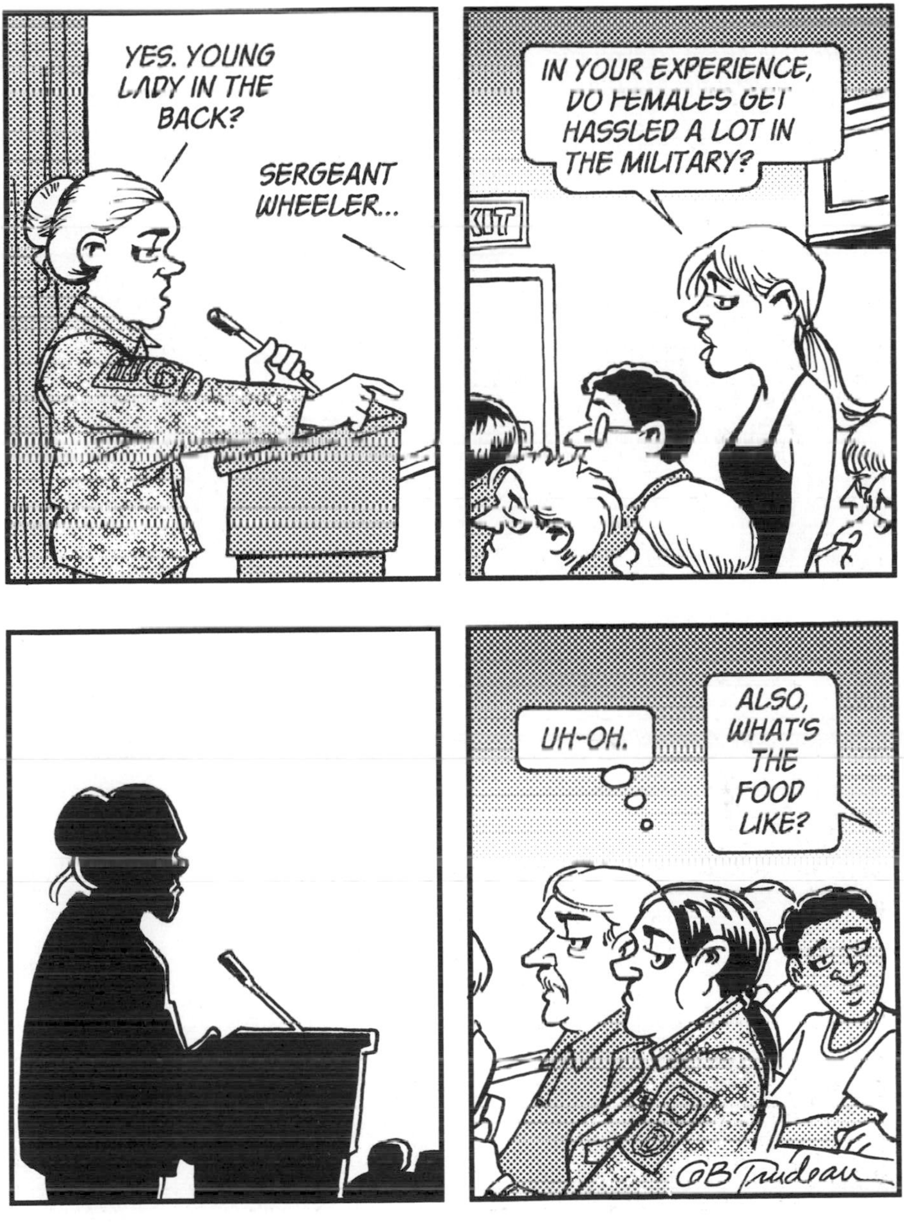
YES. YOUNG LADY IN THE BACK?
SERGEANT WHEELER...
IN YOUR EXPERIENCE, DO FEMALES GET HASSLED A LOT IN THE MILITARY?
UH-OH.
ALSO, WHAT'S THE FOOD LIKE?
©B Trudeau

ARE WOMEN "HASSLED" A LOT IN THE MILITARY? TRUTHFULLY, YES. AND FOR MANY, IT'S NOT JUST HARASSMENT.
THERE ARE NOW AN ESTIMATED 19,000 RAPES AND OTHER SEXUAL ASSAULTS EVERY YEAR. 20% OF FEMALE VETS HAVE BEEN SEXUALLY ATTACKED WHILE SERVING.
WHOA... REALLY? I'VE ALWAYS PLANNED ON JOINING...
WHAT'S THE MATH ON **NOT** GETTING RAPED?
YOU'LL HAVE TO DO IT YOURSELF.
©B Trudeau

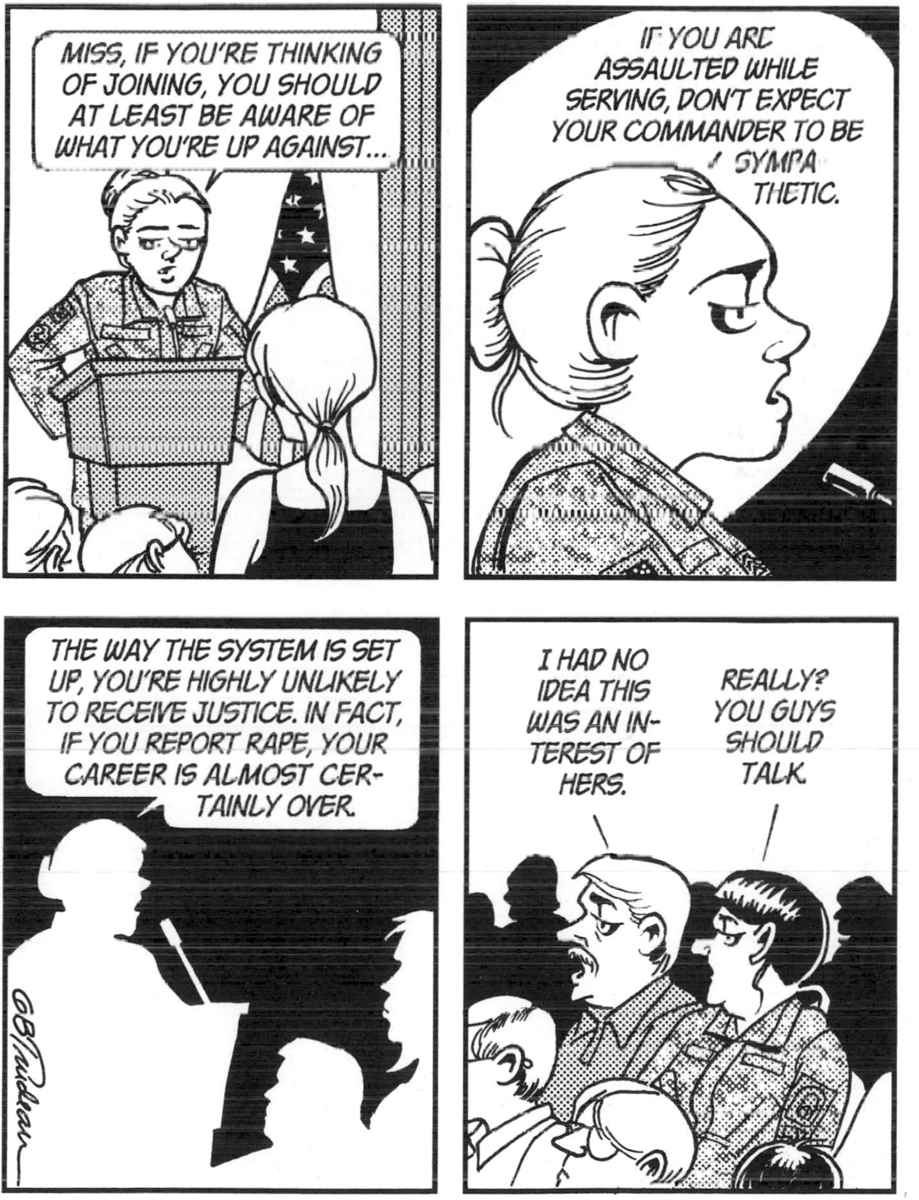
MISS, IF YOU'RE THINKING OF JOINING, YOU SHOULD AT LEAST BE AWARE OF WHAT YOU'RE UP AGAINST...
IF YOU ARE ASSAULTED WHILE SERVING, DON'T EXPECT YOUR COMMANDER TO BE SYMPATHETIC.
THE WAY THE SYSTEM IS SET UP, YOU'RE HIGHLY UNLIKELY TO RECEIVE JUSTICE. IN FACT, IF YOU REPORT RAPE, YOUR CAREER IS ALMOST CERTAINLY OVER.
I HAD NO IDEA THIS WAS AN INTEREST OF HERS.
REALLY? YOU GUYS SHOULD TALK.

SINCE ONLY A TINY PERCENTAGE ARE EVER CONVICTED, SEXUAL PREDATORS FEEL FREE TO ATTACK WITH IMPUNITY.

WHY ARE SO FEW PUNISHED? WELL, FOR ONE REASON, VICTIMS HAVE TO REPORT UP THE CHAIN OF COMMAND. SO FEW OF THEM REPORT.

WHY? 33% OF VICTIMS DON'T REPORT BECAUSE THEIR SUPERIOR IS A FRIEND OF THE RAPIST. 25% DON'T REPORT BECAUSE HE **IS** THE RAPIST!

SUCH AN INTERESTING CHOICE FOR CAREER WEEK, HARRY.

THINK I SHOULD GO PULL THE FIRE ALARM?

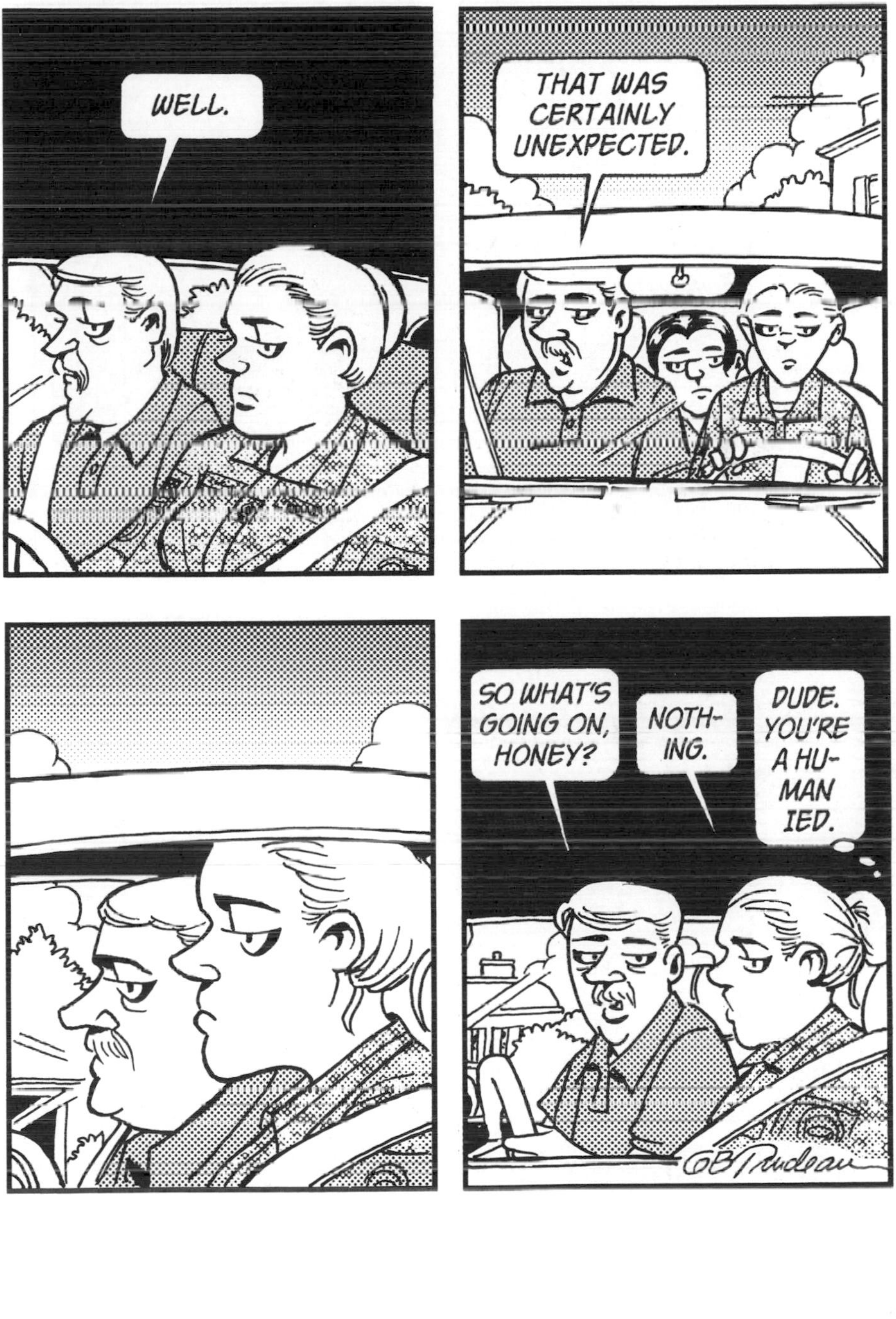
WELL.
THAT WAS CERTAINLY UNEXPECTED.
SO WHAT'S GOING ON, HONEY?
NOTH-ING.
DUDE. YOU'RE A HU-MAN IED.
GBTrudeau

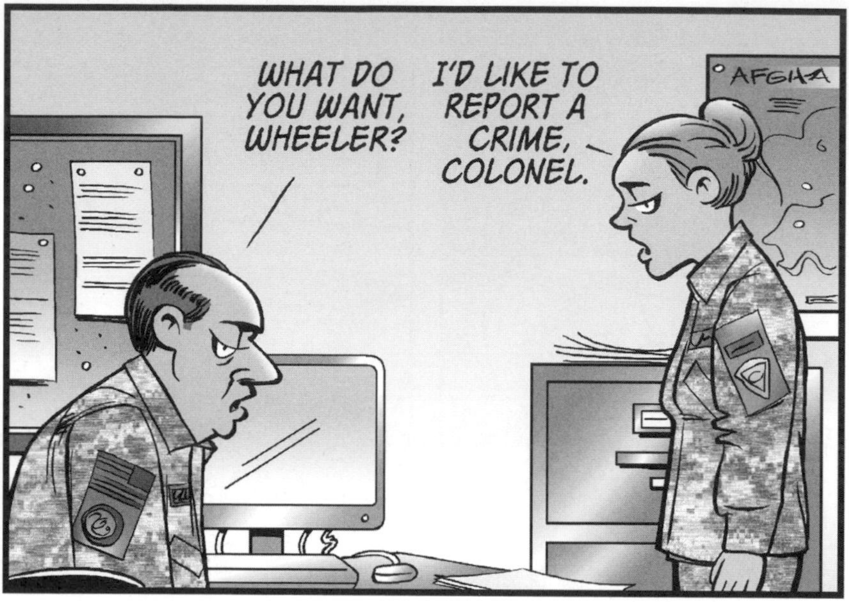
WHAT DO YOU WANT, WHEELER?
I'D LIKE TO REPORT A CRIME, COLONEL.

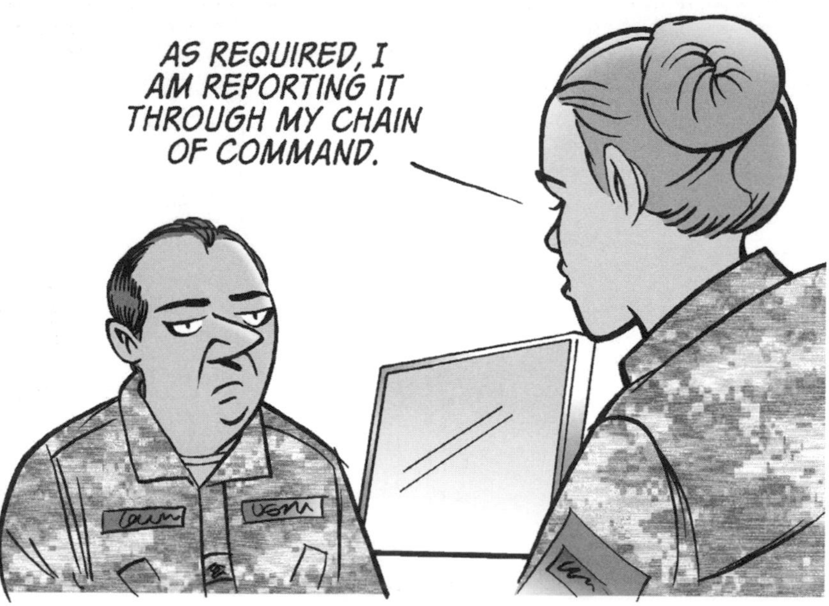
AS REQUIRED, I AM REPORTING IT THROUGH MY CHAIN OF COMMAND.

WHAT'S THE CRIME?
I WAS RAPED BY A SUPERI- OR OFFICER.
AFG
WHO'S THE ALLEGED PERPETRA- TOR?
YOU, SIR. AS YOU KNOW.

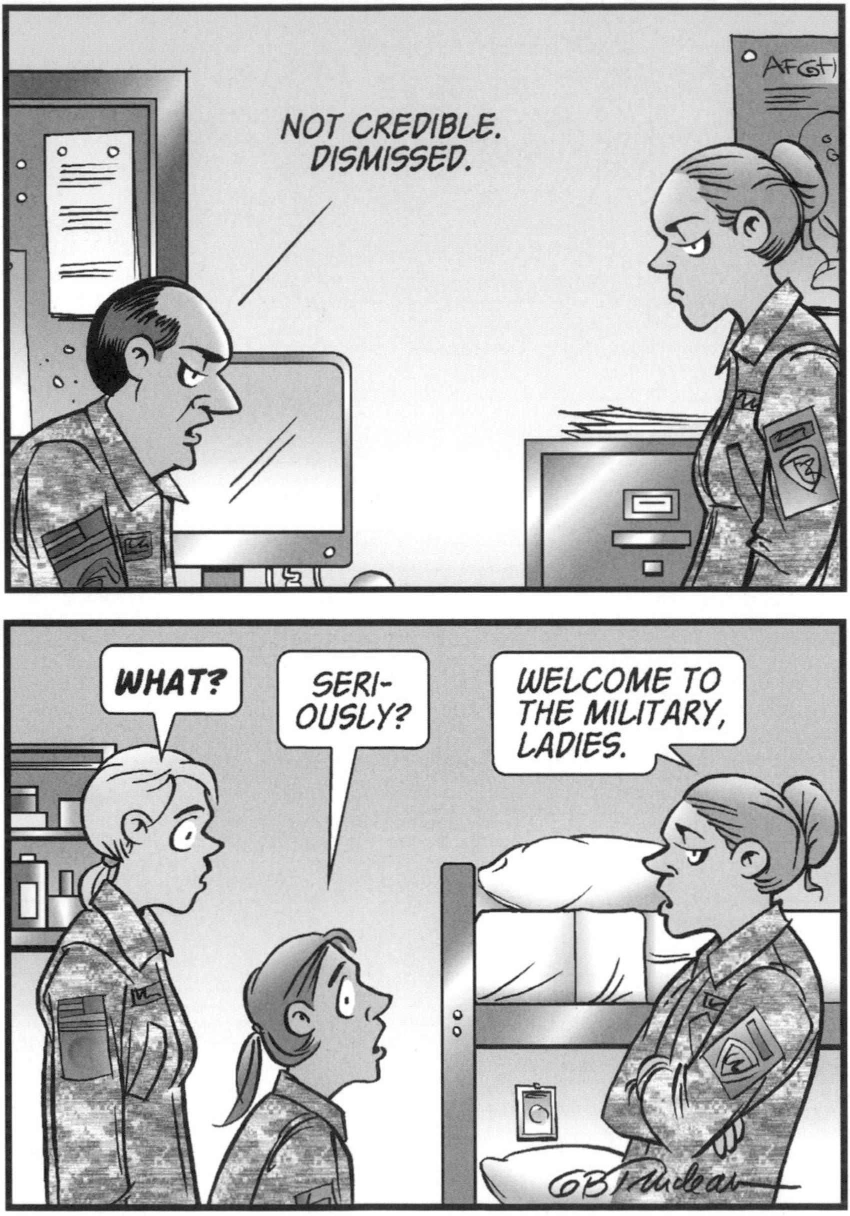
NOT CREDIBLE. DISMISSED.
WHAT?
SERI-OUSLY?
WELCOME TO THE MILITARY, LADIES.

FISHER HOUSE

because A Family's Love is Good Medicine

www.fisherhouse.org

A Fisher House is a "home away from home" for families of patients receiving medical care at major military and VA medical centers. Fisher Houses have up to 21 suites, with private bedrooms and baths. Families share a common kitchen, laundry facilities, a warm dining room, and an inviting living room. The Fisher House Foundation ensures that there is never a fee. Since inception, the program has saved military and veteran families an estimated $235 million in out-of-pocket costs for lodging and transportation. The foundation uses donated frequent flier miles to provide airline travel to reunite families of the wounded and to enable our wounded heroes to go home to convalesce, and helps cover the cost of alternative lodging when the Fisher Houses are full.

The Fisher House Foundation donates Fisher Houses to the U.S. Government. They have full-time salaried managers, but depend on volunteers and voluntary support to enhance daily operations and program expansion.

As of this printing, there are sixty-four Fisher Houses located on twenty-three military installations and twenty-four VA medical centers, plus one additional house in the United Kingdom. Another twelve houses are under construction or in design. The program began in 1990 and has offered more than 5,200,000 days of lodging to more than 220,000 families.

For further information about these programs, to find out about volunteering, or to make a tax-deductible gift, go to their Web site at:

www.fisherhouse.org

You can also obtain information by writing them at
Fisher House Foundation, Inc.
111 Rockville Pike, Suite 420
Rockville, MD 20850

Phone: (888) 294-8560
E-mail: info@fisherhouse.org

Andrews McMeel Publishing, LLC
an Andrews McMeel Universal Company
1130 Walnut Street, Kansas City, Missouri 64106
www.andrewsmcmeel.com

14 15 16 17 18 SDB 10 9 8 7 6 5 4 3 2 1

ISBN: 978-1-4494-6032-7

Library of Congress Control Number: 2014906726

DOONESBURY may be viewed on the Internet at:
www.doonesbury.com and www.GoComics.com

──────── **ATTENTION: SCHOOLS AND BUSINESSES** ────────

Andrews McMeel books are available at quantity discounts with bulk purchase for educational, business, or sales promotional use. For information, please e-mail the Andrews McMeel Publishing Special Sales Department: specialsales@amuniversal.com.